The Death Penalty
DOCUMENTS DECODED

The ABC-CLIO series *Documents Decoded* guides readers on a hunt for new secrets through an expertly curated selection of primary sources. Each book pairs key documents with in-depth analysis, all in an original and visually engaging side-by-side format. But *Documents Decoded* authors do more than just explain each source's context and significance—they give readers a front-row seat to their own investigation and interpretation of each essential document line-by-line.

Library of Congress Cataloging-in-Publication Data

Melusky, Joseph Anthony.
    The death penalty : documents decoded / Joseph A. Melusky and Keith Alan Pesto.
        p. cm. — (Documents decoded)
    Includes bibliographical references and index.
    ISBN 978-1-61069-194-9 (hardback) — ISBN 978-1-61069-195-6 (ebook)
1. Capital punishment—United States—Cases. I. Pesto, Keith A. II. Title.
    KF9227.C2M425 2013
    345.73'0773—dc23   2013023218

ISBN: 978-1-61069-194-9
EISBN: 978-1-61069-195-6

18 17 16 15 14   1 2 3 4 5

This book is also available on the World Wide Web as an eBook.
Visit www.abc-clio.com for details.

ABC-CLIO, LLC
130 Cremona Drive, P.O. Box 1911
Santa Barbara, California 93116-1911

This book is printed on acid-free paper ∞
Manufactured in the United States of America

The Death Penalty
DOCUMENTS DECODED

Joseph A. Melusky
and
Keith Alan Pesto

Documents Decoded

 ABC-CLIO

To my children, Mike and Jessica,
to my wife, Marie,
and to the memory of my dad, George, my mom,
Eleanor, and my mother-in-law, Edith.

—J.A.M.

Contents

Preface

This book provides excerpts of Supreme Court opinions from more than 30 important cases involving the death penalty. The U.S. Constitution prohibits "cruel and unusual punishments," but the exact meaning of this prohibition is somewhat open-ended. The Supreme Court has addressed various issues with an eye toward "evolving standards of decency." This is a key point. The Court ultimately defines these evolving standards of decency and tells us which practices are constitutionally permissible at a given point in history.

This book on the death penalty is part of the ABC-CLIO Documents Decoded series. References are made to Hammurabi's Code, the Hittite Code, Draco's Code, the Twelve Tables of Rome, the Bible, Justinian's Code, and other source materials, but the main document being decoded in this work is the U.S. Constitution, generally, and the Eighth Amendment along with a few other relevant constitutional provisions. This book focuses mainly on the decoding done by the Supreme Court of the United States as the justices have interpreted and applied constitutional provisions to historical and contemporary controversies. Furthermore, the excerpted judicial opinions are themselves primary-source documents, presented for your inspection and reflection.

Much has been written about capital punishment and its use in the United States. In fact, we have written two recent books on the subject ourselves. But most of these works are *about* capital punishment and are *about* important cases. Most of these works provide secondary commentaries on the subject. Outside of courtrooms and law schools, the words of the justices *themselves* are not as readily accessible to the general public. This book is designed to provide readers with a one-stop collection of the Court's main holdings in this area. The Court's actual opinions are not merely described. The opinions are excerpted and abridged to make them accessible to a general audience. In this way, readers can read the justices' *own* words and see what the justices had to say for *themselves* without relying on authors serving as intermediaries to tell them what the justices said.

The first chapter provides a brief historical overview of the debate over capital punishment and a summary of arguments favoring and opposing capital punishment. Subsequent chapters focus on relevant cases and judicial opinions. Each case is preceded by a short introduction to set the stage, provide context, and serve as a narrative bridge from the preceding case. The abridged case excerpts are brief so as to make them accessible to a wider audience. Readers are encouraged to see the original opinions in their entirety for more information.

Acknowledgments

Thanks to all the people at ABC-CLIO who worked to make this project a success. We want to thank David Paige, managing editor for Current Affairs, Politics, Government, and Law, and Denver Compton, acquisitions editor for Politics and Government, for working closely with us. We appreciate your guidance, support, encouragement, and—most of all—your patience. We also thank Senior Production Editor, Vicki Moran, and Production Editor, Nicholle Lutz, for helping us complete this project.

JOSEPH A. MELUSKY AND KEITH ALAN PESTO

Background

Chapter 1

Introduction

Whoever sheds the blood of man, by man shall his blood be shed.
—Genesis 9:6 (RSV)

Excessive bail shall not be required, nor excessive fines imposed,
nor cruel and unusual punishments inflicted.
—U.S. Constitution, Eighth Amendment

Early Death Penalty Laws and Practices

Archaeologists can, with varying degrees of confidence, reconstruct an entire extinct species from a few fragments of bone.[1] In the same way, a fairly accurate picture of human history could be reconstructed just from the documents relating to the death penalty. In his play *The Eumenides,* the great Greek dramatist Aeschylus imagined that civilized history began with the murder trial of Orestes. The goddess Athena puts an end to the anarchy of murder begetting vendetta and reprisals by appointing a jury, because "not even a goddess should decide a case of murder—murder whets the passions." Some things have changed little in 2,500 years.

The death penalty is documented from the cuneiform and hieroglyphic records of the ancient Near East. The first recorded death sentence occurred in Egypt in the 16th century BCE: a member of the nobility, accused of magic, was ordered to take his own life. During this period, nonnobles were usually killed with an ax.[2] In the 18th century BCE in Babylon, the Code of Hammurabi called for the death penalty for 25 different crimes (not including murder).[3] The death penalty was also included in the Hittite Code (14th century BCE).[4]

In 621 BCE, Draco's Code made death the penalty in Athens for even the most trivial offenses, such as stealing an apple.[5] The code was so harsh that it was said to have been written in blood instead of ink. According to Aristotle, the lawgiver Solon later retained Draco's laws for homicide but reduced the severity of punishments for lesser offenses.[6]

Rome's first written laws, the Twelve Tables, date from approximately 450 BCE. The Twelve Tables include extensive use of the death penalty for a wide variety of crimes including the publication of libels and insulting songs, the cutting or grazing of crops planted by a farmer, the burning of a house or a stack of corn near a house, cheating by a patron of his client, perjury, making disturbances at night in the city, willful murder of a freeman or a parent, and theft by a slave. Methods of execution "fit" the crime (e.g., arsonists were burned alive) and included crucifixion for slaves and noncitizens, drowning, burial alive, hanging, beating to death, and impalement. Even for cases that we would not consider criminal, such as defaulting on a debt, the law permitted the death penalty as an ultimate sanction.[7]

And of course the Bible is quoted (selectively) by death penalty proponents and opponents. In Genesis, God warned Adam of a death penalty: "In the day that you eat of [the tree of the knowledge of good and evil] you shall die."[8] The Law of Moses contained in the books of Exodus and Leviticus delineated numerous capital offenses. Murder, some assaults, rape, unchastity, perjury, blasphemy, heresy, magic, and soothsaying were punished by stoning, burning, strangling, or beheading. The book of Numbers includes references to the death penalty too. The 18th chapter of the book of Genesis even contains the earliest debate of sorts on the death penalty. There Abraham pleads with God to spare the cities of Sodom and Gomorrah. Foreshadowing modern concerns about the possibility of executing an innocent man, Abraham maintained that destruction of the cities would cause the death of the righteous as well as the wicked.[9]

As Christianity spread throughout the Roman Empire, its earliest documents, the Gospels, and the letters of St. Paul refrain from commentary on capital punishment at all. In 112 CE during one of the scattered persecutions throughout the empire, Pliny the Younger wrote to Emperor Trajan asking whether Christians should be executed as threats to public order. A century later, enough Roman officials had adopted the new religion that church fathers such as Tertullian were cautioning Christian magistrates not to order executions. By 300 CE, Lactantius was arguing that Christianity did not permit a just man even to charge anyone with a capital crime. After the official toleration announced by Emperor Constantine in 313 CE, Christian religious writers began to grapple with the problem of maintaining order within the state. Although the Catholic Church continued to regard participation in executions to be forbidden to priests and other religious offices, by 405 CE the church stopped excommunicating judges who imposed the death penalty, although St. Ambrose suggested that such officials not present themselves in churches. Ambrose's pupil, St. Augustine of Hippo, the greatest early Christian writer, wrote however that the commandment against murder was "not broken by those who wage wars on the authority of God, or those who have imposed the death penalty on criminals when representing the authority of the State in accordance with the laws of the State." Even without this apparent sanction, the legal codes of the later Roman Empire—the Theodosian Code of 438 CE and Justinian's Code of circa 530 CE—assumed the legitimacy of the death penalty not only for crimes such as murder, robbery, and rape but also for things that we consider private religious matters. Between 529 and 534 CE, Emperor Justinian ordered a compilation of Roman laws that had been published in the 1,000 years since the Twelve Tables.[10] Justinian's Code preserved the death penalty for serious crimes as well as for denial of the Trinity and rebaptizing. Crucifixion was abolished, but heretics were burned at the stake.

There things stood for another 1,000 years as Germanic tribes settled in Western Europe and the Roman tradition continued to exist only in Constantinople and the Byzantine Empire. There was no scholarly debate about whether Ambrose's or Augustine's was the better view because the new ruling class, illiterate and governed by the time-hallowed customs of the tribe, could hardly be expected to see the point. By the 10th and 11th centuries, civilization had recovered enough from depopulation and Viking incursions that renewed contact with the East revived interest in the more advanced Roman law preserved in the Byzantine Empire. The result was a more sophisticated legal system but hardly a gentler one. Whereas the Franks, Ostrogoths, or Lombards had used trial by battle or trial by ordeal, the new generation of Continental monarchs rediscovered Roman jurisprudence, including its use of torture to secure witness testimony. England, somewhat cut off from the rediscovery of Roman law by its geographic remoteness and the Norman Conquest, developed a more extensive use of the jury to find facts. William the Conqueror had brought Norman law to Britain in 1066 CE. His reforms outlawed hanging, limited penalties to blinding or castration, and also introduced the Continental concept of trial by battle. Defendants could prove their innocence by the sword or sometimes have a champion do so on their behalf. There was no appeal, because punishment was simultaneous with the verdict. Barons had drowning pits and gallows, which they used for major and minor crimes within their territories.

When the Catholic Church outlawed trial by ordeal in 1215, England went down one road toward the adversarial system and trial by jury, and the rest of Europe went down another road toward a judge-centered inquisitorial system. This was to have consequences for the death penalty debate in Europe and eventually America, but as Europe moved out of the feudal era and government became more centralized in one monarch, punishment both in England and on the Continent ceased to be a swift and matter-of-fact end to a criminal and became an elaborate ritual emphasizing the majesty of the state. From the Middle Ages through the Renaissance, capital punishment was accompanied by torture. Crucifixion had been abolished with the spread of Christianity, but Christian monarchs sentenced rebels and traitors to the equally cruel process of hanging and then drawing and quartering. Beheading was viewed as a merciful alternative for the upper classes. High treason by a woman was punished by burning. Women could also be burned for marrying a Jew or wearing a man's clothes. When a woman was burned, the executioner placed a rope around her neck when she was tied to the stake. When the flames reached her, she could be strangled from outside the ring of fire. This "chivalrous" gesture sometimes failed, leaving the condemned to be burned alive.[11] Other execution practices included boiling a person alive, breaking on the wheel, stoning, beheading, and sawing asunder.[12]

Not only had the death penalty taken on quasi-religious overtones, but it was also used to enforce political and religious orthodoxy. Theologians as orthodox as Thomas Aquinas had in the 13th century justified the death penalty for heresy by analogy to the unquestioned justice of the death penalty for counterfeiters of money. During the Reformation and the 100 years of religious wars of the 16th and mid-17th centuries, Catholics hanged Lutherans, Calvinists burned Baptists, and Anglicans disemboweled Catholics. There were a few people, such as chancellor of England Thomas More, who called for limiting the death penalty to serious crimes.

More's analysis was offered in his *Utopia,* in which he stated that hanging thieves was unjust because it was disproportionate to the crime, was ineffective because it did not attack the poverty that was the cause of theft, and was perverse because it gave the thief an incentive to kill his victim. But in the passions of the time, calm analysis of crime and punishment stood little chance of being heard. More himself was beheaded for treasonous religious opinion by Henry VIII. Luther, Calvin, and the popes of the Catholic Counter-Reformation all accepted the necessity of the death penalty.

But it was the use of death as a punishment for heresy and as a tool to induce religious conformity that launched the modern death penalty debate. In 1553, a generation after Zwingli and Luther, the physician Michael Servetus was burned at the stake in Calvin's Geneva for heresy, as prescribed by the Code of Justinian. This evoked the first significant works condemning the execution of religious dissenters, written by Sebastian Castellio in the 1550s and 1560s. In the following century, the great American Baptist minister Roger Williams's *The Bloody Tenent of Persecution* (published anonymously in 1644) called for an end to religious persecutions. Whether it was the strength of the arguments of proponents of religious toleration by thinkers such as Williams or simple exhaustion after almost a century of genocidal warfare, gradually it became accepted throughout Europe that the death penalty should be limited to the punishment of secular offenses.

The history of the English Civil War (1642–1649) provides a curious abortive attempt to limit the death penalty still further. Much like the American Civil War two centuries later, the English Civil War pitted neighbors against one another. But to the extent that there was a theme to the struggle between the parliamentary parties and the Crown, it was the demand of Protestant religious parties to govern or at least to be free of the governance of the established Anglican Church. The attempts by far-thinking reformers to use English for legal proceedings, to simplify land and inheritance law, and to limit the use of the death penalty were all associated with the more radical of Oliver Cromwell's allies; and when the monarchy was restored in 1660, the dreams of a more lenient English criminal law died too. The one permanent change from this era of English history is the almost complete end of the use of the death penalty for punishing religious dissent among Protestants. (Toleration of Catholics in England was still in the future.)

Punishment of secular offenses had not changed much in England or on the Continent even with the end of the era of religious wars. Because English judges were not authorized to use torture and because English verdicts depended to a greater extent on a potentially sympathetic jury, English law was praised or reviled depending on one's politics for its relative leniency. In the 1720s and 1740s, the French writer Montesquieu praised the relative leniency of English law, even as the English Parliament was engaged in adding to the number of capital offenses. English politicians accepted the flattery but did not let it affect their actions.

In the 18th century, penalties involving torture declined throughout Europe due to a belief that punishment and death should be swift and humane. In France, the guillotine became the preferred method of execution. Decapitation was then thought to be the least painful method of execution. Dr. Joseph Guillotin designed and built a decapitation machine to avoid human error and infliction of unnecessary pain. The first execution by guillotine took place in 1792, and the last took place in 1977.[13]

The Death Penalty and Colonial America

Capital punishment has been a feature of criminal justice in America since colonial times. Captain George Kendall was first. He was shot by a firing squad in Jamestown, Virginia, in 1608 for sowing discord and spying. The next known legal execution in the colonies also took place in Virginia 14 years later. In 1622 Daniel Frank was put to death for the crime of theft.

In New England, the Massachusetts Bay Colony adopted a criminal code that was modeled on the book of Leviticus and, in addition to punishing murder, robbery, and rape, prescribed death for idolatry and witchcraft. In 1660, Mary Dyer was hanged for defying the law banishing Quakers from the colony. In 1688, Ann Glover was hanged for being a Catholic and a witch. In 1692, 18 alleged witches were hanged after the Salem witch trials. As the 18th century went on, practice in the mother country and the colonies diverged slightly. In England, concern over vagrancy, theft, and poaching by persons dislocated by the Industrial Revolution led to scores of new capital offenses, although jury nullification and the practice of pardoning and transporting convicted criminals as indentured servants saved most capital defendants from execution.

But in 1764, history was changed by the treatise *On Crimes and Punishments* by a young Italian reformer named Cesare Beccaria. He wrote primarily to condemn the use of torture in judicial proceedings. Religious inquisitors and witch hunters had for centuries noticed that proof of witchcraft almost disappeared once suspects stopped being questioned under torture. Beccaria extended the implications of that critique to the general use of torture in Continental courtrooms to prove crimes and then turned to the question of the proper punishment once crimes had been proved. Beccaria is historically significant not only because his book took Europe by storm but also because unlike More, Williams, Castellio, and Milton, Beccaria was not arguing that the criminal did not deserve death. For the first time, Beccaria was arguing that the government should not execute even a criminal who "deserved it."

Like the English social contract theorists Hobbes and Locke, Beccaria believed that society was at its heart a contract in which the individual gave up some of his sovereignty over himself in exchange for mutual security. But no man could surrender what he did not own, Beccaria argued, namely the right to take his own life. Beccaria offered a more practical argument against the death penalty:

> It is not the intensity of punishment that has the greatest effect on the human spirit, but its duration, for our sensibility is more easily and more permanently affected by slight but repeated impressions than by a powerful but momentary action. The sway of habit is universal over every sentient being; as man speaks and walks and satisfies his needs by its aid, so the ideas of morality come to be stamped upon the mind only by long and repeated impressions. It is not the terrible yet momentary spectacle of the death of a wretch, but the long and painful example of a man deprived of liberty, who having become a beast of burden, recompenses with his labors the society he has offended, which is the strongest curb against crimes. That efficacious idea—efficacious, because very often repeated to ourselves—"I myself shall be reduced to so long and miserable a condition if I commit a similar misdeed" is far more potent than the idea of death, which men envision always at an obscure distance. . . .
>
> The death penalty becomes for the majority a spectacle and for some others an object of compassion mixed with disdain; these two sentiments rather than the

salutary fear which the laws pretend to inspire occupy the spirits of the spectators. But in moderate and prolonged punishments the dominant sentiment is the latter, because it is the only one. The limit which the legislator ought to fix on the rigor of punishments would seem to be determined by the sentiment of compassion itself, when it begins to prevail over every other in the hearts of those who are the witnesses of punishment, inflicted for their sake rather than for the criminal's.

For a punishment to be just it should consist of only such gradations of intensity as suffice to deter men from committing crimes. Now, the person does not exist who, reflecting upon it, could choose for himself total and perpetual loss of personal liberty, no matter how advantageous a crime might seem to be. Thus the intensity of the punishment of a life sentence of servitude, in place of the death penalty, has in it what suffices to deter any determined spirit. It has, let me add, even more. Many men are able to look calmly and with firmness upon death—some from fanaticism, some from vanity, which almost always accompanies man even beyond the tomb, some from a final and desperate attempt either to live no longer or to escape their misery. But neither fanaticism nor vanity can subsist among fetters or chains, under the rod, under the yoke, in a cage of iron, where the desperate wretch does not end his woes but merely begins them. Our spirit resists violence and extreme but momentary pains more easily than it does time and incessant weariness, for it can, so to speak, collect itself for a moment to repel the first, but the vigor of its elasticity does not suffice to resist the long and repeated action of the second. . . .

But he who foresees a great number of years, or even a whole lifetime to be spent in servitude and pain, in sight of his fellow citizens with whom he lives in freedom and friendship, slave of the laws which once afforded him protection, makes a useful comparison of all this with the uncertainty of the result of his crimes, and the brevity of the time in which he would enjoy their fruits. The perpetual example of those whom he actually sees the victims of their own carelessness makes a much stronger impression upon him than the spectacle of a punishment that hardens more than it corrects him.

The death penalty cannot be useful, because of the example of barbarity it gives men. If the passions or the necessities of war have taught the shedding of human blood, the laws, moderators of the conduct of men, should not extend the beastly example, which becomes more pernicious since the inflicting of legal death is attended with much study and formality. It seems to me absurd that the laws, which are an expression of the public will, which detest and punish homicide, should themselves commit it, and that to deter citizens from murder, they order a public one.[14]

Beccaria was stating ideas whose times had come. He was praised by philosophers such as David Hume in England and Voltaire in France and was quoted by English judge and legal writer William Blackstone as well as by American lawyers such as John Adams, in his defense of the British soldiers charged for their role in the 1770 Boston Massacre, and Thomas Jefferson, in his "Bill for Proportioning Crimes and Punishments" (1779), an unsuccessful attempt to revise the laws of Virginia to limit capital punishment to cases of treason and murder. More important, Empress Maria Teresa and Grand Duke Leopold actually repealed death penalty laws within the Austria-Hungarian Empire and in Tuscany. Beccaria's argument that deterrence and not retribution should dictate the measure of punishment was attractive to the style of the Enlightenment era because it avoided appeal to any religious belief and because its balancing of crime against punishment was secular, logical, almost algebraic.

Law in the colonies was anything but logical. The United States is a common-law country whose legal system was inherited from the English tradition that developed after the Norman conquest and relied on judges (who were in theory the alter egos of the king, who could not do justice in person) giving reasons for their decisions that were then used as precedent in the next similar case and by the next judge. On the Continent, the contrasting system was the so-called civil law system based on the prevailing influence of Justinian's Code, which (again in theory) covered all cases and needed only to be consulted without a judicial gloss. Common-law judges, even if they would describe their role as merely finding the law and not making it, see themselves as independent lawgivers and not just servants of the legislator.

In England, the struggle by Parliament for independence and then supremacy led to a push in the 17th and 18th centuries (e.g., in 1679 for habeas corpus reform and in 1701 for tenure during good behavior) for separation of the judicial power from the executive power because the judges were perceived as allies of the Crown and dangerous to liberty. The United States was settled predominantly by colonists who for religious, political, or economic reasons did not get along with the way things were in England, which meant that most of them in theory believed in parliamentary supremacy. Parliament legislated rarely in the colonies—its attempts to do so after the Seven Years' War (1756–1763) sparked the American Revolution—but royal judges, particularly the admiralty judges who enforced customs laws, were a daily presence. One of the reasons that the Articles of Confederation omitted any judicial system for the new United States and the Constitution sketched only the barest outlines of a national judiciary was the historic fear of judges as the natural allies of tyranny.

The Eighth Amendment, banning cruel and unusual punishments, was intended as a check on federal judges acting like English judges of the past and on Congress giving judges excessive power. As Patrick Henry said in opposing Virginia's ratification of the Constitution without a Bill of Rights:

> What has distinguished our ancestors?—That they would not admit of tortures, or cruel and barbarous punishment. But Congress may introduce the practice of the civil law, in preference to that of the common law. They may introduce the practice of France, Spain, and Germany—of torturing, to extort a confession of the crime.[15]

Abraham Holmes said virtually the same thing in opposing ratification in the Massachusetts convention:

> They are nowhere restrained from inventing the most cruel and unheard-of punishments, and annexing them to crimes; and there is no constitutional check on them, but that *racks* and *gibbets* may be amongst the most mild instruments of their discipline.[16]

Of the states that ratified the Constitution, Pennsylvania, Virginia, New York, and North Carolina expressly called for a Bill of Rights banning cruel and unusual punishments.

The founding fathers of the United States were profoundly attached to the idea that English liberty had been achieved through conscious struggle against monarchy and that the Revolution was necessary to prevent the encroachment by the Crown and its ministers on that liberty. In framing the Constitution and the

Bill of Rights, the founding fathers looked back to history as a guide and were not radicals who wished to make an entirely new start. Though attracted by Beccaria's arguments, they were not willing to discard seven centuries of English criminal law for Beccaria's single book, and the new American states and the federal government all maintained the traditional punishment of death for treason, murder, piracy, rape, and other felonies.

Nevertheless, Beccaria's ideas landed on American soil well prepared to receive it. Pennsylvania in particular, with its Quaker heritage, retained the death penalty for fewer crimes than any other state. Beccaria came to American lawyers filtered through the most influential law book in the colonies, Blackstone's *Commentaries on the Laws of England* (1765–1769):

> We may farther observe that sanguinary laws are a bad symptom of the distemper of any state, or at least of it's [*sic*] weak constitution. The laws of the Roman kings, and the twelve tables of the *decemviri,* were full of cruel punishments: the Porcian law, which exempted all citizens from sentence of death, silently abrogated them all. In this period the republic flourished: under the emperors severe punishments were revived; and then the empire fell.[17]

That American governments took Blackstone's cautions against "sanguinary" laws to heart was recognized by Alexis de Tocqueville, who visited America in the 1830s to write about the American prison system. In *Democracy in America,* the French writer explained:

> In no country is criminal justice administered with more mildness than in the United States. While the English seem disposed carefully to retain the bloody traces of the dark ages in their penal legislation, the Americans have almost expunged capital punishment from their codes. North America is, I think, the only one country upon earth in which the life of no one citizen has been taken for a political offense in the course of the last fifty years.[18]

As de Tocqueville was writing, American punishment for crime was indeed changing for the milder. Throughout the previous two centuries, the most common reason an Englishman or an American might end up in jail was for indebtedness. By the 1830s, federal and state legislators were finally abolishing imprisonment for debt. The public spectacle of executions had become obnoxious or even frightening to civic leaders, as the previous solemnity of a public hanging had taken on the atmosphere of a carnival. Beginning in the 1830s, executions were moved out of the public square and into the penitentiary with only a few official witnesses, a development that would continue for a century. In the 1840s and 1850s, some of the states of the Old Northwest Territory, notably Michigan and Wisconsin, abolished the death penalty.

The total abolition of the death penalty was a step that most were not prepared to take. John Stuart Mill, an influential 19th-century liberal, delivered a speech before Parliament on April 21, 1868, in favor of capital punishment. English abolitionists proposed a ban on capital punishment. They rejected retribution as a justification for the death penalty, maintaining that it is absurd to teach respect for life by destroying it. Mill disagreed. He said that the system inflicts suffering on criminals so they will not inflict suffering on the innocent. Fining a criminal does not show disrespect for property. Imprisoning a criminal does not show disrespect for personal freedom. It follows that executing a murderer does not show disrespect for human life. On the contrary, it underscores our regard for human life by enforcing a rule that he who takes a life shall forfeit his own.

> Much has been said of the sanctity of human life, and the absurdity of supposing that we can teach respect for life by ourselves destroying it. But . . . this argument . . . might be brought against any punishment whatever. . . . Does fining a criminal show want of respect for property, or imprisoning him, for personal freedom? Just as unreasonable is it to think that to take the life of a man who has taken that of another is to show want of regard for human life. We show, on the contrary, most emphatically our regard for it, by the adoption of a rule that he who violates that right in another forfeits it for himself, and that while no other crime that he can commit deprives him of his right to live, this shall.[19]

Abolitionists also criticized the death penalty as cruel and inhumane. Mill countered that it is the *least* cruel method of deterring murderers. Life imprisonment places the criminal in "a living tomb" long after the crime has faded from memory. A long life of imprisonment and arduous toil may be crueler that the "short pang of rapid death":

> When there has been brought home to any one, by conclusive evidence, the greatest crime known to the law; and when the attendant circumstances suggest no palliation of the guilt, no hope that the culprit may even yet not be unworthy to live among mankind, nothing to make it probable that the crime was an exception to his general character rather than a consequence of it, then I confess it appears to me that to deprive the criminal of the life of which he has proved himself to be unworthy—solemnly to blot him out from the fellowship of mankind and from the catalogue of the living—is the most appropriate as it is certainly the most impressive, mode in which society can attach to so great a crime the penal consequences which for the security of life it is indispensable to annex to it. I defend this penalty, when confined to atrocious cases, on the very ground on which it is commonly attacked—on that of humanity to the criminal; as beyond comparison the least cruel mode in which it is possible adequately to deter from the crime. . . . What comparison can there really be, in point of severity, between consigning a man to the short pang of a rapid death, and immuring him in a living tomb, there to linger out what may be a long life in the hardest and most monotonous toil, without any of its alleviations or rewards—debarred from all pleasant sights and sounds, and cut off from all earthly hope . . . ?[20]

Where was the Eighth Amendment's ban on cruel and unusual punishments in all this? As with the rest of the Bill of Rights, it was regarded as a restraint on the federal government only, not on the states, and as an unnecessary restraint at that. As Supreme Court justice Joseph Story wrote in his text *Commentaries on the Constitution* (1833):

> This is an exact transcript of a clause in the bill of rights, framed at the revolution of 1688. The provision would seem to be wholly unnecessary in a free government, since it is scarcely possible, that any department of such a government should authorize, or justify such atrocious conduct. It was, however, adopted as an admonition to all departments of the national government, to warn them against such violent proceedings, as had taken place in England in the arbitrary reigns of some of the Stuarts.[21]

The Eighth Amendment, in other words, had been copied from the English Bill of Rights of 1689 as a symbol of continuity, not as a change in the law. There is no doubt that Justice Story was right. Beccaria's deterrence rationale for punishment, and not the Eighth Amendment, remained the polestar for death penalty abolitionists in America until the 20th century. In that century, arguments over the death penalty would take place in new venues, in academic disciplines and legal institutions not even dreamed of by the framers of the Eighth Amendment. But the Eighth Amendment would become the rallying cry of death penalty abolitionists and retentionists alike.

The Constitution was ratified in 1787, the Fifth Amendment in 1791, and the Fourteenth Amendment in 1868. They reflect an acceptance of the legitimacy of the death penalty, providing that no person shall be deprived of "life, liberty, or property, without due process of law." Persons can be deprived of their *lives* if they receive due process of law.

But the death penalty is constitutionally impermissible if it is inflicted in a "cruel or unusual fashion." Methods of execution change. Methods of execution matter. What is "cruel and unusual" today may have been regarded as "humane and commonplace" yesterday. Courts apply such concepts with an eye toward "evolving standards of decency."

In 1972 the Supreme Court struck down a death penalty law in *Furman v. Georgia* (408 U.S. 238, 1972). The divided Court objected to the appearance of racial bias or arbitrariness in the *application* of the death penalty. Responding to *Furman,* many states revised their death penalty laws to reduce jury sentencing discretion. In 1976 in *Gregg v. Georgia* (428 U.S. 153, 1976) and two companion cases, *Proffitt v. Florida* (428 U.S. 242, 1976) and *Jurek v. Texas* (428 U.S. 262, 1976), the Court ruled that modified death penalty laws successfully addressed the *Furman* objections. Announcing the decision of the majority and writing for a plurality of three justices in *Gregg,* Justice Potter Stewart said that the Eighth Amendment draws its meaning from "the evolving standards of decency that mark the progress of a maturing society" (quoting *Trop v. Dulles,* 356 U.S. 86, 1958). "Excessive" punishments that inflict unnecessary pain or that are grossly disproportionate to the severity of the crime are prohibited. But capital punishment for the crime of murder is not invariably disproportionate. It is an extreme sanction suitable to the most extreme crimes.

"Humane capital punishment" may appear to be an oxymoron to some, but some methods of execution are crueler than others. Burning at the stake, breaking on the wheel, pressing under stones, drawing and quartering, boiling in oil, disembowelment, crucifixion, and beheading were once common and usual. Today, they are rejected as incompatible with contemporary standards of decency. Standards of decency evolve, and questions about the relevance of the Eighth Amendment to capital punishment evolve as well from questions about what methods of execution are forbidden, to what crimes deserve the death penalty, to who can be executed, to how guilt can be proved and how errors should be corrected, to the question whether we continue to employ capital punishment at all. This point is explored in the following chapters in cases decided by the Supreme Court.

To understand the law of capital punishment in the United States, one must read Supreme Court opinions. They can be difficult to read, and because their style changes over time, it is important to be able to pick out the common features of opinions from different eras. Not every opinion has all the same elements in the same order, but most begin with a statement of the specific facts of the case.

This is not just good literary style: because the justices' review of cases is almost completely discretionary, the facts of the case chosen for review often signal which way the Court is going to rule. For instance, *Coker v. Georgia* (1977) struck down the death penalty for rape. The defendant in the case they chose to announce this rule was serving a sentence for murder, two rapes, kidnapping, and aggravated assault and was at large after an escape when he committed the rape that earned him the death sentence. The Court did not choose a close case or one in which the defendant merited even a description of mitigating factors. This indicates how strong the support on the Court was for the principle that no crime less than murder merits the death penalty. The two dissenting opinions, by contrast, spent far more time explaining the circumstances of the crime to illustrate why they thought the Court was making a mistake on the law and choosing a particularly undeserving defendant to benefit.

Another reason why the facts are important is the principle that the Supreme Court, like all federal courts, has limited jurisdiction. This is not just a modest slogan. Unlike many European courts and even several state courts that have the power to render advisory opinions—statements as to how the law might apply in hypothetical situations—Article III of the Constitution limits federal courts to deciding "Cases and Controversies." This means that an issue cannot be decided if it does not affect the life or liberty of a real person. I cannot ask a court what might happen to me if I were convicted of murder in the course of a robbery, even though I did not kill anyone or anticipate that anyone might be killed; only someone convicted who wishes to challenge his or her sentence can. As a result, the development of the law proceeds in what looks from the outside like lurches followed by long pauses. Furthermore, I cannot normally ask a federal court for a ruling if I have already served a prison sentence (or been executed), because the answer to my question is an academic exercise only: the case is moot. Because it is not always apparent to the Court what the facts of a case are, the Court sometimes grants review only to find that the issue it wanted to review is not properly presented, and in such cases the writ of certiorari may be dismissed as improvidently granted.

The next section of a Supreme Court opinion to look for is the explanation of the prior proceedings. This is a set of facts involving not the defendant or the crime but the decisions of the lower federal and/or state courts. Particularly in the modern era, the Court will often not grant review to a legal issue until several courts of appeal have considered it and ruled in conflicting fashion. The choice of court from which review was granted offers few hints as to how the justices will rule, although in recent decades when the Supreme Court grants review of a ruling from the Ninth Circuit Court of Appeals, it is safe to predict a reversal. In the 1980s when Justice O'Connor joined the Court and Justice William Rehnquist became chief justice, the Court continued to reverse death penalty cases and overturn state laws on direct review but became increasingly deferential to state court decisions when it reviewed habeas corpus decisions. As a result, to understand a decision one must know whether the Supreme Court is reviewing a ruling of a state's highest court or the grant or denial of a writ of habeas corpus by a federal court after the state courts have finished considering a matter.

In most appellate opinions, a court will announce the precise legal issue or two issues that it believes are the focus of the case. In Supreme Court jurisprudence, the legal issue is normally phrased in the form of a question, often in the precise wording of the petition for a writ of certiorari that the Court granted. How the Court phrases the question presented can render its conclusion self-evident, at least to the majority. That is why the dissent often quarrels not with the majority's presentation of the facts but instead with its formulation of the issues.

The holding is the shortest part of the opinion: for example, "the stay of execution is vacated, and the decision denying the petitioner a writ of *habeas corpus* is affirmed." Obviously, this is the most important part of the case to the litigants, particularly to the condemned defendant on death row. The Court attempts to give broad guidance and does not sit to correct each error committed in earlier proceedings. But holdings have this legal importance: they state legal principles or precedents that bind lower courts in future cases. Additional statements of legal principles not necessary to support the holding are sometimes offered. These statements are called obiter dicta ("something said in passing") that is above and beyond what was necessary to decide the case. Whether a point of law is dictum or not may be unclear. For example, in *Coker v. Georgia,* the Court stated that rape "of an adult woman" could not be punished by death. In 2008 the Court heard *Kennedy v. Louisiana,* a case involving rape of a child. A significant part of the argument in the *Kennedy* case concerned whether the adjective "adult" was part of *Coker's* holding or merely dictum.

The statement of the rationale explains the holding. This part of the case makes it an authoritative precedent for future cases and not merely a decision of importance to the disputing parties in the case at hand. As such, the rationale is often the most memorable aspect of a case: "Separate is inherently unequal"; "The power to tax is the power to destroy"; "One person, one vote"; and "Free speech would not protect falsely shouting 'fire' in a crowded theater." These legal sound bites are famous, but many lawyers could not describe the facts of the cases from which they are taken (*Brown v. Board of Education, McCulloch v. Maryland, Reynolds v. Sims,* and *Schenck v. United States,* respectively) or even their holdings. How the rationale is framed and phrased influences how controversial the ruling will be and how many justices will join in support.

In a common-law system, the notion of stare decisis means that the precedent established by one case should apply to future similar cases. A matter once decided by a majority of the Court should ordinarily be accepted as a rule in the next case even by the justices who originally dissented. The justices are often accused, in Hamlet's phrase, of honoring this custom "more in the breach" (William Shakespeare, *Hamlet, Prince of Denmark,* Act 1, Scene 4). It is true, as you will read, that the justices have sometimes reversed course with enough haste that it looks like the only reason for the change was the change in the roster of the justices. One common feature of recent Senate confirmation hearings is to see a prospective justice grilled about his or her respect for stare decisis by a senator from the party opposite the president, as the senator throws up a controversial legal issue on which the new justice might conceivably have an impact. But all of the justices, regardless of their political position, regard stare decisis as less binding in decisions involving constitutional interpretation because they consider the Court to be the final arbiter of what the Constitution requires. Unlike the Court's interpretation of statutes, its "incorrect" interpretation of the Constitution cannot be corrected by Congress or a state legislature.

Such constitutional interpretations can be modified through the enactment of constitutional amendments or by the Court itself as it revisits and reinterprets constitutional provisions. In the death penalty area, it has not been unusual for the Court to limit rationales, backtrack, and even reverse previous decisions.

One must also take into account the separate opinions of the justices. In English and colonial practice when several judges sat together, each would announce his opinion of what the law was, and only after each one explained would it be clear what the court had decided. The importance of an individual judge's views was limited when practicing before anyone but that judge. Beginning with John Marshall, the fourth chief justice of the Supreme Court (1801–1835), the Court began announcing an "opinion of the Court." A justice who disagreed with the majority was free to pen a dissent, and one who agreed with the result but not the reasoning of the majority could write a concurrence. Although the law is what today's majority says it is, concurrences and dissents are still important: when a decision gains only the support of a plurality of the Supreme Court, lower courts look to the narrowest concurrence for guidance about what the decision really means. And, of course, with the replacement of a justice, today's dissent is sometimes tomorrow's majority opinion.

Notes

1. More extensive treatment of some of the material from this section appeared in Joseph A. Melusky and Keith A. Pesto, *The Capital Punishment Debate* (Santa Barbara, CA: Greenwood, 2011). For a related but expanded discussion of different methods of execution, see Melusky, "From Burning at the Stake to Lethal Injection: Evolving Standards of Decency and Methods of Execution," a paper delivered at a meeting of the National Social Science Association, Las Vegas, NV (April 17–19, 2011).

2. Michael H. Reggio, "History of the Death Penalty," PBS.org, http://www.pbs.org/wgbh/pages/frontline/shows/execution/readings/history.html.

3. "Ancient History Sourcebook: Code of Hammurabi, c. 1780 BCE," Fordham University, http://www.fordham.edu/halsall/ancient/hamcode.asp.

4. "Ancient History Sourcebook: The Code of the Nesilim, c. 1650–1500 BCE," Fordham University, http://www.fordham.edu/halsall/ancient/1650nesilim.asp.

5. For excerpts from the Code of Draco, see Joseph A. Melusky and Keith A. Pesto, *Cruel and Unusual Punishment: Rights and Liberties under the Law* (Santa Barbara, CA: ABC-CLIO, 2003), 201–202.

6. Aristotle, *The Athenian Constitution,* translated by P. J. Rhodes (London: Penguin, 1984), 48.

7. "Ancient History Sourcebook: The Twelve Tables, c. 450 BCE," Fordham University, http://www.fordham.edu/halsall/ancient/12tables.asp. Creditors could "cut pieces" from the debtor.

8. Genesis 2:17, RSV.

9. Genesis 18:25, RSV.

10. The resulting *Corpus Juris Civilis* (Body of Civil Law) was in use in the Byzantine Empire for the next 900 years. See "Medieval Sourcebook: The Institutes, 535 CE," Fordham University, http://www.fordham.edu/halsall/basis/535institutes.asp.

11. Reggio, "History of the Death Penalty."

12. Robert L. Heilbroner, *The Worldly Philosophers* (New York: Simon and Schuster, 1961), 18.

13. "The History of Execution Methods," Russian Information Network, http://istina .rin.ru/eng/ufo/text/296.html.

14. Cesare Baccaria, *On Crimes and Punishments,* translated by Henry Paolucci (1764; Englewood Cliffs, NJ: Prentice Hall, 1963), 46–50.

15. Neil H. Cogan, ed., *The Complete Bill of Rights* (New York: Oxford University Press, 1997), 619.

16. Ibid.

17. William Blackstone, *Commentaries on the Laws of England,* Vol. 4, *Of Public Wrongs* (1769; Chicago: University of Chicago Press, 1979), 17.

18. Alexis de Tocqueville, *Democracy in America,* translated by Henry Reeve, edited by Henry Steele Commager (1840; New York: Oxford University Press, 1947), 368.

19. John Stuart Mill, "Speech in Favor of Capital Punishment," Ethics Update, http:// ethics.sandiego.edu/Books/Mill/Punishment/index.html.

20. Ibid.

21. Joseph Story, *Commentaries on the Constitution of the United States* (1833; Durham, NC: Carolina Academic press, 1987), 710–711.

Cases: Evolving Standards of Decency and the U.S. Supreme Court's Responses to the Death Penalty

Chapter 2
The Road from *Wilkerson to Furman:* 1878–1971

Death by Firing Squad

Wilkerson v. Utah
March 17, 1879

INTRODUCTION

The Supreme Court's first discussion of the death penalty in *Wilkerson v. Utah* did not occur until almost 100 years after the drafting of the Constitution. Wilkerson was convicted of murder and was sentenced to be put to death by a firing squad. The unanimous Court concluded that death by firing squad did not violate the Constitution's ban on cruel and unusual punishment.

At this time Utah was a territory, and Congress provided that an appeal would be available to criminal defendants sentenced to capital punishment. Wilkerson challenged the judge's authority to order him to be executed by firing squad. The federal government and most states used hanging as the method of execution.

JUSTICE CLIFFORD announced the judgment of the Court.

[T]he presiding justice in open court sentenced the prisoner as follows: That "you be taken from hence to some place in this Territory, where you shall be safely kept until . . . the last-named day [when] you [will] be taken from your place of confinement to some place within this district, and that you there be publicly shot until you are dead."

. . . Territories are invested with legislative power . . . [to] define offences and prescribe the punishment of the offenders, subject to the prohibition of the Constitution that

cruel and unusual punishments shall not be inflicted.

... Different statutory regulations existed in the Territory for nearly a quarter of a century, and the usages of the army to the present day are that sentences ... may in certain cases be executed by shooting, and in others by hanging. ...

[T]he authorities referred to are quite sufficient to show that the punishment of shooting as a mode of executing the death penalty for the crime of murder in the first degree is not [cruel and unusual punishment] within the meaning of the eighth amendment.

Soldiers convicted of capital military offences are in the great majority of cases sentenced to be shot, and the ceremony for such occasions is given in great fullness by the writers upon the subject of courts-martial.

... Difficulty would attend the effort to define with exactness the extent of the constitutional provision which provides that cruel and unusual punishments shall not be inflicted; but

it is safe to affirm that punishments of torture ... and all others in the same line of unnecessary cruelty, are forbidden by that amendment to the Constitution.

The Supreme Court here cited the text by Justice Joseph Story that is quoted in chapter 1.

The death penalty was part of the criminal law of the federal government from the very first crime bill passed by Congress in 1790. The only controversy over that bill was whether the corpses of executed criminals should be made available to medical schools for dissection. Congress provided that they would be.

The Court cited several legal treatises, including the writings of William Blackstone, an English judge and legal professor who between 1765 and 1769 wrote the four-volume *Commentaries on the Laws of England*. Blackstone's convenient summary of centuries of law made *Commentaries* a best seller in the colonies and before the American Civil War were the foundation of a legal education for young lawyers such as Abraham Lincoln. Blackstone disapproved of the excessive use of the death penalty in English law in his time.

The Supreme Court's conclusion that the Eighth Amendment's ban on "cruel and unusual punishments" barred torture but not executions remained the accepted wisdom for another century. The Court also cited Justice Thomas Cooley's work *A Treatise on the Constitutional Limitations Which Rest upon the Legislative Power of the States of the American Union* (1868). Justice Cooley, a Michigan Supreme Court justice from 1865 to 1885, was America's most influential legal writer in the latter half of the 19th century. He suggested that punishments such as beheading were "unusual" and therefore were barred by the Eighth Amendment because they had fallen out of regular use.

Death by Electrocution

In re Kemmler

May 23, 1890

INTRODUCTION

A decade later the Supreme Court considered execution by electrocution, then a brand-new technology. William Kemmler was the first person sentenced to die by electrocution. In 1885 Governor Grover Cleveland of New York, just before resigning to become president, recommended that a commission be appointed to study whether scientific advances could replace hanging, "which has come down to us from the dark ages," by "a less barbarous manner" of execution. In 1888 the state legislature provided that "[t]he punishment of death must, in every case, be inflicted by causing to pass through the body of the convict a current of electricity of sufficient intensity to cause death, and the application of such current must be continued until such convict is dead." The state legislature had determined that electrocution was "a more humane method" than hanging and would produce an "instantaneous" and "painless" death. Kemmler argued that electrocution was cruel and unusual punishment.

CHIEF JUSTICE FULLER delivered the opinion of the Court.

The Supreme Court had decided in 1833 that the Bill of Rights restrained only the federal government, not the states. The Fourteenth Amendment, ratified in 1868, prohibited states from denying "liberty" without due process of law. In the late 19th century, jurists began to argue that this provision—the Due Process Clause—had the effect of extending either all or parts of the Bill of Rights to the states as well. The idea of extending the Bill of Rights by way of the Fourteenth Amendment was called "incorporation." In this case, the Court considered whether the Eighth Amendment's ban on cruel and unusual punishment was included as part of the Fourteenth Amendment's Due Process Clause.

. . . The eighth amendment . . . [prohibits] cruel and unusual punishments. . . . [T]he fourteenth amendment . . . provides[s] that . . . [n]o state shall . . . deprive any person of life, liberty, or property without due process of law. . . . It is . . . urged that . . . the state [is prohibited] from the imposition of cruel and unusual punishments by inclusion in the term "due process of law." . . .

It is not contended, as it could not be, that the Eighth Amendment was intended to apply to the States, but it is urged that the . . . Fourteenth Amendment . . . is a prohibition on the State from the imposition of

The source of the Eighth Amendment was the language of the English Bill of Rights, drafted by Parliament and presented to William of Orange and Mary in 1689 as a condition of their holding the throne after the Glorious Revolution that ousted James II.

cruel and unusual punishments,

and that such punishments are . . . prohibited by inclusion in the term "due process of law." . . .

. . . This declaration of rights had reference to the acts of the executive and judicial departments of the government of England; but the language in question, as used in the

Constitution of the State of New York, was intended particularly to operate upon the legislature of the state, to whose control the punishment of crime was almost wholly confided. So that, if the punishment prescribed for an offense against the laws of the State were manifestly cruel and unusual as burning at the stake, crucifixion, breaking on the wheel, or the like, it would be the duty of the courts to adjudge such penalties to be within the constitutional prohibition. And we think this equally true of the eighth amendment, in its application to Congress. . . .

Punishments are cruel when they involve torture or a lingering death; but the punishment of death is not cruel within the meaning of that word as used in the Constitution. It implies there something inhuman and barbarous— something more than the mere extinguishment of life. The courts of New York held that the mode adopted in this instance might be said to be unusual because it was new, but that it could not be assumed to be cruel in the light of that common knowledge which has stamped certain punishments as such; that it was for the legislature to say in what manner sentence of death should be executed [and] that this act was passed in the effort to devise a more humane method of reaching the result. . . .

The Court asserts two principles of law: that the death penalty is not itself cruel and that the phrase "cruel and unusual" means "cruel" rather than "unusual."

. . . [The Fourteenth Amendment] was not designed to interfere with the power of the state to protect the lives, liberties, and property of its citizens, and to promote their health, peace, morals, education, and good order. The enactment of this statute was, in itself, within the legitimate sphere of the legislative power of the state, and in the observance of those general rules prescribed by our systems of jurisprudence; and the legislature of the state of New York determined that it did not inflict cruel and unusual punishment, and its courts have sustained that determination.

We cannot perceive that the state has thereby abridged the privileges or immunities of the petitioner, or deprived him of due process of law. . . .

The Supreme Court's opinion that Kemmler could be electrocuted was unanimous. Notwithstanding the legislative optimism that death would be instantaneous and therefore painless, Kemmler's execution was sufficiently gruesome that future executions were closed to witnesses and the electric chair itself was moved from the model penitentiary at Auburn to Sing Sing.

Second Attempts at Execution

Louisiana ex rel. Francis v. Resweber

January 13, 1947

INTRODUCTION

The question of whether the Eighth Amendment applied to states by way of the Fourteenth Amendment's Due Process Clause returned to the Court in 1947 in a case involving Willie Francis. By the end of the New Deal, President Franklin D. Roosevelt had appointed justices who believed that the Court had a special duty to scrutinize legislation or practices that affected criminal prosecutions and civil rights generally. Because even today more than 95 percent of criminal prosecutions are state prosecutions, the Supreme Court had many more opportunities to examine the application of the Bill of Rights to state and local law enforcement practices.

Willie Francis was sentenced to die in the electric chair for a murder committed when he was 15. Instead of sending the condemned to death row, at this time Louisiana sent its electric chair with a portable generator by truck to the individual parish (county) jail when it was time to execute a criminal. The first attempt to electrocute Francis failed when the chair malfunctioned. Would a second electrocution attempt be cruel and unusual punishment? The majority of the Court found no constitutional violation.

The Fifth Amendment forbids double jeopardy, or trying someone twice for the same crime: "nor shall any person be subject for the same offence to be twice put in jeopardy of life or limb." The justices were also asked to consider whether issuing a second death warrant for the same crime created a case of double jeopardy.

JUSTICE REED announced the judgment of the Court in an opinion in which THE CHIEF JUSTICE [VINSON], JUSTICE BLACK and JUSTICE JACKSON join.

. . . The petitioner, Willie Francis, is a colored citizen of Louisiana. He was duly convicted of murder, and, in September, 1945, sentenced to be electrocuted for the crime. Upon a proper death warrant, Francis was prepared for execution and on May 3, 1946, pursuant to the warrant, was placed in the official electric chair of the State of Louisiana in the presence of the authorized witnesses.

The executioner threw the switch, but, presumably because of some mechanical difficulty, death did not result. He was thereupon removed from the chair and returned to prison, where he now is. A new death warrant was issued by the Governor of Louisiana, fixing the execution for May 9, 1946. . . .

To determine whether or not the execution of the petitioner may fairly take place after the experience through which he passed, we shall examine the circumstances under the assumption, but without so deciding, that

violation of the principles of the Fifth and Eighth Amendments as to double jeopardy and cruel and unusual punishment would be violative of the Due Process Clause of the Fourteenth Amendment.

23

As nothing has been brought to our attention to suggest the contrary, we must and do assume that the state officials carried out their duties under the death warrant in a careful and humane manner. Accidents happen for which no man is to blame. We turn to the question as to whether the proposed enforcement of the criminal law of the state is offensive to any constitutional requirements to which reference has been made.

First. Our minds rebel against permitting the same sovereignty to punish an accused twice for the same offense. . . . When an accident, with no suggestion of malevolence, prevents the consummation of a sentence, the state's subsequent course in the administration of its criminal law is not affected on that account by any requirement of due process under the Fourteenth Amendment. We find no double jeopardy here which can be said to amount to a denial of federal due process in the proposed execution.

Second. We find nothing in what took place here which amounts to cruel and unusual punishment in the constitutional sense. The case before us does not call for an examination into any punishments except that of death. . . . The traditional humanity of modern Anglo-American law forbids the infliction of unnecessary pain in the execution of the death sentence. Prohibition against the wanton infliction of pain has come into our law from the Bill of Rights of 1688. The identical words appear in our Eighth Amendment. The Fourteenth would prohibit by its Due Process Clause execution by a state in a cruel manner. . . .

"Prohibition against the wanton infliction of pain has come into our law from the Bill of Rights of 1688."

Petitioner's suggestion is that, because he once underwent the psychological strain of preparation for electrocution, now to require him to undergo this preparation again subjects him to a lingering or cruel and unusual punishment. Even the fact that petitioner has already been subjected to a current of electricity does not make his subsequent execution any more cruel in the constitutional sense than any other execution. The cruelty against which the Constitution protects a convicted man is cruelty inherent in the method of punishment, not the necessary suffering involved in any method employed to extinguish life humanely. The fact that an unforeseeable accident prevented the prompt consummation of the sentence cannot, it seems to us, add an element of cruelty to a subsequent execution. There is no purpose to inflict unnecessary pain, nor any unnecessary pain involved in the proposed execution. The situation of the unfortunate victim of this accident is just as though he had suffered the identical amount of mental anguish and physical pain in any other occurrence, such as, for example, a fire in the cell block. We cannot agree that the hardship imposed upon the petitioner rises to that level of hardship denounced as denial of due process because of cruelty. . . .

JUSTICE FRANKFURTER, concurring.

When four members of the Court find that a State has denied to a person the due process which the Fourteenth Amendment safeguards, it seems to me important to be explicit regarding the criteria by which the State's duty of obedience to the Constitution must be judged. Particularly is this so when life is at stake. . . .

In an impressive body of decisions, this Court has decided that the Due Process Clause of the Fourteenth Amendment expresses a demand for civilized standards which are not defined by the specifically enumerated guarantees of the Bill of Rights. . . .

. . . In short,

the Due Process Clause of the Fourteenth Amendment did not withdraw the freedom of a State to enforce its own notions of fairness in the administration of criminal justice unless, as it was put for the Court by Mr. Justice Cardozo, "in so doing, it offends some principle of justice so rooted in the traditions and conscience of our people as to be ranked as fundamental." . . .

Once we are explicit in stating the problem before us in terms defined by an unbroken series of decisions, we cannot escape acknowledging that it involves the application of standards of fairness and justice very broadly conceived. They are not the application of merely personal standards, but the impersonal standards of society which alone judges, as the organs of Law, are empowered to enforce. . . .

I cannot bring myself to believe that for Louisiana to leave to executive clemency, rather than to require, mitigation of a sentence of death duly pronounced upon conviction for murder because a first attempt to carry it out was an innocent misadventure, offends a principle of justice "rooted in the traditions and conscience of our people." Short of the compulsion of such a principle, this Court must abstain from

---

Justice Felix Frankfurter had written a classic work on the trial and executions of Nicola Sacco and Bartolemeo Vanzetti and as a law professor had called for the abolition of the death penalty. He reasoned that since the first failure was unintentional, a second attempt would be constitutionally permissible. Justice Frankfurter's opinions often illustrated the conflict between the justice's liberal personal views and his legal philosophy that the judiciary should defer to the political branches of government. In Justice Frankfurter's deciding vote, this concept of judicial restraint prevailed over his personal opposition to executions.

Justice Frankfurter succeeded Justice Benjamin Cardozo on the Court. In *Palko v. Connecticut* (1937), Cardozo articulated the above test for determining which provisions of the Bill of Rights were so "fundamental" that they should be incorporated into the Fourteenth Amendment and applied to the states as well. The *Palko* test became this era's mainstream theory of incorporation, although later justices from both the Left and the Right criticized its subjectivity, with some complaining that it allowed justices to import their personal preferences into the Constitution and others complaining that the Fourteenth Amendment should make the entire Bill of Rights applicable to states just as it applied to the federal government.

interference with State action no matter how strong one's personal feeling of revulsion against a State's insistence on its pound of flesh. . . . I cannot rid myself of the conviction that, were I to hold that Louisiana would transgress the Due Process Clause if the State were allowed, in the precise circumstances before us, to carry out the death sentence, I would be enforcing my private view, rather than that consensus of society's opinion which, for purposes of due process, is the standard enjoined by the Constitution. . . .

JUSTICE BURTON, with whom JUSTICE DOUGLAS, JUSTICE MURPHY and JUSTICE RUTLEDGE concur, dissenting.

. . . [Francis] asks this Court to stay his execution on the ground that it will violate the due process of law guaranteed to him by the Constitution of the United States. We believe that the unusual facts before us require that the judgment of the Supreme Court of Louisiana be vacated, and that this cause be remanded for further proceedings not inconsistent with this opinion. . . .

. . . Taking human life by unnecessarily cruel means shocks the most fundamental instincts of civilized man. It should not be possible under the constitutional procedure of a self-governing people. Abhorrence of the cruelty of ancient forms of capital punishment has increased steadily until, today, some states have prohibited capital punishment altogether. It is unthinkable that any state legislature in modern times would enact a statute expressly authorizing capital punishment by repeated applications of an electric current separated by intervals of days or hours until finally death shall result. The Legislature of Louisiana did not do so. . . .

In determining whether the proposed procedure is unconstitutional, we must measure it against a lawful electrocution. The contrast is that between instantaneous death and death by installments—caused by electric shocks administered after one or more intervening periods of complete consciousness of the victim. . . .

"The contrast is that between instantaneous death and death by installments . . ."

The all-important consideration is that the execution shall be so instantaneous and substantially painless that the punishment shall be reduced, as nearly as possible, to no more than that of death itself. Electrocution has been approved only in a form that eliminates suffering.

The Louisiana statute . . . does not provide for electrocution by interrupted or repeated applications of electric current at intervals of several days or even minutes. It does not provide for the application of electric current of intensity less than that sufficient to cause death. It prescribes expressly and solely for the application of a current of sufficient intensity to cause death and for the continuance of that application until death results. Prescribing capital punishment, it should be construed strictly. There can be no implied provision for a second, third or multiple application of the current. There is no statutory or judicial precedent upholding a delayed process of electrocution. . . .

If the state officials deliberately and intentionally had placed [Francis] in the electric chair five times and, each time, had applied electric current to his body in a manner not sufficient, until the final time, to kill him, such a form of torture would rival that of burning at the stake. Although the failure of the first attempt, in the present case, was unintended, the reapplication of the electric current will be intentional. How many deliberate and intentional reapplications of electric current does it take to produce a cruel, unusual and unconstitutional punishment? While five applications would be more cruel and unusual than one, the uniqueness of the present case demonstrates that, today, two separated applications are sufficiently "cruel and unusual" to be prohibited. If five attempts would be "cruel and unusual," it would be difficult to draw the line between two, three, four and five. . . .

Lack of intent that the first application be less than fatal is not material. The intent of the executioner cannot lessen the torture or excuse the result. It was the statutory duty of the state officials to make sure that there was no failure. . . .

We believe that . . . the proposed action is unconstitutional. . . .

The dissenting members of the Court argued that the intent of authorities to carry out the execution the first time was irrelevant and that what counted was the effect of their actions. Because it would be torture to pretend to execute a prisoner multiple times, the dissent argued that it was also torture to do so even it this was not the officials' intent. Francis was executed at age 17.

Other Types of Cruel and Unusual Punishment

Trop v. Dulles

March 31, 1958

INTRODUCTION

This case considered how a penalty of loss of citizenship should be measured against the protections of the Eighth Amendment.

Non–death penalty sentences can also violate constitutional protections against cruel and unusual punishment. For example, in *Weems v. United States* (1910), Paul Weems, a Coast Guard official in the U.S. government of the Philippine Islands, was convicted in the territorial courts of embezzling 612 pesos. He was sentenced to 15 years of incarceration. Conditions included that he be chained from wrist to ankle and compelled to work at "hard and painful labor." Writing for the majority, Justice McKenna concluded that such a severe penalty for a relatively minor crime constituted cruel and unusual punishment. Over a dissent by Justices White and Holmes, the Court overturned the conviction in its entirety.

During the Cold War, the Court increasingly began to clash with Congress over civil rights and with state and local governments over discrimination against black citizens. Use of the death penalty declined through the 1950s, more due to fewer prosecutions in which the penalty was sought than as a direct result of action by the Supreme Court. After Willie Francis's case, the Court avoided examination of the death penalty and declined to review the espionage conviction and federal death sentences imposed on Julius and Ethel Rosenberg, who were electrocuted at Sing Sing in June 1953. The Court also avoided examination of California's death penalty in the case of Caryl Chessman, who spent an unprecedented 12 years on death row challenging his conviction in 1948 of a series of sexual assaults and kidnappings on California highways. Chessman pretended to be a police officer and tricked his victims into stopping by flashing a red light from his automobile. The first death row celebrity, Chessman filed repeated petitions in the Supreme Court (16 in all, a record for the time) until even Justice Douglas wrote in *Chessman v. Teets* (1957) that "Chessman is playing a game with the courts, stalling for time." Despite international appeals for a commuted sentence, Chessman was executed in 1960.

CHIEF JUSTICE WARREN announced the judgment of the Court and delivered an opinion, in which JUSTICE BLACK, JUSTICE DOUGLAS, and JUSTICE WHITTAKER join.

The petitioner in this case, a native-born American, is declared to have lost his United States citizenship . . . for wartime desertion.

As in *Perez v. Brownell,* the issue before us is whether this forfeiture of citizenship comports with the Constitution.

Perez v. Brownell, decided the same day, held that an American could lose his or her citizenship by voting in a foreign election.

In 1944 petitioner was a private in the United States Army, serving in French Morocco. On May 22, he escaped from a stockade at Casablanca, where he had been confined following a previous breach of discipline. The next day petitioner and a companion were walking along a road . . . in the general direction back to Casablanca, when an Army truck approached and stopped. A witness testified that petitioner boarded the truck willingly and that no words were spoken. In Rabat petitioner was turned over to military police. Thus ended petitioner's "desertion." He had been gone less than a day and had willingly surrendered to an officer on an Army vehicle while he was walking back towards his base. He testified that at the time he and his companion were picked up by the Army truck, "we had decided to return to the stockade. The going was tough. We had no money to speak of, and at the time we were on foot and we were getting cold and hungry." A general court-martial convicted petitioner of desertion and sentenced him to three years at hard labor, forfeiture of all pay and allowances, and a dishonorable discharge.

In 1952 petitioner applied for a passport. His application was denied on the ground that under the provisions of . . . the Nationality Act of 1940 . . . he had lost his citizenship by reason of his conviction and dishonorable discharge for wartime desertion. . . .

. . . The Solicitor General informed the Court that during World War II, according to Army estimates, approximately 21,000 soldiers and airmen were convicted of desertion and given dishonorable discharges. . . . Over this group of men, enlarged by whatever the corresponding figures may be for the Navy and Marines, the military has been given the power to grant or withhold citizenship. . . .

. . . We conclude that the judgment in this case must be reversed for the following reasons.

. . . [W]e must face the question whether the Constitution permits the Congress to take away citizenship as a punishment for crime. If it is assumed that the power of Congress extends to divestment of citizenship, the problem still remains as to this statute whether denationalization is a cruel and unusual punishment within the meaning of the Eighth Amendment. Since wartime desertion is punishable by death, there can be no argument that the penalty of denationalization is excessive in relation to the gravity

"Since wartime desertion is punishable by death, there can be no argument that the penalty of denationalization is excessive in relation to the gravity of the crime."

of the crime. The question is whether this penalty subjects the individual to a fate forbidden by the principle of civilized treatment guaranteed by the Eighth Amendment.

At the outset, let us put to one side the death penalty as an index of the constitutional limit on punishment.

Whatever the arguments may be against capital punishment, both on moral grounds and in terms of accomplishing the purposes of punishment—and they are forceful—the death penalty has been employed throughout our history, and, in a day when it is still widely accepted, it cannot be said to violate the constitutional concept of cruelty. But it is equally plain that the existence of the death penalty is not a license to the Government to devise any punishment short of death within the limit of its imagination.

The plurality had quietly substituted "disproportionate" as a synonym for "cruel and unusual." The four dissenters, Justices Frankfurter, Burton, Clark, and Harlan, argued that even if this is what the Eighth Amendment meant, ever since 1776 American law provided that a deserting soldier could be shot. Therefore, loss of citizenship could not be excessive. Chief Justice Warren's reply to this argument signaled to all interested observers that there was a bloc on the Court that would vote to strike down the death penalty, too.

The exact scope of the constitutional phrase "cruel and unusual" has not been detailed by this Court. . . . The basic concept underlying the Eighth Amendment is nothing less than the dignity of man. While the State has the power to punish, the Amendment stands to assure that this power be exercised within the limits of civilized standards. Fines, imprisonment and even execution may be imposed depending upon the enormity of the crime, but any technique outside the bounds of these traditional penalties is constitutionally suspect. . . . The Court [has] recognized . . . that the words of the Amendment are not precise, and that their scope is not static.

The Amendment must draw its meaning from the evolving standards of decency that mark the progress of a maturing society.

The plurality cited *Weems v. United States* as its only support for this theory. It was the first time in decades that *Weems* had even been mentioned in the Supreme Court.

We believe . . . that use of denationalization as a punishment is barred by the Eighth Amendment. . . .

A plurality of four justices voted to overturn Trop's loss of citizenship because of the Eighth Amendment. Justice Brennan concurred with the result but on the grounds that forfeiture of citizenship for desertion was not within Congress's war powers.

Changing Court Opinion

Justice Arthur Goldberg,
Memorandum to the Conference

October term, 1963

INTRODUCTION

President John F. Kennedy's two appointees, Justices Byron White and Arthur Goldberg, joined the Supreme Court in 1962. They formed a majority with Chief Justice Warren and Justices Douglas and Brennan to incorporate virtually all of the criminal law provisions of the Bill of Rights into the Due Process Clause, thus applying them to the states. In *Robinson v. California* (1962), the Court formally held that the Eighth Amendment applied to the states, ruling that California could not make narcotics addiction a crime. In the autumn of 1963, Justice Goldberg circulated a memorandum to the justices calling for the Court to strike down the death penalty as cruel and unusual punishment. Admitting that none of the lawyers in the six capital cases on the docket had made such an argument and that public opinion still supported the death penalty, Goldberg cited *Weems v. United States* as support for the Court's deciding the issue even without a request. Although the Court denied review in all six cases that term, in a memoir 25 years later Goldberg noted that his position encouraged the bar to begin challenging the legality of all capital punishment and that this led to a de facto moratorium on executions from 1968 to 1976.

. . . It may be suggested that since the death penalty is a mode of punishment "about which opinion is fairly divided" a state does not violate the Constitution when it "treats [the prisoner] by [such] a mode." *Louisiana ex rel. Francis v. Resweber* (Frankfurter, J. concurring). With all deference, this reasoning does not seem persuasive here. In certain matters—especially those relating to fair procedures in criminal trials—this Court traditionally has guided rather than followed public opinion in the process of articulating and establishing progressively civilized standards of decency. If only punishments already overwhelmingly condemned by public opinion came within the cruel and unusual punishment proscription, the Eighth Amendment would be a dead letter; for such punishments would presumably be abolished by the legislature. The Eighth Amendment, like the others in the Bill of Rights, was intended as a countermajoritarian limitation on governmental action; it should be applied to nurture rather than to retard our "evolving standards of decency." Can there be any doubt that if this court condemns the death penalty as cruel and unusual—whatever the initial effect—before too long that penalty will no longer "be a mode of punishment about which opinion is fairly divided." . . .

Selection of Jurors

Witherspoon v. Illinois

June 3, 1968

INTRODUCTION

Having made the prediction that the Court could settle political controversy over the death penalty simply by abolishing it, Justice Goldberg left the Court to become ambassador to the United Nations in 1965. The Supreme Court continued to address death penalty issues in non–capital punishment cases. *Fay v. Noia* (1963) reversed the life sentence imposed on Charles Noia for a 1942 murder on the grounds that his confession had been coerced. Noia was granted a writ of habeas corpus and released despite the objection that he had not even appealed on that ground in the state court. Justice Brennan wrote for the Court that as long as he had not "deliberately bypassed" an issue, a defendant in state custody could claim in federal court that his conviction violated the U.S. Constitution. As a result, a death row inmate could be almost certain that his execution would be stayed indefinitely even if the state courts rejected his appeals, because he could file a petition before federal district judges followed by a second round of appeals to the federal appellate courts and then followed by a petition to the Supreme Court. There was no limit on the number of times an inmate could file a petition and no requirement that the first federal habeas corpus petition be filed until the inmate actually faced an execution date. In 1966 there was one execution in the nation; in 1967 there were two. While states continued to sentence defendants to death at the rate of about 100 per year, there were no executions from 1968 onward. The Court continued to issue opinions tinkering with the death penalty, including *United States v. Jackson* (1968), which held that the federal death penalty for kidnapping was unconstitutional because it coerced a defendant into giving up the right to a jury trial: sloppy legislative drafting permitted a death sentence after trial but limited a judge to imposing a life sentence if a defendant pleaded guilty. In keeping with a decades-long concern that capital punishment was being disproportionately used on black defendants, *Boykin v. Alabama* (1969) overturned the death sentence imposed on a young black man who had pleaded guilty to five armed robberies on the grounds that the defendant did not make a knowing and voluntary waiver of his rights. In *Witherspoon v. Illinois* (1968), the Court held that states could not exclude from juries all persons opposed to the death penalty because doing so would produce juries that were not fairly representative of the community. Exclusion of jurors was permissible only if it could be shown that a juror's personal opposition to the death penalty was so strong as to prevent him or her from making an impartial decision on the defendant's guilt. A jury consisting of people who meet these specifications is said to be death-qualified.

JUSTICE STEWART delivered the opinion of the Court.

The petitioner was brought to trial in 1960 in Cook County, Illinois, upon a charge of murder. The jury found him guilty and fixed his penalty at death. At the time of his trial an Illinois statute provided: "In trials for murder it shall be a cause for challenge of any juror who shall, on being examined, state that he has conscientious scruples against capital punishment, or that he is opposed to the same."

Through this provision the State of Illinois armed the prosecution with unlimited challenges for cause in order to exclude those jurors who, in the words of the State's highest court, "might hesitate to return a verdict inflicting [death]." At the petitioner's trial, the prosecution eliminated nearly half the *venire* of prospective jurors by challenging, under the authority of this statute, any[one] who expressed qualms about capital punishment. From those who remained were chosen the jurors who ultimately found the petitioner guilty and sentenced him to death. The Supreme Court of Illinois denied post-conviction relief, and we granted *certiorari* to decide whether the Constitution permits a State to execute a man pursuant to the verdict of a jury so composed.

The issue before us is a narrow one. It does not involve the right of the prosecution to challenge for cause those prospective jurors who state that their reservations about capital punishment would prevent them from making an impartial decision as to the defendant's guilt. Nor does it involve the State's assertion of a right to exclude from the jury in a capital case those who say that they could never vote to impose the death penalty or that they would refuse even to consider its imposition in the case before them. For the State of Illinois did not stop there, but authorized the prosecution to exclude as well all who said that they were opposed to capital punishment and all who indicated that they had conscientious scruples against inflicting it.

"Let's get these conscientious objectors out of the way, without wasting any time on them."

In the present case the tone was set when the trial judge said early in the *voir dire,* "Let's get these conscientious objectors out of the way, without wasting any time on them." . . .

The petitioner contends that a State cannot confer upon a jury selected in this manner the power to determine guilt. He maintains that such a jury, unlike one chosen at random from a cross-section of the community, must necessarily be biased in favor of conviction, for the kind of juror who would be unperturbed by the prospect of sending a man to his death, he contends, is the kind of juror who would too readily ignore the presumption of the defendant's innocence, accept the prosecution's version of the facts, and return a verdict of guilt. . . .

The data adduced by the petitioner, however, are too tentative and fragmentary to establish that jurors not opposed to the death penalty tend to favor the prosecution in the determination of guilt. We simply cannot conclude, either on the basis of the record now before us or as a matter of judicial notice, that the exclusion of jurors opposed to capital punishment results in an unrepresentative jury on the issue of guilt or substantially increases the risk of conviction. In light of the presently available information, we are not prepared to announce a *per se* constitutional rule requiring the reversal of every conviction returned by a jury selected as this one was.

It does not follow, however, that the petitioner is entitled to no relief. For in this case the jury was entrusted with two distinct responsibilities: first, to determine whether the petitioner was innocent or guilty; and second, if guilty, to determine whether his sentence should be imprisonment or death. It has not been shown that this jury was biased with respect to the petitioner's guilt. But it is self-evident that, in its role as arbiter of the punishment to be imposed, this jury fell woefully short of that impartiality to which the petitioner was entitled under the Sixth and Fourteenth Amendments. . . .

The Court focused on the role of the jury in assigning a punishment rather than in making a conviction. For the justices, excluding not only those opposed to the death penalty but also all of those who were reluctant to impose it meant that the jury was not representative of a nation divided over capital punishment.

A man who opposes the death penalty, no less than one who favors it, can make the discretionary judgment entrusted to him by the State and can thus obey the oath he takes as a juror. But a jury from which all such men have been excluded cannot perform the task demanded of it. Guided by neither rule nor standard, "free to select or reject as it [sees] fit," a jury that must choose between life imprisonment and capital punishment can do little more—and must do nothing less—than express the conscience of the community on the ultimate question of life or death. Yet, in a nation less than half of whose people believe in the death penalty, a jury composed exclusively of [those favoring the death penalty] cannot speak for the community. Culled of all who harbor doubts about the wisdom of capital punishment—of all who would be reluctant to pronounce the extreme penalty—such a jury can speak only for a distinct and dwindling minority. . . . [W]hen it swept from the jury all who expressed conscientious or religious scruples against capital punishment and all who opposed it in principle, the State crossed the line of neutrality. In its quest for a jury capable of imposing the death penalty, the State produced a jury uncommonly willing to condemn a man to die. . . .

Is a death penalty jury a hanging jury? Consider California, which has the largest death row population in the United States by far but rarely executes anyone. Prosecutors in California (and elsewhere) know that the chances that an execution will be carried out are minimal but nevertheless keep seeking capital convictions. Even if it is not carried out, the death penalty serves as a bargaining chip, and prosecutors, defense counsel, and judges alike believe that jurors who would be prepared to impose the death sentence are more likely to convict in the first place. This is the flip side of Blackstone's argument that being reluctant to impose a mandatory death penalty makes jurors more likely to acquit. Like other opposites, the theory that death-qualified juries are conviction prone is not a logically necessary one. Because only one jury sits in any given trial, there is no possible way of running a controlled experiment to measure whether or how much of an effect *Witherspoon* has on convictions. Some food for thought may be provided by a 1990 study funded by the National Science Foundation in which one researcher reported that almost half of the 634 capital case jurors interviewed already had an opinion on whether death was the appropriate sentence before the penalty phase even began. Ninety-five percent of these jurors reported that they were either absolutely convinced or were pretty sure of the correctness of their decision. Three-fourths of all jurors believed that the judge's instructions only provided a framework for the decision that most jurors had already made.

Whatever else might be said of capital punishment, it is at least clear that its imposition by a hanging jury cannot be squared with the Constitution. The State of Illinois has stacked the deck against the petitioner. To execute this death sentence would deprive him of his life without due process of law. . . .

JUSTICE DOUGLAS, concurring in part.

My difficulty with the opinion of the Court is a narrow but important one. The Court permits a State to eliminate from juries some of those who have conscientious scruples against the death penalty; but it allows those to serve who have no scruples against it as well as those who, having such scruples, nevertheless are deemed able to determine after a finding of guilt whether the death penalty or a lesser penalty should be imposed. I fail to see or understand the constitutional dimensions of those distinctions.

The constitutional question is whether the jury must be "impartially drawn from a cross-section of the community," or whether it can be drawn with systematic and intentional exclusion of some qualified groups. . . .

The idea that a jury should be "impartially drawn from a cross-section of the community" certainly should not mean a selection of only those with a predisposition to impose the severest sentence or with a predisposition to impose the least one that is possible. . . .

A fair cross-section of the community may produce a jury almost certain to impose the death penalty if guilt were found; or it may produce a jury almost certain not to impose it. The conscience of the community is subject to many variables, one of which is the attitude toward the death sentence. . . .

I see no constitutional basis for excluding those who are so opposed to capital punishment that they would never inflict it on a defendant. Exclusion of them means the selection of jurors who are either protagonists of the death penalty or neutral concerning it. That results in a systematic exclusion of qualified groups, and the deprivation to the accused of a cross-section of the community for decision on both his guilt and his punishment. . . .

In the present case . . . the wholesale exclusion of a class that makes up a substantial portion of the population produces an unrepresentative jury. . . .

JUSTICE BLACK, with whom JUSTICE HARLAN and JUSTICE WHITE join, dissenting.

The Court closes its reversal of this murder case with the following graphic paragraph:

> Whatever else might be said of capital punishment, it is at least clear that its imposition by a hanging jury cannot be squared with the Constitution. The State of Illinois has stacked the deck against the petitioner. To execute this death sentence would deprive him of his life without due process of law.

I think this charge against the Illinois courts is completely without support in the record. . . . It seems particularly unfortunate to me that this Court feels called upon to charge that [the Illinois Supreme Court] would let a man go to his death after the trial court had contrived a "hanging jury" and, in this Court's language, "stacked the deck" to bring about the death sentence for petitioner.

With all due deference it seems to me that one might much more appropriately charge that this Court has today written the law in such a way that the States are being forced to try their murder cases with biased juries. If this Court is to hold capital punishment unconstitutional, I think it should do so forthrightly, not by making it impossible for States to get juries that will enforce the death penalty. . . .

The Court decided the flipside of *Witherspoon* in *Morgan v. Illinois* (1992), holding that a defendant may attempt to life-qualify a jury. That is, a capital defendant can ask specifically whether prospective jurors would automatically vote for death upon conviction of a capital offense and can challenge for cause any juror who replies in the affirmative.

The *Witherspoon* decision seems to permit the prosecutor to stack the deck by death-qualifying the jury. In fact, *Witherspoon* must be seen against the contemporary practice in most states for prosecutors to remove for cause any prospective juror who agreed that he had religious or conscientious objections or reservations about the death penalty, even if he could put them aside and follow the court's instructions. *Witherspoon* limited this exclusion to two specified cases: a juror who would vote against the death penalty regardless of the law or evidence and a juror who would not be impartial about guilt because he wished to avoid the death penalty issue.

We say "he" because the Constitution was not seen as requiring that women be eligible to serve on a criminal jury until the Supreme Court's decision in *Taylor v. Louisiana* (1975). In Louisiana, women could serve on a jury if they registered as volunteers, which resulted in jury pools being about 99 percent men. Five other states had a variation, automatically exempting women from service on request. This practice also violated the Sixth Amendment, the Supreme Court held in *Duren v. Missouri* (1979), a case argued for Duren by future justice Ruth Bader Ginsburg. But what about other exemptions? Most jurisdictions still automatically excuse persons over 70 years of age. Does that violate a defendant's right to a jury from a fair cross section of the community? We are unlikely to find out, because defense attorneys generally perceive older jurors as more likely to convict or impose a death sentence and so are unlikely to challenge that exemption.

Standardizing the Death Penalty

McGautha v. California

May 3, 1971

INTRODUCTION

The American Law Institute (ALI) was established in 1923 with the goal of improving American law. The ALI's founding came during an era that saw attempts to develop uniform laws in the 48 states in areas such as the sale of goods, banking, and commercial transactions. Eventually every state would adopt some of the ALI's proposed uniform laws. Another ALI project that began in the 1930s was the drafting of Restatements, comprehensive treatments of the laws of contracts, property, and torts designed to synthesize cases throughout the nation and explain the policy choices thought to underlie the variety of state legal rules. In time, every state's highest court would refer to the Restatements as authoritative sources of law. In the 1950s, the ALI commissioned constitutional scholar Herbert Wechsler of Columbia University to draft a Model Penal Code. Professor Wechsler was assisted by the sociologist Thorsten Sellin of the University of Pennsylvania, who had worked on the Royal Commission that successfully recommended the abolition of capital punishment in Great Britain. The Model Penal Code, completed in 1962, recommended that the death penalty be reserved only for murder with aggravating circumstances and prescribed a two-part process for capital cases in which the jury would first decide on guilt and then the jury or a judge would determine the sentence after hearing aggravating and mitigating evidence not necessarily presented at trial. The Model Penal Code approach was acclaimed by death penalty opponents, and variations on the Model Penal Code's procedure were adopted in several states. In *McGautha v. California* (1971), the Supreme Court, by a vote of 6–3, rejected the argument that due process required the Model Penal Code approach and upheld traditional state laws that gave juries complete discretion over whether or not the death penalty would be imposed on a particular defendant.

JUSTICE HARLAN delivered the opinion of the Court.

. . . McGautha . . . [was] convicted of murder in the first degree in . . . California . . . and sentenced to death pursuant to the statutes of th[e] State. . . . [T]he decision whether the defendant should live or die was left to the absolute discretion of the jury. In McGautha's case the jury, in accordance with California law, determined punishment in a separate proceeding following the trial on the issue of guilt. . . . We granted *certiorari* in the McGautha case limited to the question whether petitioner's constitutional rights were infringed by permitting the jury to impose the death penalty without any governing standards. . . . For the reasons that follow, we find no constitutional infirmity in the conviction of [the] petitioner, and we affirm. . . .

It will put the constitutional issues in clearer focus to begin by setting out the course which [the] trial took.

A. McGautha's Guilt Trial

McGautha and his co-defendant Wilkinson were charged with committing two armed robberies and a murder on February 14, 1967. In accordance with California procedure in capital cases, the trial was in two stages, a guilt stage and a punishment stage. At the guilt trial the evidence tended to show that the defendants, armed with pistols, entered the market of Mrs. Pon Lock early in the afternoon of the murder. While Wilkinson kept a customer under guard, McGautha trained his gun on Mrs. Lock and took almost $300. Roughly three hours later, McGautha and Wilkinson held up another store, this one owned by Mrs. Benjamin Smetana and operated by her with her husband's assistance. While one defendant forcibly restrained a customer, the other struck Mrs. Smetana on the head. A shot was fired, fatally wounding Mr. Smetana. Wilkinson's former girl friend testified that shortly after the robbery McGautha told her he had shot a man and showed her an empty cartridge in the cylinder of his gun. Other evidence at the guilt stage was inconclusive on the issue as to who fired the fatal shot. The jury found both defendants guilty of two counts of armed robbery and one count of first-degree murder as charged.

B. McGautha's Penalty Trial

At the penalty trial, which took place on the following day but before the same jury, the State waived its opening, presented evidence of McGautha's prior felony convictions and sentences . . . and then rested. Wilkinson testified in his own behalf . . . [and] called several witnesses in his behalf. . . .

McGautha also testified in his own behalf at the penalty hearing. . . . He called no witnesses in his behalf.

The jury was instructed in the following language:

"in this part of the trial the law does not forbid you from being influenced by pity for the defendants and you may be governed by mere sentiment and sympathy for the defendants in arriving at a proper penalty in this case; however, the law does forbid you from being governed by mere conjecture, prejudice, public opinion or public feeling."

"The defendants in this case have been found guilty of the offense of murder in the first degree, and it is now your duty to determine which of the penalties provided by law should be

". . . McGautha told her he had shot a man and showed her an empty cartridge in the cylinder of the gun."

imposed on each defendant for that offense. Now, in arriving at this determination you should consider all of the evidence received here in court presented by the People and defendants throughout the trial before this jury. You may also consider all of the evidence of the circumstances surrounding the crime, of each defendant's background and history, and of the facts in aggravation or mitigation of the penalty which have been received here in court. However, it is not essential to your decision that you find mitigating circumstances on the one hand or evidence in aggravation of the offense on the other hand. . . ."

". . . Notwithstanding facts, if any, proved in mitigation or aggravation, in determining which punishment shall be inflicted, you are entirely free to act according to your own judgment, conscience, and absolute discretion. That verdict must express the individual opinion of each juror."

. . . Late in the afternoon of August 25 the jury returned verdicts fixing Wilkinson's punishment at life imprisonment and McGautha's punishment at death.

The trial judge . . . pronounced the death sentence. McGautha's conviction was unanimously affirmed by the California Supreme Court. His contention that standardless jury sentencing is unconstitutional was rejected on the authority of an earlier case, *In re Anderson,* in which that court had divided narrowly on the issue. . . .

Before proceeding to a consideration of the issues before us, it is important to recognize and underscore the nature of our responsibilities in judging them. Our function is not to impose on the States, *ex cathedra,* what might seem to us a better system for dealing with capital cases. Rather, it is to decide whether the Federal Constitution proscribes the present procedures. . . .

The defendant argued that not giving the jury specific guidelines regarding when the death penalty should be imposed gave jurors too much freedom in selecting a punishment and was therefore a violation of the guarantee of an impartial legal process.

We consider first McGautha's . . . claim: that the absence of standards to guide the jury's discretion on the punishment issue is constitutionally intolerable . . . and . . . violates the basic command of the Fourteenth Amendment that no State shall deprive a person of his life without due process of law. Despite the undeniable surface appeal of the proposition, we conclude that the courts below correctly rejected it.

[A] . . . significant discussion of standardless jury sentencing in capital cases in our decisions is found in *Witherspoon v. Illinois.* In reaching its conclusion that persons with conscientious scruples against the death penalty could not be automatically excluded from sentencing juries in capital cases, the Court relied heavily on the fact that such juries "do little more—and must do nothing less—than express the conscience of the community on the ultimate question of life or death." The Court noted that "one of the most important functions any jury can perform in making such a selection is to maintain a link between contemporary community values and the penal system—a link without which the determination of punishment could hardly reflect 'the evolving standards of decency that mark the progress of a maturing society.' "

The inner quotation is from the opinion of Mr. Chief Justice Warren for four members of the Court in *Trop v. Dulles.*

In recent years academic and professional sources have suggested that jury sentencing discretion should be controlled by standards of some sort. The American Law Institute first published such a recommendation in 1959. Several States have enacted new criminal codes in the intervening 12 years, some adopting features of the Model Penal Code. Other States have modified their laws with respect to murder and the death penalty in other ways. None of these States have followed the Model Penal Code and adopted statutory criteria for imposition of the death penalty. In recent years, challenges to standardless jury sentencing have been presented to many state and federal appellate courts. No court has held the challenge good. . . .

In light of history, experience, and the present limitations of human knowledge, we find it quite impossible to say that committing to the untrammeled discretion of the jury the power to pronounce life or death in capital cases is offensive to anything in the Constitution.

The States are entitled to assume that jurors confronted with the truly awesome responsibility of decreeing death for a fellow human will act with due regard for the consequences of their decision and will consider a variety of factors, many of which will have been suggested by the evidence or by the arguments of defense counsel. For a court to attempt to catalog the appropriate factors in this elusive area could inhibit rather than expand the scope of consideration, for no list of circumstances would ever be really complete. The infinite variety of cases and facets to each case would make general standards either meaningless "boiler-plate" or a statement of the obvious that no jury would need. . . . Affirmed. . . .

One year later after Justices Harlan and Black retired, this decision was reversed in *Furman v. Georgia.* Only months before *Furman,* the California Supreme Court ruled in *People v. Anderson* that under California law the death penalty was cruel and unusual and therefore unconstitutional. This ruling took infamous murderers such as Sirhan Sirhan and Charles Manson off death row. It also sparked a new political movement to remove elected state court judges from the bench for their anti–death penalty rulings.

Chapter 3
From *Furman* to *Gregg*: 1972–1976

Suspending the Death Penalty

Furman v. Georgia
June 29, 1972

INTRODUCTION

Attacks on the death penalty as a form of "cruel and unusual" punishment continued during the 1960s. Executions declined. Reservations grew about the legality of capital punishment. During the 1970s, the death penalty was invalidated and later reinstated. In 1972, the Supreme Court appeared to eliminate capital punishment when it struck down Georgia's death penalty statute in *Furman v. Georgia*. The challenged statute gave juries complete discretion in imposing the death sentence. The Court held that such unguided jury discretion violated the Eighth Amendment's ban on cruel and unusual punishment. But the death penalty itself was not dealt a death blow by *Furman*.

The case, decided by a 5–4 vote, revealed a badly divided Court. The majority was unable to agree on a single opinion. Five separate concurring opinions were issued by Justices Douglas, Brennan, Stewart, White, and Marshall. Only Brennan and Marshall concluded that the death penalty *itself* had become constitutionally impermissible. The others took issue with how it had been *applied*. The four Nixon appointees—Chief Justice Burger and Justices Powell, Rehnquist, and Blackmun—dissented.

The immediate effect of the ruling was to strike down existing death penalty statutes in 40 states. *Furman* established that certain death penalty laws were unconstitutional if they were arbitrary, disproportionate to the crime, offended society's sense of justice, or were not more effective than less-severe penalties. However, as Burger pointed out in dissent, the Court's decision permitted states to make a "thorough re-evaluation" of the subject and to enact new death penalty laws that limited jury discretion.

JUSTICE DOUGLAS, JUSTICE BRENNAN, JUSTICE STEWART, JUSTICE WHITE, and JUSTICE MARSHALL have filed separate opinions in support of the judgments. THE CHIEF JUSTICE, JUSTICE BLACKMUN, JUSTICE POWELL, and JUSTICE REHNQUIST have filed separate dissenting opinions.

JUSTICE DOUGLAS, concurring.

In these three cases the death penalty was imposed, one of them for murder, and two for rape. In each the determination of whether the penalty should be death or a lighter punishment was left by the State to the discretion of the judge or of the jury. In each of the three cases the trial was to a jury. . . . [We consider] whether the . . . death penalty constitute[s] "cruel and unusual punishment" within the meaning of the Eighth Amendment as applied to the States by the Fourteenth. I vote to vacate each judgment, believing that . . . the death penalty does violate the Eighth and Fourteenth Amendments. . . .

The words "cruel and unusual" certainly include penalties that are barbaric. But the words, at least when read in light of the English proscription against selective and irregular use of penalties, suggest that it is "cruel and unusual" to apply the death penalty—or any other penalty—selectively to minorities whose numbers are few, who are outcasts of society, and who are unpopular, but whom society is willing to see suffer though it would not countenance general application of the same penalty across the board. . . .

There is increasing recognition . . . that the basic theme of equal protection is implicit in "cruel and unusual" punishments. "A penalty . . . should be considered 'unusually' imposed if it is administered arbitrarily or discriminatorily."

The Fourteenth Amendment, passed to protect newly free slaves in the wake of the Civil War, guarantees that everyone will receive "equal protection under the law." During the 1960s and 1970s, critics of the death penalty as well as of the justice system as a whole were increasingly able to show that harsh punishments were more likely to be imposed on blacks and the poor.

. . . The President's Commission on Law Enforcement and Administration of Justice recently concluded: "Finally there is evidence that the imposition of the death sentence . . . follow[s] discriminatory patterns. The death sentence is disproportionately imposed and carried out on the poor, the Negro, and the members of unpopular groups." A study of capital cases in Texas from 1924 to 1968 [concluded]: "Application of the death penalty is unequal: most of those executed were poor, young, and ignorant. . . ."

Seventy-five of the 460 cases involved co-defendants, who, under Texas law, were given separate trials. In several instances where a white and a Negro were co-defendants, the white was sentenced to life imprisonment or a term of years, and the Negro was given the death penalty. "Another ethnic disparity is found in the type of sentence imposed for rape. The Negro convicted of rape is far more likely to get the death penalty than a term sentence, whereas whites and Latins are far more likely to get a term sentence than the death penalty."

Warden Lewis E. Lawes of Sing Sing said: "Not only does capital punishment fail in its justification, but no punishment could be invented with so many inherent defects.

It is an unequal punishment in the way it is applied to the rich and to the poor. The defendant of wealth and position never goes to the electric chair or to the gallows. Juries do not intentionally favor the rich, the law is theoretically impartial, but the defendant with ample means is able to have his case presented with every favorable aspect, while the poor defendant often has a lawyer assigned by the court. Sometimes such assignment is considered part of political patronage; usually the lawyer assigned has had no experience whatever in a capital case."

Former Attorney General Ramsey Clark has said, "It is the poor, the sick, the ignorant, the powerless and the hated who are executed." . . .

Furman, a black, killed a householder while seeking to enter the home at night. Furman shot the deceased through a closed door. He was 26 years old and had finished the sixth grade in school. Pending trial, he was committed to the Georgia Central State Hospital for a psychiatric examination on his plea of insanity tendered by court-appointed counsel. The superintendent reported that a unanimous staff diagnostic conference had concluded . . . that "at present the patient is not psychotic, but he is not capable of cooperating with his counsel in the preparation of his defense"; and the staff believed "that he is in need of further psychiatric hospitalization and treatment." . . .

We cannot say from facts disclosed in these records that these defendants were sentenced to death because they were

---

Warden Lawes was president of the American Correctional Association, formerly the American Prison Association. Wardens, despite stereotypical portrayals to the contrary, were often vocal opponents of capital punishment. When the Federal Bureau of Prisons was established in 1930 during President Herbert Hoover's administration, it was strongly committed to rehabilitation as the primary goal of imprisonment. Therefore, wardens of federal prisons typically opposed the death penalty as a retributive punishment.

Ramsey Clark testified before Congress in opposition to the death penalty in 1968. He argued that it was used in a racially discriminatory way. Clark's father, Justice Tom Clark, who had voted with Douglas to affirm sentences in death penalty cases, stepped down from the Supreme Court in 1967 in part to avoid the appearance of impropriety in issuing rulings on federal government cases. President Johnson appointed Thurgood Marshall, a death penalty opponent, to replace Justice Clark.

black. Yet our task is not restricted to an effort to divine what motives impelled these death penalties. Rather, we deal with a system of law and of justice that leaves to the uncontrolled discretion of judges or juries the determination whether defendants committing these crimes should die or be imprisoned. Under these laws no standards govern the selection of the penalty. People live or die, dependent on the whim of 1 man or of 12. . . .

In a Nation committed to equal protection of the laws there is no permissible "caste" aspect of law enforcement. Yet we know that the discretion of judges and juries in imposing the death penalty enables the penalty to be selectively applied, feeding prejudices against the accused if he is poor and despised, and lacking political clout, or if he is a member of a suspect or unpopular minority, and saving those who by social position may be in a more protected position. . . .

The high service rendered by the "cruel and unusual" punishment clause of the Eighth Amendment is to require legislatures to write penal laws that are evenhanded, nonselective, and nonarbitrary, and to require judges to see to it that general laws are not applied sparsely, selectively, and spottily to unpopular groups. . . .

. . . [T]hese discretionary statutes are unconstitutional in their operation. They are pregnant with discrimination . . . not compatible with the idea of equal protection of the laws that is implicit in the ban on "cruel and unusual" punishments. . . .

I concur in the judgments of the Court.
JUSTICE BRENNAN, concurring.

The test . . . will ordinarily be a cumulative one: If a punishment is unusually severe, if there is a strong probability that it is inflicted arbitrarily, if it is substantially rejected by contemporary society, and if there is no reason to believe that it serves any penal purpose more effectively than some less severe punishment, then the continued infliction of that punishment violates the command of the Clause that the State may not inflict inhuman and uncivilized punishments upon those convicted of crimes. . . .

In comparison to all other punishments today, then, the deliberate extinguishment of human life by the State is uniquely degrading to human dignity. . . .

William Brennan, one of the most liberal justices on the Supreme Court in the 1950s and 1960s, eventually took the position that all use of capital punishment was constitutionally invalid—despite references to capital crimes in the text of the Constitution itself—because the Constitution was a "living document." This philosophy had been hinted at in *Weems v. U.S.* and suggested in *Trop v. Dulles,* but Justices Brennan and Marshall became its most famous champions.

In sum . . . [d]eath is an unusually severe and degrading punishment; there is a strong probability that it is inflicted arbitrarily; its rejection by contemporary society is virtually total; and there is no reason to believe that it serves any penal purpose more effectively than the less severe punishment of imprisonment. . . [T]hese principles . . . enable a court to determine whether a punishment comports with human dignity. Death, quite simply, does not. . . .

JUSTICE STEWART, concurring.

. . . These death sentences are cruel and unusual in the same way that being struck by lightning is cruel and unusual. For, of all the people convicted of rapes and murders in 1967 and 1968, many just as reprehensible as these, the petitioners are among a capriciously selected random handful upon whom the sentence of death has in fact been imposed. . . .

Potter Stewart's position leads to the paradox that if reserving capital punishment for unusually horrific crime makes it "capricious" and impermissible, then more frequent executions would make capital punishment constitutionally acceptable. The political history of the country has usually trended toward less use of capital punishment, so it is unlikely that Stewart's thesis will ever be tested.

[T]he Eighth and Fourteenth Amendments cannot tolerate the infliction of a sentence of death under legal systems that permit this unique penalty to be so wantonly and so freakishly imposed.

JUSTICE WHITE, concurring.

. . . I begin with what I consider a near truism: that the death penalty could so seldom be imposed that it would cease to be a credible deterrent or measurably to contribute to any other end. . . . It is perhaps true that no matter how infrequently those convicted of rape or murder are executed, the penalty so imposed is not disproportionate to the crime and those executed may deserve exactly what they received. It would also be clear that executed defendants are finally and completely incapacitated from again committing rape or murder or any other crime. But when imposition of the penalty reaches a certain degree of infrequency, it would be very doubtful that any existing general need for retribution would be measurably satisfied. Nor could it be said with confidence that society's need for specific deterrence justifies death for so few when for so many in like circumstances life imprisonment or shorter prison terms are judged sufficient, or that community values are measurably reinforced by authorizing a penalty so rarely invoked.

Most important, a major goal of the criminal law—to deter others by punishing the convicted criminal—would not be substantially served where the penalty is so seldom invoked that it ceases to be the credible threat essential to influence the conduct of others. For present purposes I accept the morality and utility of punishing one person to influence another. I accept also the effectiveness of punishment generally and need not reject the death penalty as a more effective deterrent than a lesser punishment.

But common sense and experience tell us that seldom-enforced laws become ineffective measures for controlling human conduct and that the death penalty, unless imposed with sufficient frequency, will make little contribution to deterring those crimes for which it may be exacted.

The imposition and execution of the death penalty are obviously cruel in the dictionary sense. But the penalty has not been considered cruel and unusual punishment in the constitutional sense because it was thought justified by the social ends it was deemed to serve. At the moment that it ceases realistically to further these purposes, however, the emerging question is whether its imposition . . . would violate the Eighth Amendment. It is my view that it would, for its imposition would then be the pointless and needless extinction of life with only marginal contributions to any discernible social or public purposes. A penalty with such negligible returns to the State would be patently excessive and cruel and unusual punishment violative of the Eighth Amendment. . . .

For Byron White, a former deputy attorney general appointed to the Court by President Kennedy, the commonly accepted reasons for punishment are retribution, rehabilitation, deterrence of the offender (or interdiction), and deterrence of others. White generally accepted retribution as justifying capital punishment. For interdiction and rehabilitation, however, White reasoned that if punishments less than death worked equally well, capital punishment lost its justification. Regarding deterrence, or preventing future crimes, White found that a penalty so rarely applied was not a credible deterrent. White was a member of the middle bloc of justices. In close votes, his opinion could swing the outcome. Consequently, White's focus made evidence concerning the deterrent effects of capital punishment a key issue in post-*Furman* cases.

JUSTICE MARSHALL, concurring.

. . . Perhaps the most important principle in analyzing "cruel and unusual" punishment questions is one that is reiterated again and again in the prior opinions of the Court: i.e., the cruel and unusual language "must draw its meaning from the evolving standards of decency that mark the progress of a maturing society." Thus, a penalty that was permissible at one time in our Nation's history is not necessarily permissible today. . . .

Marshall, like Brennan, saw the Constitution as a living document. Like Justice Goldberg, Marshall believed that it was the Court's duty to lead public opinion and therefore the political processes by interpreting the Constitution. Marshall maintained that if properly informed, the public would abolish the death penalty. In his view, some things (such as segregation and capital punishment) are inherently evil, and no amount of popular support can make them legally acceptable.

. . . [H]istory demonstrates that capital punishment was carried from Europe to America but, once here, was tempered considerably. At times in our history, strong abolitionist movements have existed. But, they have never been completely successful, as no more than one-quarter of the States of the Union have, at any one time, abolished the death penalty. They have had partial success, however, especially in reducing the number of capital crimes, replacing mandatory death sentences with jury discretion, and developing more humane methods of conducting executions.

. . . The question now to be faced is whether American society has reached a point where abolition . . . is demanded by the Eighth Amendment. . . .

There is but one conclusion that can be drawn from all of this—i.e., the death penalty is an excessive and unnecessary punishment that violates the Eighth Amendment. The statistical evidence is . . . persuasive. . . . [F]or more than 200 years men have labored to demonstrate that capital punishment serves no purpose that life imprisonment could not serve equally well. . . . Little, if any, evidence has been adduced to prove the contrary. . . . There is no rational basis for concluding that capital punishment is not excessive. It therefore violates the Eighth Amendment.

"[F]or more than 200 years men have labored to demonstrate that capital punishment serves no purpose that life imprisonment could not serve equally well."

In addition, even if capital punishment is not excessive, it nonetheless violates the Eighth Amendment because it is morally unacceptable to the people of the United States at this time in their history. . . .

While a public opinion poll obviously is of some assistance in indicating public acceptance or rejection of a specific penalty, its utility cannot be very great. This is because whether or not a punishment is cruel and unusual depends, not on whether its mere mention "shocks the conscience and sense of justice of the people," but on whether people who were fully informed as to the purposes of the penalty and its liabilities would find the penalty shocking, unjust, and unacceptable.

In other words, the question with which we must deal is not whether a substantial proportion of American citizens would today, if polled, opine that capital punishment is barbarously cruel, but whether they would find it to be so in the light of all information presently available. . . .

Assuming knowledge of all the facts presently available regarding capital punishment, the average citizen would, in my opinion, find it shocking to his conscience and sense of justice. For this reason alone capital punishment cannot stand. . . .

CHIEF JUSTICE BURGER, with whom JUSTICE BLACKMUN, JUSTICE POWELL, and JUSTICE REHNQUIST join, dissenting.

. . . Since there is no majority of the Court on the ultimate issue presented in these cases, the future of capital punishment in this country has been left in an uncertain limbo. Rather than providing a final and unambiguous answer on the basic constitutional question, the collective impact of the majority's ruling is to demand an undetermined measure of change from the various state legislatures and the Congress. While I cannot endorse . . . today's result . . . , I am not altogether displeased that legislative bodies have been given the opportunity, and indeed unavoidable responsibility, to make a thorough re-evaluation of the entire subject of capital punishment. If today's opinions demonstrate nothing else, they starkly show that this is an area where legislatures can act far more effectively than courts.

The legislatures are free to eliminate capital punishment for specific crimes or to carve out limited exceptions to a general abolition of the penalty, without adherence to the conceptual strictures of the Eighth Amendment. The legislatures can and should make an assessment of the deterrent influence of capital punishment, both generally and as affecting the commission of specific types of crimes. If legislatures come to doubt the efficacy of capital punishment, they can abolish it, either completely or on a selective basis. If new evidence persuades them that they have acted unwisely, they can reverse their field and reinstate the penalty to the extent it is thought warranted. An Eighth Amendment ruling by judges cannot be made with such flexibility or discriminating precision. . . .

Since Reconstruction, the Court has had nine justices. The resulting two maxims of Supreme Court politics are that "it takes five votes to get anything done" and "with five votes you can do almost anything." Nevertheless, the value of an opinion as legal precedent depends on the opinion's intrinsic cogency and the cohesion of the group of justices who agree with it. Each of the four dissenting justices in *Furman* published his own opinion, but all were united behind Chief Justice Burger in emphasizing that capital punishment itself was not being abolished and could be salvaged if legislatures would make some procedural improvements. State legislators responded.

Reinstating the Death Penalty

Gregg v. Georgia
July 2, 1976

INTRODUCTION

Furman struck down existing death penalty laws. Subsequently, 35 states responded to the invitation in Burger's dissent by passing revised death penalty statutes. Ten states attempted to eliminate jury discretion by making the death penalty mandatory for certain crimes. Twenty-five states implemented the two-stage procedure that had been recommended in the Model Penal Code in capital cases but not required by *McGautha*: the first stage of the trial would determine guilt or innocence, and the second stage would determine punishment. The question now became whether such modified death penalty laws met the objections of the *Furman* majority.

In 1976, the Supreme Court reviewed new death penalty laws in *Gregg v. Georgia* and two companion cases, *Proffitt v. Florida* and *Jurek v. Texas*. The Court upheld modified death penalty laws in Georgia, Florida, and Texas and refused to declare that the death penalty is unconstitutional in all cases. Justice Stewart announced the Court's judgment that the death penalty itself was constitutionally permissible as long as its application avoided the defects described in *Furman*. In strong dissents, Justices Brennan and Marshall reaffirmed their *Furman* positions that the death penalty was constitutionally impermissible "for whatever crime and under all circumstances."

The unofficial moratorium on executions that began with *Witherspoon* in 1968 ended when Gary Gilmore was executed by a firing squad in Utah on January 17, 1977. Gilmore did not challenge his death sentence. His last recorded words were "Let's do it." Capital punishment was back.

Judgment of the Court, and opinion of JUSTICE STEWART, JUSTICE POWELL, and

JUSTICE STEVENS, announced by JUSTICE STEWART.

The issue in this case is whether the imposition of the sentence of death for the crime of murder under the law of Georgia violates the Eighth and Fourteenth Amendments.

The petitioner, Troy Gregg, was charged with committing armed robbery and murder. In accordance with Georgia procedure in capital cases, the trial was in two stages, a guilt stage and a sentencing stage. The evidence at the guilt trial established that on November 21, 1973, the petitioner and a traveling companion, Floyd Allen, while hitchhiking north in Florida were picked up by Fred Simmons and Bob Moore. . . . [T]he four men interrupted their journey for a rest stop along the highway. The next morning the bodies of Simmons and Moore were discovered in a ditch nearby.

. . . [T]he petitioner and Allen, while in Simmons' car, were arrested in Asheville, N.C. In the search incident to the arrest a .25-caliber pistol, later shown to be that used to kill Simmons and Moore, was found in the petitioner's pocket.

After receiving the warnings required by *Miranda v. Arizona*, and signing a written waiver of his rights, the petitioner signed a statement in which he admitted shooting, then robbing Simmons and Moore. He justified the slayings on grounds of self-defense. . . .

In *Miranda v. Arizona* (1966), the Court addressed the Fifth Amendment's protections against forced incrimination. The Court created the now famous *Miranda* warning by ruling that suspects in custody must be informed that they have the right to remain silent and the right to have an attorney present before being interrogated by police.

The trial judge submitted the murder charges . . . [and] the robbery case to the jury. . . . The jury found the petitioner guilty of two counts of armed robbery and two counts of murder.

At the penalty stage, which took place before the same jury, neither the prosecutor nor the petitioner's lawyer offered any additional evidence. Both counsel, however, made lengthy arguments dealing generally with the propriety of capital punishment under the circumstances and with the weight of the evidence of guilt. The trial judge instructed the jury that it could recommend either a death sentence or a life prison sentence on each count. The judge further charged the jury that in determining what sentence was appropriate the jury was free to consider the facts and circumstances, if any, presented by the parties in mitigation or aggravation.

Finally, the judge instructed the jury that it "would not be authorized to consider [imposing] the penalty of death" unless it first found beyond a reasonable doubt one of these aggravating circumstances:

"One—That the offense of murder was committed while the offender was engaged in the commission of two other capital felonies, to-wit the armed robbery of [Simmons and Moore].

"Two—That the offender committed the offense of murder for the purpose of receiving money and the automobile described in the indictment.

"Three—The offense of murder was outrageously and wantonly vile, horrible and inhuman, in that they [*sic*] involved the depravity of [the] mind of the defendant."

Finding the first and second of these circumstances, the jury returned verdicts of death on each count.

The Supreme Court of Georgia affirmed the convictions and the imposition of the death sentences for murder. . . . The death sentences imposed for armed robbery, however, were vacated on the grounds that the death penalty had rarely been imposed in Georgia for that offense and that the jury improperly considered the murders as aggravating circumstances for the robberies after having considered the armed robberies as aggravating circumstances for the murders. . . .

It is clear from . . . precedents that the Eighth Amendment has not been regarded as a static concept. As Mr. Chief Justice Warren said, in an oft-quoted phrase, "[t]he Amendment must draw its meaning from the evolving standards of decency that mark the progress of a maturing society." *Trop v. Dulles.* Thus, an assessment of contemporary values concerning the infliction of a challenged sanction is relevant to the application of the Eighth Amendment. . . . [T]his assessment does not call for a subjective judgment. It requires, rather, that we look to objective indicia that reflect the public attitude toward a given sanction.

But our cases also make clear that public perceptions of standards of decency with respect to criminal sanctions are not conclusive.

A penalty also must accord with "the dignity of man," which is the "basic concept underlying the Eighth Amendment." This means, at least, that the punishment not be "excessive." When a form of punishment in the abstract (in this case, whether capital punishment may ever be imposed as a sanction for murder) rather than in the particular (the propriety of death as a penalty to be applied to a specific defendant for a specific crime) is under consideration, the inquiry into "excessiveness" has two aspects. First, the punishment must not involve the unnecessary and wanton infliction of pain. . . . Second, the punishment must not be grossly out of proportion to the severity of the crime. *Trop v. Dulles.* . . .

Of course, the requirements of the Eighth Amendment must be applied with an awareness of the limited role to be played by the courts. . . .

Therefore, in assessing a punishment selected by a democratically elected legislature against the constitutional measure, we presume its validity. We may not require the

Although accepting Brennan and Marshall's "evolving standards of decency" principle, the plurality emphasized that the Court should not incautiously substitute its judgment for that of the elected legislatures. The role of the Court, they stressed, was to provide an outer boundary for the severity of punishments, and because the death penalty was expressly provided for in the Fifth and Fourteenth Amendments, it was a permissible sanction for the crime of murder. Unlike the previous Georgia practice of having the jury engage in the decision between life and death without guidance, Georgia's revised two-phase approach required the jury, after finding a defendant guilty of murder, to consider evidence of aggravating and mitigating circumstances before imposing a sentence of death and, more important, to specify what factors it relied on in reaching its decision. Furthermore, the Georgia Supreme Court was required to review those findings and determine whether the death penalty was disproportionate.

legislature to select the least severe penalty possible so long as the penalty selected is not cruelly inhumane or disproportionate to the crime involved. And a heavy burden rests on those who would attack the judgment of the representatives of the people. . . .

. . . We now consider specifically whether the sentence of death for the crime of murder is a *per se* violation of the Eighth and Fourteenth Amendments to the Constitution. We note first that history and precedent strongly support a negative answer to this question.

The imposition of the death penalty for the crime of murder has a long history of acceptance both in the United States and in England. . . .

It is apparent from the text of the Constitution itself that the existence of capital punishment was accepted by the Framers. At the time the Eighth Amendment was ratified, capital punishment was a common sanction in every State. Indeed, the First Congress of the United States enacted legislation providing death as the penalty for specified crimes. . . .

"It is apparent from the text of the Constitution itself that the existence of capital punishment was accepted by the Framers."

And the Fourteenth Amendment, adopted over three-quarters of a century later, similarly contemplates the existence of the capital sanction in providing that no State shall deprive any person of "life, liberty, or property" without due process of law. . . .

Four years ago, the petitioners in *Furman* and its companion cases predicated their argument primarily upon the asserted proposition that standards of decency had evolved to the point where capital punishment no longer could be tolerated. The petitioners in those cases said, in effect, that the evolutionary process had come to an end, and that standards of decency required that the Eighth Amendment be construed finally as prohibiting capital punishment for any crime regardless of its depravity and impact on society. This view was accepted by two Justices. Three other Justices were unwilling to go so far; focusing on the procedures by which convicted defendants were selected for the death penalty rather than on the actual punishment inflicted, they joined in the conclusion that the statutes before the Court were constitutionally invalid.

The petitioners in the capital cases before the Court today renew the "standards of decency" argument, but developments

"The legislatures of at least 35 States have enacted new statutes that provide for the death penalty for at least some crimes that result in the death of another person."

during the four years since *Furman* have undercut substantially the assumptions upon which their argument rested. . . .

The most marked indication of society's endorsement of the death penalty for murder is the legislative response to *Furman.* The legislatures of at least 35 States have enacted new statutes that provide for the death penalty for at least some crimes that result in the death of another person. And the Congress of the United States, in 1974, enacted a statute providing the death penalty for aircraft piracy that results in death. These recently adopted statutes have attempted to address the concerns expressed by the Court in *Furman* primarily (i) by specifying the factors to be weighed and the procedures to be followed in deciding when to impose a capital sentence, or (ii) by making the death penalty mandatory for specified crimes. But all of the post-*Furman* statutes make clear that capital punishment itself has not been rejected by the elected representatives of the people.

In the only statewide referendum occurring since *Furman* and brought to our attention, the people of California adopted a constitutional amendment that authorized capital punishment, in effect negating a prior ruling by the Supreme Court of California . . . that the death penalty violated the California Constitution. . . .

The jury also is a significant and reliable objective index of contemporary values because it is so directly involved. . . . It may be true that evolving standards have influenced juries in recent decades to be more discriminating in imposing the sentence of death. But the relative infrequency of jury verdicts imposing the death sentence does not indicate rejection of capital punishment *per se.* Rather, the reluctance of juries in many cases to impose the sentence may well reflect the humane feeling that this most irrevocable of sanctions should be reserved for a small number of extreme cases. . . .

As we have seen, however, the Eighth Amendment demands more than that a challenged punishment be acceptable to contemporary society. The Court also must ask whether it comports with the basic concept of human dignity at the core of the Amendment. . . .

The death penalty is said to serve two principal social purposes: retribution and deterrence of capital crimes by prospective offenders.

In part, capital punishment is an expression of society's moral outrage at particularly offensive conduct. This function may be unappealing to many, but it is essential in an ordered society that asks its citizens to rely on legal processes rather than self-help to vindicate their wrongs. . . .

The plurality accepted that retribution was not a forbidden objective. Justice Stewart approved the view that "certain crimes are themselves so grievous an affront to humanity that the only adequate response may be the penalty of death." In contrast, Justice Marshall thought that capital punishment denied the inalienable dignity and worth of even a guilty wrongdoer.

Statistical attempts to evaluate the worth of the death penalty as a deterrent to crimes by potential offenders have occasioned a great deal of debate. The results simply have been inconclusive. . . .

Although the plurality remarked that the evidence that the death penalty acted as a deterrent was "inconclusive," the Court was familiar with a 1975 study by University of Chicago professor Isaac Ehrlich. Ehrlich estimated that between 1933 and 1967, each capital execution deterred eight murders. U.S. solicitor general Robert Bork appeared and argued in favor of the constitutionality of the death penalty, heavily emphasizing Ehrlich's study. During the 1970s, the economic analysis of law movement centered at the University of Chicago began profoundly reshaping many fields of law and public policy. *Gregg v. Georgia* signals the first major influence of this analytical approach on the Supreme Court.

In sum, we cannot say that the judgment of the Georgia Legislature that capital punishment may be necessary in some cases is clearly wrong. . . .

Finally, we must consider whether the punishment of death is disproportionate in relation to the crime for which it is imposed. There is no question that death as a punishment is unique in its severity and irrevocability. . . . But we are concerned here only with the imposition of capital punishment for the crime of murder, and when a life has been taken deliberately by the offender, we cannot say that the punishment is invariably disproportionate to the crime. It is an extreme sanction, suitable to the most extreme of crimes.

We hold that the death penalty is not a form of punishment that may never be imposed, regardless of the circumstances of the offense, regardless of the character of the offender, and regardless of the procedure followed in reaching the decision to impose it.

We now consider whether Georgia may impose the death penalty on the petitioner in this case. . . .

Furman mandates that where discretion is afforded a sentencing body on a matter so grave as the determination of whether a human life should be taken or spared, that discretion must be suitably directed and limited so as to minimize the risk of wholly arbitrary and capricious action. . . .

Jury sentencing has been considered desirable in capital cases in order "to maintain a link between contemporary community values and the penal system—a link without which the determination of punishment could hardly reflect 'the evolving standards of decency that mark the progress of a maturing society.'" But it creates special problems. . . . Those who have studied the question suggest that a bifurcated procedure—one in which the question of sentence is not considered until the determination of guilt has been made—is the best answer. . . .

> *"While some have suggested that standards to guide a capital jury's sentencing deliberation are impossible to formulate, the fact is that such standards have been developed."*

While some have suggested that standards to guide a capital jury's sentencing deliberation are impossible to formulate, the fact is that such standards have been developed. . . . While such standards are by necessity somewhat general, they do provide guidance to the sentencing authority and thereby reduce the likelihood that it will impose a sentence that fairly can be called capricious or arbitrary. Where the sentencing authority is required to specify the factors it relied upon in reaching its decision, the further safeguard of meaningful appellate review is available to ensure that death sentences are not imposed capriciously or in a freakish manner.

In summary, the concerns expressed in *Furman* that the penalty of death not be imposed in an arbitrary or capricious manner can be met by a carefully drafted statute that ensures that the sentencing authority is given adequate information and guidance. As a general proposition these concerns are best met by a system that provides for a bifurcated proceeding at which the sentencing authority is apprised of the information relevant to the imposition of sentence and provided with standards to guide its use of the information. . . .

We now turn to consideration of the constitutionality of Georgia's capital-sentencing procedures. In the wake of *Furman,* Georgia amended its capital punishment statute, but chose not to narrow the scope of its murder provisions. Thus, now as before *Furman,* in Georgia "[a] person commits murder when he unlawfully and with malice aforethought, either express or implied, causes the death of another human being." All persons convicted of murder "shall be punished by death or by imprisonment for life."

Georgia did act, however, to narrow the class of murderers subject to capital punishment by specifying statutory aggravating circumstances, one of which must be found by the jury to exist beyond a reasonable doubt before a death sentence can ever be imposed. In addition, the jury is authorized to consider any other appropriate aggravating or mitigating circumstances. The jury is not required to find any mitigating circumstance in order to make a recommendation of mercy that is binding on the trial court, but it must find a statutory aggravating circumstance before recommending a sentence of death.

These procedures require the jury to consider the circumstances of the crime and the criminal before it recommends sentence. No longer can a Georgia jury do as *Furman's* jury did: reach a finding of the defendant's guilt and then, without guidance or direction, decide whether he should live or die. Instead, the jury's attention is directed to the specific circumstances of the crime: Was it committed in the course of another capital felony? Was it committed for money? Was it committed upon a peace officer or judicial officer? Was it committed in a par-ticularly heinous way or in a manner that endangered the lives of many persons? In addition, the jury's attention is focused on the characteristics of the person who committed the crime: Does he have a record of prior convictions for capital offenses? Are there any special facts about this defendant that mitigate against imposing capital punishment (e.g., his youth, the extent of his cooperation with the police, his emotional state at the time of the crime)? As a result, while some jury discretion still exists, "the discretion to be exercised is controlled by clear and objective standards so as to produce non-discriminatory appli-cation." . . .

Finally, the Georgia statute has an additional provision designed to assure that the death penalty will not be imposed on a capriciously selected group of convicted defendants. The new sentencing procedures require that the State Supreme Court review every death sentence. . . .

It is apparent that the Supreme Court of Georgia has taken its review responsibilities seriously. . . . [A]lthough armed rob-bery is a capital offense under Georgia law, the Georgia court concluded that the death sentences imposed in this case for that crime were "unusual in that they are rarely imposed for [armed robbery]. Thus, under the test provided by statute . . . they must be considered to be excessive or disproportionate to the penalties imposed in similar cases." The court there-fore vacated Gregg's death sentences for armed robbery and has followed a similar course in every other armed robbery death penalty case to come before it.

The provision for appellate review in the Georgia capital-sentencing system serves as a check against the random or arbitrary imposition of the death penalty. . . .

"The provision for appellate review in the Georgia capital-sentencing system serves as a check against the random or arbitrary imposition of the death penalty."

For the reasons expressed in this opinion, we hold that the statutory system under which Gregg was sentenced to death does not violate the Constitution. Accordingly, the judgment of the Georgia Supreme Court is affirmed. . . .

JUSTICE WHITE, with whom THE CHIEF JUSTICE and JUSTICE REHNQUIST join, concurring in the judgment. [Omitted]

JUSTICE BLACKMUN, concurring in the judgment. [Omitted]

JUSTICE BRENNAN, dissenting.

The Cruel and Unusual Punishments Clause "must draw its meaning from the evolving standards of decency that mark the progress of a maturing society." The [majority] opinions . . . hold that "evolving standards of decency" require focus not on the essence of the death penalty itself but primarily upon the procedures employed by the State to single out persons to suffer the penalty of death. Those opinions hold further that, so viewed, the Clause invalidates the mandatory infliction of the death penalty but not its infliction under sentencing procedures that . . . adequately safeguard against the risk that the death penalty was imposed in an arbitrary and capricious manner.

In *Furman v. Georgia,* I read "evolving standards of decency" as requiring focus upon the essence of the death penalty itself and not primarily or solely upon the procedures under which the determination to inflict the penalty upon a particular person was made. . . .

Justice White's concurrence stuck to a narrow focus on the text of the Georgia statute, emphasizing that it provided a list of aggravating factors that a jury could consider and from which a jury had to unanimously find at least one before imposing the death sentence. Most important, the new statute provided for mandatory judicial review to determine whether the death sentence was imposed in a discriminatory or standardless fashion.

Brennan took his dissent to the level of principle. Quoting American sociologist Thorsten Sellin and French writer Albert Camus, Brennan asserted that capital punishment denied the humanity of the defendant.

This Court inescapably has the duty, as the ultimate arbiter of the meaning of our Constitution, to say whether . . . "moral concepts" require us to hold that the law has progressed to the point where we should declare that the punishment of death, like punishments on the rack, the screw, and the wheel, is no longer morally tolerable in our civilized society. My opinion in *Furman v. Georgia* concluded that our civilization and the law had progressed to this point and that therefore the punishment of death, for whatever crime and under all circumstances, is "cruel and unusual" in violation of the Eighth and Fourteenth Amendments of the Constitution. . . .

The fatal constitutional infirmity in the punishment of death is that it treats "members of the human race as nonhumans, as objects to be toyed with and discarded. [It is] thus inconsistent with the fundamental premise of the Clause that even the vilest criminal remains a human being possessed of common human dignity." As such it is a penalty that "subjects the individual to a fate forbidden by the principle of civilized treatment guaranteed by the [Clause]." I therefore would hold, on that ground alone, that death is today a cruel and unusual punishment prohibited by the Clause. "Justice of this kind is obviously no less shocking than the crime itself, and the new 'official' murder, far from offering redress for the offense committed against society, adds instead a second defilement to the first." . . .

JUSTICE MARSHALL, dissenting.

. . . In *Furman* I concluded that the death penalty is constitutionally invalid for two reasons. First, the death penalty is excessive. And second,

the American people, fully informed as to the purposes of the death penalty and its liabilities, would in my view reject it as morally unacceptable.

Between *Furman* and *Gregg*, at least 460 persons were sentenced to death under reenacted capital punishment statutes. Nevertheless, Marshall did not focus on whether a procedure was popular, or formally correct, but instead focused on whether it reflected a knowing, intelligent, and voluntary decision. Framing the issue this way, Marshall continued to assert that the reenactment of death penalty statutes reflected a failure of the public to be fully informed about the death penalty.

Since the decision in *Furman*, the legislatures of 35 States have enacted new statutes authorizing the imposition of the death sentence for certain crimes, and Congress has enacted a law providing the death penalty for air piracy resulting in death. I would be less than candid if I did not acknowledge that these developments have a significant bearing on a realistic assessment of the moral acceptability of the death penalty to the American people. But if the constitutionality of the death penalty turns, as I have urged, on the opinion of an informed citizenry, then even the enactment of new death statutes cannot be viewed as conclusive. In *Furman*, I observed that the American people are largely unaware of the information critical to a judgment on the morality of the death penalty, and concluded that if they were better informed they would consider it shocking, unjust, and unacceptable. A recent study, conducted after the enactment of the post-*Furman* statutes, has confirmed that the American people know little about the death penalty, and that the opinions of an informed public would differ significantly from those of a public unaware of the consequences and effects of the death penalty. . . .

Chapter 4

After *Gregg*: 1976–1982

Mandatory Death Penalties

Woodson v. North Carolina

July 2, 1976

INTRODUCTION

Executions resumed in the United States following the Supreme Court's decision in *Gregg*. Public debate intensified. Some supporters maintained that capital punishment deters crime. However, a study of capital punishment from 1976 through 1989 concluded that the death penalty does little to deter capital crime. Using statistics from the FBI's *Uniform Crime Report,* the study concluded that regions that use the death penalty the least are the safest for police officers. On the other hand, police officers are most at risk in the South, where executions are carried out most frequently.[1]

In a number of cases decided between 1976 and 1982, the Supreme Court found fault with death penalty practices and applications. In *Woodson v. North Carolina* (1976), the Court struck down mandatory death sentences for convicted murderers if the character of the defendant and the circumstances of the crime were not taken into account. In *Coker v. Georgia* (1977), the Court held that a death sentence for rape of an adult woman is disproportionate to the crime. In *Lockett v. Ohio* (1978), the Court invalidated a death sentence where the jury had not been permitted to consider all relevant mitigating circumstances. In *Godfrey v. Georgia* (1980), the Court struck down as too vague a state law that called for the death penalty for "outrageous or wantonly vile" crimes. In *Eddings v. Oklahoma* (1982), the Court again struck down a death sentence because relevant mitigating circumstances had not been considered.

In *Woodson v. North Carolina* and the companion case, *Roberts v. Louisiana,* the Court struck down state laws that made the death penalty mandatory for first-degree murder. The Court voted 5–4, with Justices Brennan, Marshall, Stewart, Powell, and Stevens in the majority. Chief Justice Burger and Justices Blackmun, White, and Rehnquist were in the minority.

**Judgment of the Court, and opinion of JUSTICE STEW-
ART, JUSTICE POWELL, and JUSTICE STEVENS,
announced by JUSTICE STEWART.**

**The question in this case is whether the imposition of
a death sentence for the crime of first-degree murder
under the law of North Carolina violates the Eighth and
Fourteenth Amendments. . . .**

Four men participated in an armed robbery of a convenience food store: James Tyrone Woodson, Luby Waxton, Leonard Tucker, and Johnnie Lee Carroll. During the robbery, a cashier was killed and a customer was seriously wounded. The petitioners were convicted of first-degree murder.

The evidence for the prosecution established that the four
men had been discussing a possible robbery for some time.
On the fatal day Woodson had been drinking heavily. About
9:30 p.m., Waxton and Tucker came to the trailer where
Woodson was staying. When Woodson came out of the
trailer, Waxton struck him in the face and threatened to kill
him in an effort to make him sober up and come along on
the robbery. . . . Upon arriving at their destination Tucker
and Waxton went into the store while Carroll and Woodson
remained in the car as lookouts. Once inside the store, Tucker
purchased a package of cigarettes from the woman cashier.
Waxton then also asked for a package of cigarettes, but as
the cashier approached him he pulled the derringer out of his
hip pocket and fatally shot her at point-blank range. Waxton
then took the money tray from the cash register and gave it to
Tucker, who carried it out of the store, pushing past an entering
customer as he reached the door. After he was outside, Tucker
heard a second shot from inside the store, and shortly thereafter Waxton emerged, carrying a handful of paper money.
Tucker and Waxton got in the car and the four drove away.

The petitioners' testimony agreed in large part with this version
of the circumstances of the robbery. It differed diametrically in
one important respect: Waxton claimed that he never had a gun,
and that Tucker had shot both the cashier and the customer.

**During the trial Waxton asked to be allowed to plead
guilty to the same lesser offenses to which Tucker had
pleaded guilty, but the solicitor refused to accept the
pleas. Woodson, by contrast, maintained throughout
the trial that he had been coerced by Waxton, that he
was therefore innocent, and that he would not consider
pleading guilty to any offense. . . .**

The petitioners, James Woodson and Luby Waxton, were found guilty. State law required a death sentence. The judge and jury had no choice. On appeal, the North Carolina Supreme Court affirmed. The U.S. Supreme Court agreed to consider whether the imposition of the death penalties in this case violated the Eighth and Fourteenth Amendments. Stewart did not find that the death penalty is cruel and unusual punishment in all cases. But mandatory death sentences were problematic.

The history of mandatory death penalty statutes in the United
States thus reveals that the practice of sentencing to death all

" At least since the Revolution, American jurors have, with some regularity, disregarded their oaths and refused to convict defendants where a death sentence was the automatic consequence of a guilty verdict."

persons convicted of a particular offense has been rejected as unduly harsh and unworkably rigid. The two crucial indicators of evolving standards of decency respecting the imposition of punishment in our society—jury determinations and legislative enactments—both point conclusively to the repudiation of automatic death sentences. At least since the Revolution, American jurors have, with some regularity, disregarded their oaths and refused to convict defendants where a death sentence was the automatic consequence of a guilty verdict. . . . Thereafter, continuing evidence of jury reluctance to convict persons of capital offenses in mandatory death penalty jurisdictions resulted in legislative authorization of discretionary jury sentencing. . . .

It is now well established that the Eighth Amendment draws much of its meaning from "the evolving standards of decency that mark the progress of a maturing society." *Trop v. Dulles.* . . . [O]ne of the most significant developments in our society's treatment of capital punishment has been the rejection of the common-law practice of inexorably imposing a death sentence upon every person convicted of a specified offense. North Carolina's mandatory death penalty statute for first-degree murder departs markedly from contemporary standards respecting the imposition of the punishment of death and thus cannot be applied consistently with the Eighth and Fourteenth Amendments' requirement that the State's power to punish "be exercised within the limits of civilized standards." . . .

It is argued that North Carolina has remedied the inadequacies of the death penalty statutes held unconstitutional in *Furman* by withdrawing all sentencing discretion from juries in capital cases. But when one considers the long and consistent American experience with the death penalty in first-degree murder cases, it becomes evident that mandatory statutes enacted in response to *Furman* have simply papered over the problem of unguided and unchecked jury discretion. . . .

[Another] constitutional shortcoming of the North Carolina statute is its failure to allow the particularized consideration of relevant aspects of the character and record of each convicted defendant before the imposition upon him of a sentence of death. . . . A process that accords no significance to relevant facets of the character and record of the individual offender or the circumstances of the particular offense excludes from consideration in fixing the ultimate punishment of death the possibility of compassionate or mitigating factors stemming from the diverse frailties of humankind. It treats all persons convicted of a designated offense not as uniquely individual human beings, but as members of a faceless, undifferentiated mass to be subjected to the blind infliction of the penalty of death.

. . . While the prevailing practice of individualizing sentencing determinations generally reflects simply enlightened policy rather than a constitutional imperative, we believe that in capital cases the fundamental respect for humanity underlying the Eighth Amendment requires consideration of the character and record of the individual offender and the circumstances of the particular offense as a constitutionally indispensable part of the process of inflicting the penalty of death. . . .

For the reasons stated, we conclude that the death sentences imposed upon the petitioners under North Carolina's mandatory death sentence statute violated the Eighth and Fourteenth Amendments and therefore must be set aside. . . .

Despite the concern of Justice White in *Furman* that allowing juries discretion ran a greater risk of arbitrary death penalties, the Court has made it clear that mandatory death penalty provisions will be struck down. In *Sumner v. Shuman* (1987), the Court invalidated a Nevada statute mandating the death penalty for inmates who commit a murder while already serving a life sentence.

Note

1. See William C. Bailey and Ruth D. Peterson, "Murder, Capital Punishment, and Deterrence: A Review of Evidence and an Examination of Police Killings," *Journal of Social Issues* 50(2) (Summer 1994): 53–74, cited in "Law Enforcement and the Death Penalty," Death Penalty Information Center, http://www.deathpenaltyinfo.org/law-enforcement-views-deterrence.

Death Penalty for Rape

Coker v. Georgia

June 29, 1977

INTRODUCTION

In *Coker v. Georgia,* the Court reviewed state laws that made rape a capital offense. The Court ruled that although rape is a reprehensible crime, death is a "disproportionate and excessive punishment" for a rapist who does not take human life. Justice White, joined by Justices Stewart, Blackmun, and Stevens, announced the judgment of the Court. White cited history and objective evidence, noting that Georgia was the only state that "authorizes a sentence of death when the rape victim is an adult woman, and only two other jurisdictions provide capital punishment when the victim is a child." Justices Brennan and Marshall concurred, repeating their position from *Gregg* that the death penalty is always a cruel and unusual form of punishment. Justice Powell concurred in part and dissented in part. Chief Justice Burger, joined by Justice Rehnquist, dissented.

JUSTICE WHITE announced the judgment of the Court and filed an opinion in which JUSTICE STEWART, JUSTICE BLACKMUN, and JUSTICE STEVENS, joined.

Georgia Code Ann. 26-2001 (1972) provides that "[a] person convicted of rape shall be punished by death or by imprisonment for life, or by imprisonment for not less than one nor more than 20 years." Punishment is determined by a jury in a separate sentencing proceeding in which at least one of the statutory aggravating circumstances must be found before the death penalty may be imposed.

On September 2, 1974, Coker escaped from the Ware Correctional Institution near Waycross, Georgia. He had been serving six separate sentences, including two terms of life imprisonment for assault, kidnapping, rape, and murder. At about 11:00 p.m., he entered the house of Allen and Enita Carver through an unlatched kitchen door. He attacked the married couple he found inside. He tied up Mr. Carver and took his money and car keys. Then he raped the 16-year-old Mrs. Carver at knife point and forced her to accompany him as he continued his flight in the couple's car. The police arrested Coker.

Petitioner Coker was convicted of rape and sentenced to death. Both the conviction and the sentence were affirmed by the Georgia Supreme Court. Coker was granted a *writ of certiorari,* limited to the single claim, rejected by the Georgia court, that the punishment of death for rape violates the Eighth Amendment, which proscribes "cruel and unusual punishments" and which must be observed by the States as well as the Federal Government.

[Coker] was charged with escape, armed robbery, motor vehicle theft, kidnaping, and rape. . . . The jury returned a verdict of guilty, rejecting his general plea of insanity.

A sentencing hearing was then conducted in accordance with the procedures dealt with at length in *Gregg v. Georgia*. . . . The jury was instructed that it could consider as aggravating circumstances whether the rape had been committed by a person with a prior record of conviction for a capital felony and whether the rape had been committed in the course of committing another capital felony, namely, the armed robbery of Allen Carver. The court also instructed, pursuant to statute, that even if aggravating circumstances were present, the death penalty need not be imposed if the jury found they were outweighed by mitigating circumstances, that is, circumstances not constituting justification or excuse for the offense in question, "but which, in fairness and mercy, may be considered as extenuating or reducing the degree" of moral culpability or punishment. The jury's verdict on the rape count was death by electrocution. Both aggravating circumstances on which the court instructed were found to be present by the jury.

. . . It is now settled that the death penalty is not invariably cruel and unusual punishment within the meaning of the Eighth Amendment; it is not inherently barbaric or an unacceptable mode of punishment for crime; neither is it always disproportionate to the crime for which it is imposed. It is also established that imposing capital punishment, at least for murder, in accordance with the procedures provided under the Georgia statutes saves the sentence from the infirmities which led the Court to invalidate the prior Georgia capital punishment statute in *Furman v. Georgia*.

In sustaining the imposition of the death penalty in *Gregg,* however, the Court firmly [noted] . . . that the Eighth Amendment bars not only those punishments that are "barbaric" but also those that are "excessive" in relation to the crime committed. Under *Gregg,* a punishment is "excessive" and unconstitutional if it (1) makes no measurable contribution to acceptable goals of punishment and hence is nothing more than the purposeless and needless imposition of pain and suffering; or (2) is grossly out of proportion to the severity of the crime. A punishment might fail the test on either ground. . . . [T]hese Eighth Amendment judgments should not be . . . merely the subjective views of individual Justices; judgment should be informed by objective factors. . . . To this end, attention must be given to the public attitudes concerning a particular sentence—history and precedent, legislative attitudes, and the response of juries reflected in their

"It is now settled that the death penalty is not invariably cruel and unusual punishment within the meaning of the Eighth Amendment . . ."

"We have concluded that a sentence of death is grossly disproportionate and excessive punishment for the crime of rape . . ."

sentencing decisions are to be consulted. In *Gregg,* after giving due regard to such sources, the Court's judgment was that the death penalty for deliberate murder was neither the purposeless imposition of severe punishment nor a punishment grossly disproportionate to the crime. But the Court reserved the question of the constitutionality of the death penalty when imposed for other crimes.

That question, with respect to rape of an adult woman, is now before us. We have concluded that a sentence of death is grossly disproportionate and excessive punishment for the crime of rape and is therefore forbidden by the Eighth Amendment as cruel and unusual punishment.

As advised by recent cases, we seek guidance in history and from the objective evidence of the country's present judgment concerning the acceptability of death as a penalty for rape of an adult woman. At no time in the last 50 years have a majority of the States authorized death as a punishment for rape. . . . *Furman* then invalidated most of the capital punishment statutes in this country, including the rape statutes, because, among other reasons, of the manner in which the death penalty was imposed and utilized under those laws.

With their death penalty statutes for the most part invalidated, the States were faced with the choice of enacting modified capital punishment laws in an attempt to satisfy the requirements of *Furman* or of being satisfied with life imprisonment as the ultimate punishment for any offense. Thirty-five States immediately reinstituted the death penalty for at least limited kinds of crime. . . .

But if the "most marked indication of society's endorsement of the death penalty for murder is the legislative response to *Furman," Gregg v. Georgia,* it [is] . . . telling . . . that the public judgment with respect to rape, as reflected in the statutes providing the punishment for that crime, has been dramatically different. In reviving death penalty laws to satisfy *Furman's* mandate, none of the States that had not previously authorized death for rape chose to include rape among capital felonies. . . .

It should be noted that Florida, Mississippi, and Tennessee also authorized the death penalty in some rape cases, but only where the victim was a child and the rapist an adult. The Tennessee statute has since been invalidated because the death sentence was mandatory. The upshot is that Georgia is the sole jurisdiction in the United States at the present time that authorizes a sentence of death when the rape victim is an adult woman, and only two other jurisdictions provide capital punishment when the victim is a child.

The current judgment with respect to the death penalty for rape is not wholly unanimous among state legislatures, but it obviously weighs very heavily on the side of rejecting capital punishment as a suitable penalty for raping an adult woman.

It was also observed in *Gregg* that "[t]he jury . . . is a significant and reliable objective index of contemporary values. . . ."

According to the factual submissions in this Court, out of all rape convictions in Georgia since 1973 . . . in the vast majority of cases, at least 9 out of 10, juries have not imposed the death sentence.

These recent events evidencing the attitude of state legislatures and sentencing juries do not wholly determine this controversy, for the Constitution contemplates that in the end our own judgment will be brought to bear on the question of the acceptability of the death penalty under the Eighth Amendment. Nevertheless, the legislative rejection of capital punishment for rape strongly confirms our own judgment, which is that death is indeed a disproportionate penalty for the crime of raping an adult woman.

We do not discount the seriousness of rape as a crime. It is highly reprehensible, both in a moral sense and in its almost total contempt for the personal integrity and autonomy of the female victim and for the latter's privilege of choosing those with whom intimate relationships are to be established. Short of homicide, it is the "ultimate violation of self." It is also a violent crime because it normally involves force, or the threat of force or intimidation, to overcome the will and the capacity of the victim to resist. Rape is very often accompanied by physical injury to the female and can also inflict mental and psychological damage. Because it undermines the community's sense of security, there is public injury as well.

"We do not discount the seriousness of rape as a crime."

Rape is without doubt deserving of serious punishment; but in terms of moral depravity and of the injury to the person and to the public, it does not compare with murder, which does involve the unjustified taking of human life. Although it may be accompanied by another crime, rape by definition does not include the death of or even the serious injury to another person. The murderer kills; the rapist, if no more than that, does not. Life is over for the victim of the murderer; for the rape victim, life may not be nearly so happy as it was, but it is not over and normally is not beyond repair.

We have the abiding conviction that the death penalty, which "is unique in its severity and irrevocability," is an excessive penalty for the rapist who, as such, does not take human life. . . .

Since the 18th century, observers such as William Blackstone and Pennsylvania attorney general William Bradford had observed that juries were reluctant to convict defendants of crimes less than murder when the penalty could be death. Some prosecutors applauded *Coker v. Georgia* because they believed that the death penalty made juries less likely to convict rapists. For example, Linda Fairstein, director of the Sex Crimes Unit in the Manhattan district attorney's office, pointed out that the conviction rate in rape cases greatly increased during the 1980s and 1990s.

JUSTICE BRENNAN, concurring in the judgment.

Adhering to my view that the death penalty is in all circumstances cruel and unusual punishment prohibited by the Eighth and Fourteenth Amendments, *Gregg v. Georgia* (dissenting opinion), I concur in the judgment of the Court setting aside the death sentence imposed under the Georgia rape statute.

JUSTICE MARSHALL, concurring in the judgment.

In *Gregg v. Georgia* (dissenting opinion), I stated: "In *Furman v. Georgia* (concurring opinion), I set forth at some length my views on the basic issue presented to the Court in these cases. The death penalty, I concluded, is a cruel and unusual punishment prohibited by the Eighth and Fourteenth Amendments. That continues to be my view." . . .

JUSTICE POWELL, concurring in the judgment in part and dissenting in part.

I concur in the judgment of the Court on the facts of this case, and also in the plurality's reasoning supporting the view that ordinarily death is disproportionate punishment for the crime of raping an adult woman. Although rape invariably is a reprehensible crime, there is no indication that petitioner's offense was committed with excessive brutality or that the victim sustained serious or lasting injury. The plurality, however, does not limit its holding to the case before us or to similar cases. Rather, in an opinion that ranges well beyond what is necessary, it holds that capital punishment always—regardless of the circumstances—is a disproportionate penalty for the crime of rape. . . .

Today, in a case that does not require such an expansive pronouncement, the plurality draws a bright line between murder and all rapes—regardless of the degree of brutality of the rape or the effect upon the victim. I dissent because I am not persuaded that such a bright line is appropriate. As noted in *Snider v. Peyton,* "[t]here is extreme variation in the degree of culpability of rapists." The deliberate viciousness of the rapist may be greater than that of the murderer. Rape is never an act committed accidentally. Rarely can it be said to be unpremeditated. There also is wide variation in the effect on the victim. The plurality opinion says that "[l]ife is over for the victim of the murderer; for the rape victim, life may not be nearly so happy as it was, but it is not over and normally is not beyond repair." But there is indeed "extreme variation" in the crime of rape. Some victims are so grievously injured physically or psychologically that life is beyond repair.

Thus, it may be that the death penalty is not disproportionate punishment for the crime of aggravated rape. Final resolution of the question must await careful inquiry into objective indicators of society's "evolving standards of decency," particularly legislative enactments and the responses of juries in capital cases. . . . The plurality properly examines [precedents] which do support the conclusion that society finds the death penalty unacceptable for the crime of rape in the absence of excessive brutality or severe injury. But it has not been shown that society finds the penalty disproportionate for all rapes. . . . To this extent, I respectfully dissent.

CHIEF JUSTICE BURGER, with whom JUSTICE REHNQUIST joins, dissenting.

In a case such as this, confusion often arises as to the Court's proper role in reaching a decision.

Our task is not to give effect to our individual views on capital punishment; rather, we must determine what the Constitution permits a State to do under its reserved powers.

The Tenth Amendment reserves powers not granted to the federal government or prohibited in the Constitution to the states. Burger argues that the ban on disproportional punishment as cruel and unusual does not apply in this case, and therefore the Court should not interfere with the state law in the case.

In striking down the death penalty imposed upon the petitioner in this case, the Court has overstepped the bounds of proper constitutional adjudication by substituting its policy judgment for that of the state legislature. I accept that the Eighth Amendment's concept of disproportionality bars the death penalty for minor crimes. But rape is not a minor crime; hence the Cruel and Unusual Punishments Clause does not give the Members of this Court license to engraft their conceptions of proper public policy onto the considered legislative judgments of the States. Since I cannot agree that Georgia lacked the constitutional power to impose the penalty of death for rape,

Future Supreme Court justice Ruth Bader Ginsburg filed an amicus curiae brief in *Coker.* Responding to questions during her own Supreme Court confirmation hearings 16 years later, she reiterated her support for the Court's decision in this case.

I dissent from the Court's judgment. . . .

Unlike the plurality, I would narrow the inquiry in this case to the question actually presented: Does the Eighth Amendment's ban against cruel and unusual punishment prohibit the State of Georgia from executing a person who has, within the space of three years, raped three separate women, killing one and attempting to kill another, who is serving prison terms exceeding his probable lifetime and who has not hesitated to escape confinement at the first available opportunity? Whatever one's view may be as to the State's constitutional power to impose the death penalty upon a rapist who stands before a court convicted for the first time, this case reveals a chronic rapist whose continuing danger to the community is abundantly clear. . . .

Mitigating Factors

Lockett v. Ohio

July 3, 1978

INTRODUCTION

An Ohio statute allowed judges in capital cases to consider only three mitigating factors. If none of these factors was found, the defendant had to be sentenced to death. The Supreme Court struck down this death penalty law because it did not permit consideration of a wider range of relevant mitigating factors. In another case decided on the same day (*Bell v. Ohio*), the Court also held that a judge must be permitted to consider relevant mitigating factors. In Chief Justice Burger's words, a state law cannot preclude a trial judge "from considering as a mitigating factor, any aspect of the defendant's character or record and any of the circumstances of the offense that the defendant proffers."

CHIEF JUSTICE BURGER announced the Court's judgment and delivered an opinion of the Court with respect to Parts I and II, in which JUSTICES STEWART, WHITE, BLACKMUN, POWELL, REHNQUIST, and STEVENS joined, and an opinion with respect to Part III, in which JUSTICES STEWART, POWELL, and STEVENS joined. JUSTICE BLACKMUN filed an opinion concurring in part and concurring in the judgment. JUSTICE MARSHALL filed an opinion concurring in the judgment. JUSTICE WHITE filed an opinion concurring in part, concurring in the judgment, and dissenting in part. JUSTICE REHNQUIST filed an opinion concurring in part and dissenting in part. JUSTICE BRENNAN took no part in the consideration or decision of the case. . . .

We granted *certiorari* in this case to consider . . . whether Ohio violated the Eighth and Fourteenth Amendments by sentencing Sandra Lockett to death pursuant to a statute that narrowly limits the sentencer's discretion to consider the circumstances of the crime and the record and character of the offender as mitigating factors.

> Lockett was charged with aggravated murder "with aggravating specifications" and aggravated robbery and was sentenced to death.

I

. . . [A]ggravating specifications [included] (1) that the murder was "committed for the purpose of escaping detection, apprehension, trial, or punishment" for aggravated robbery, and (2) that the murder was "committed while . . . committing, attempting to commit, or fleeing immediately after committing or attempting to commit . . . aggravated robbery." That offense was punishable by death in Ohio. . . . She was also charged with aggravated robbery. The State's case against her depended largely upon the testimony of a coparticipant, one Al Parker, who gave the following account of her participation in the robbery and murder.

Lockett became acquainted with Parker and Nathan Earl Dew while she and a friend, Joanne Baxter, were in New Jersey. Parker and Dew then accompanied Lockett, Baxter, and Lockett's brother back to Akron, Ohio, Lockett's hometown. After they arrived in Akron, Parker and Dew needed money for the trip back to New Jersey. Dew suggested that he pawn his ring. Lockett . . . felt that the ring was too beautiful to pawn, and suggested instead that they could get some money by robbing a grocery store and a furniture store in the area. She warned that the grocery store's operator was a "big guy" who carried a "45" and that they would have "to get him real quick." She also volunteered to get a gun from her father's basement to aid in carrying out the robberies, but by that time, the two stores had closed and it was too late to proceed with the plan to rob them.

. . . Lockett's brother suggested a plan for robbing a pawnshop. He and Dew would enter the shop and pretend to pawn a ring. Next Parker, who had some bullets, would enter the shop, ask to see a gun, load it, and use it to rob the shop. No one planned to kill the pawnshop operator in the course of the robbery. Because she knew the owner, Lockett was not to be among those entering the pawnshop, though she did guide the others to the shop that night.

The next day Parker, Dew, Lockett, and her brother gathered at Baxter's apartment. Lockett's brother asked if they were "still going to do it," and everyone, including Lockett, agreed to proceed. . . . The robbery proceeded according to plan until the pawnbroker grabbed the gun when Parker announced the "stickup." The gun went off with Parker's finger on the trigger, firing a fatal shot into the pawnbroker.

Parker, who actually fired the fatal shot, accepted a plea bargain, agreeing to testify against the others in return for reduced charges and thereby eliminating the possibility that Parker could receive the death penalty.

Parker went back to the car where Lockett waited with the engine running. While driving away from the pawnshop, Parker told Lockett what had happened. She took the gun from the pawnshop and put it into her purse. Lockett and Parker drove to Lockett's aunt's house and called a taxicab. Shortly thereafter, while riding away in a taxicab, they were stopped by the police. . . .

Lockett's brother and Dew were later convicted of aggravated murder with specifications. Lockett's brother was sentenced to death, but Dew received a lesser penalty because . . . "of mental deficiency," one of the three mitigating circumstances specified in the Ohio death penalty statute. . . .

At trial, the opening argument of Lockett's defense counsel summarized . . . Lockett's version of the events leading to the killing. He asserted . . . that, as far as Lockett knew, Dew and her brother had planned to pawn Dew's ring for $100 to obtain money for the trip back to New Jersey. . . .

[At trial], [t]he court instructed the jury that, before it could find Lockett guilty, it had to find that she purposely had killed the pawnbroker while committing or attempting to commit aggravated robbery.

The jury instructions included the concept of vicarious liability, that is, the idea that although she had not shot the victim, she was responsible for the actions of her coconspirators.

The jury was further charged that one who

> purposely aids, helps, associates himself or herself with another for the purpose of committing a crime is regarded as if he or she were the principal offender and is just as guilty as if the person performed every act constituting the offense. . . .

Regarding the intent requirement, the court instructed:

> A person engaged in a common design with others to rob by force and violence an individual or individuals of their property is presumed to acquiesce in whatever may reasonably be necessary to accomplish the object of their enterprise. . . .
>
> If the conspired robbery and the manner of its accomplishment would be reasonably likely to produce death, each plotter is equally guilty with the principal offender as an aider and abettor in the homicide. . . . An intent to kill by an aider and abettor may be found to exist beyond a reasonable doubt under such circumstances.

The jury found Lockett guilty as charged.

Once a verdict of aggravated murder with specifications had been returned, the Ohio death penalty statute required the trial judge to impose a death sentence unless, after "considering the nature and circumstances of the offense" and Lockett's "history, character, and condition," he found by a preponderance of the evidence that (1) the victim had induced or facilitated the offense, (2) it was unlikely that Lockett would have committed the offense but for the fact that she "was under duress, coercion, or strong provocation," or (3) the offense was "primarily the product of [Lockett's] psychosis or mental deficiency."

In accord with the Ohio statute, the trial judge requested a presentence report as well as psychiatric and psychological reports. The reports contained detailed information about Lockett's intelligence, character, and background. The psychiatric and psychological reports described her as a 21-year-old with low-average or average intelligence, and not suffering from a mental deficiency. One of the psychologists reported that "her prognosis for rehabilitation" if returned to society was favorable. The presentence report showed that Lockett had committed no major offenses although she had a record of several minor ones as a juvenile and two minor offenses as an adult. It also showed that she had once used heroin but was receiving treatment at a drug abuse clinic and seemed to be "on the road to success" as far as her drug problem was concerned. It concluded that Lockett suffered no psychosis and was not mentally deficient.

After considering the reports and hearing argument on the penalty issue, the trial judge concluded that the offense had not been primarily the product of psychosis or mental deficiency. Without specifically addressing the other two statutory mitigating factors, the judge said that he had "no alternative, whether [he] like[d] the law or not" but to impose the death penalty. He then sentenced Lockett to death. . . .

III

. . . We find it necessary to consider only [Lockett's] contention that her death sentence is invalid because the statute under which it was imposed did not permit the sentencing judge to consider, as mitigating factors, her character, prior record, age, lack of specific intent to cause death, and her relatively minor part in the crime. . . .

. . . Essentially [Lockett] contends that the Eighth and Fourteenth Amendments require that the sentencer be given a full opportunity to consider mitigating circumstances in capital cases and that the Ohio statute does not comply with that requirement. . . .

Chief Justice Burger next discussed the relevance of *Woodson v. North Carolina* to this case.

We begin by recognizing that the concept of individualized sentencing in criminal cases generally, although not constitutionally required, has long been accepted in this country. . . .

Although legislatures remain free to decide how much discretion in sentencing should be reposed in the judge or jury in noncapital cases, the plurality opinion in *Woodson,* after reviewing the historical repudiation of mandatory sentencing in capital cases, concluded that

> in capital cases the fundamental respect for humanity underlying the Eighth Amendment . . . requires consideration of the character and record of the individual offender and the circumstances of the particular offense as a constitutionally indispensable part of the process of inflicting the penalty of death.

That declaration rested "on the predicate that the penalty of death is qualitatively different" from any other sentence. . . . [T]his qualitative difference between death and other penalties calls for a greater degree of reliability when the death sentence is imposed. The mandatory death penalty statute in *Woodson* was held invalid because it permitted no consideration of "relevant facets of the character and record of the individual offender or the circumstances of the particular offense." The plurality did not attempt to indicate, however, which facets of an offender or his offense it deemed "relevant" in capital sentencing or what degree of consideration of "relevant facets" it would require.

So "which facets of an offender or his offense" are relevant in capital sentencing? Burger goes on to argue that any aspect of a defendant's record or character or of the offense may be relevant and that capital cases should not exclude mitigating factors that might be considered when judging lesser crimes.

We are now faced with those questions and we conclude that the Eighth and Fourteenth Amendments require that the sentence . . . not be precluded from considering, as a mitigating factor, any aspect of a defendant's character or record and any of the circumstances of the offense that the defendant proffers as a basis for a sentence less than death. We recognize that, in noncapital cases, the established practice of individualized sentences rests not on constitutional commands, but on public policy enacted into statutes. The considerations that account for the wide acceptance of individualization of sentences in noncapital cases surely cannot be thought less important in capital cases. Given that the imposition of death by public authority is so profoundly different from all other penalties, we cannot avoid the conclusion that an individualized decision is essential in capital cases. The need for treating each defendant in a capital case with that degree of respect due the uniqueness of the individual is far more important than in noncapital cases. . . .

There is no perfect procedure for deciding in which cases governmental authority should be used to impose death. But a statute that prevents the sentencer in all capital cases from giving independent mitigating weight to aspects of the defendant's character and record and to circumstances of the offense proffered in mitigation creates the risk that the death penalty will be imposed in spite of factors which may call for a less severe penalty. When the choice is between life and death, that risk is unacceptable and incompatible with the commands of the Eighth and Fourteenth Amendments.

The Ohio death penalty statute does not permit the type of individualized consideration of mitigating factors we now hold to be required by the Eighth and Fourteenth Amendments in capital cases. . . .

The limited range of mitigating circumstances which may be considered by the sentencer under the Ohio statute is incompatible with the Eighth and Fourteenth Amendments. To meet constitutional requirements, a death penalty statute must not preclude consideration of relevant mitigating factors. Accordingly, the judgment under review is reversed to the extent that it sustains the imposition of the death penalty, and the case is remanded for further proceedings.

JUSTICE BRENNAN took no part in the consideration or decision of this case. . . .

JUSTICE BLACKMUN, concurring in part and concurring in the judgment. [Omitted]

JUSTICE MARSHALL, concurring in the judgment.

I continue to adhere to my view that the death penalty is, under all circumstances, a cruel and unusual punishment prohibited by the Eighth Amendment. . . . This case, as well, serves to reinforce my view.

"Under the Ohio death penalty statue, this 21-year-old Negro woman was sentenced to death for a killing that she did not actually commit or intend to commit."

When a death sentence is imposed under the circumstances presented here, I fail to understand how any of my Brethren . . . can disagree that it must be vacated. Under the Ohio death penalty statute, this 21-year-old Negro woman was sentenced to death for a killing that she did not actually commit or intend to commit. She was convicted under a theory of vicarious liability. The imposition of the death penalty for this crime totally violates the principle of proportionality embodied in the Eighth Amendment's prohibition; it makes no distinction between a willful and malicious murderer and an accomplice to an armed robbery in which a killing unintentionally occurs. . . .

JUSTICE WHITE, concurring in part, dissenting in part, and concurring in the judgments of the Court....

... It is clear from recent history that the infliction of death under circumstances where there is no purpose to take life has been widely rejected as grossly out of proportion to the seriousness of the crime.

The value of capital punishment as a deterrent to those lacking a purpose to kill is extremely attenuated. Whatever questions may be raised concerning the efficacy of the death penalty as a deterrent to intentional murders—and that debate rages on—its function in deterring individuals from becoming involved in ventures in which death may unintentionally result is even more doubtful. . . .

Under those circumstances the conclusion is unavoidable that the infliction of death upon those who had no intent to bring about the death of the victim is not only grossly out of proportion to the severity of the crime but also fails to contribute significantly to acceptable or, indeed, any perceptible goals of punishment. . . .

JUSTICE REHNQUIST, concurring in part and dissenting in part. [Omitted]

Aggravating Factors

Godfrey v. Georgia

May 19, 1980

INTRODUCTION

Furman, Gregg, and *Woodson* established that states could retain the death penalty if there were aggravating circumstances, that a defendant was permitted to present all evidence of mitigating factors, and that properly instructed juries did not act arbitrarily. In *Godfrey v. Georgia,* the Court focused on aggravating factors. A Georgia law permitted a death sentence if the crime was "outrageous or wantonly vile." The law was struck down as unconstitutionally vague. Justice Stewart, joined by Justices Blackmun, Powell, and Stevens, announced the judgment of the Court. Stewart stated that "[t]here is no principled way to distinguish this case, in which the death penalty was imposed, from the many cases in which it was not." Justices Brennan and Marshall concurred, again reiterating their belief that "the death penalty is in all circumstances cruel and unusual punishment." Chief Justice Burger and Justice White, joined by Justice Rehnquist, dissented.

One evening in 1977, Godfrey and his wife had a heated argument after he had been drinking. Godfrey threatened her with a knife and damaged her clothing. She told him that she was leaving him, left to stay with relatives, and secured a warrant charging him with aggravated assault. A few days later, she filed for divorce. Godfrey believed that his mother-in-law was undermining him by discouraging his wife from considering reconciliation. On September 20 after another heated argument over the telephone, Godfrey took his shotgun to his mother-in-law's trailer. There he fatally shot his wife, struck his fleeing 11-year-old daughter with the gun barrel, reloaded the gun, and fatally shot his mother-in-law. Godfrey then called the sheriff, surrendered, and confessed. Upon arrival, the police found Godfrey sitting on a chair near the driveway. He told a police officer "they're dead, I killed them" and showed the officer where he had put the murder weapon. Later Godfrey said, "I've done a hideous crime . . . but I have been thinking about it for eight years. . . . I'd do it again."

JUSTICE STEWART announced the judgment of the Court and delivered an opinion, in which JUSTICE BLACKMUN, JUSTICE POWELL, and JUSTICE STEVENS joined.

Under Georgia law, a person convicted of murder may be sentenced to death if it is found beyond a reasonable doubt that the offense "was outrageously or wantonly vile, horrible or inhuman in that it involved torture, depravity of mind, or an aggravated battery to the victim." In *Gregg v. Georgia,* the Court held that this statutory aggravating circumstance is not unconstitutional on its face. Responding to the argument that the language of the provision is "so broad that capital punishment could be imposed in any murder case," the joint opinion said:

> "It is, of course, arguable that any murder involves depravity of mind or an aggravated battery. But this language need not be construed in this way, and there is no reason to assume that the Supreme Court of Georgia will adopt such an open-ended construction."

. . . The issue now before us is whether, in affirming the imposition of the sentences of death in the present case, the Georgia Supreme Court has adopted such a broad and vague construction of the **aggravating circumstance** as to violate the Eighth and Fourteenth Amendments to the United States Constitution. . . .

The petitioner was subsequently indicted on two counts of murder and one count of aggravated assault. He pleaded not guilty and relied primarily on a defense of temporary insanity at his trial. The jury returned verdicts of guilty on all three counts.

The sentencing phase of the trial was held before the same jury. . . . [T]he trial judge instructed the jury . . . [and] . . . quoted to the jury the statutory language of . . . aggravating circumstance in its entirety.

The jury imposed sentences of death on both of the murder convictions. As to each, the jury specified that the aggravating circumstance they had found beyond a reasonable doubt was "that the offense of murder was outrageously or wantonly vile, horrible and inhuman."

In accord with Georgia law in capital cases, the trial judge prepared a report in the form of answers to a questionnaire for use on appellate review. One question on the form asked whether or not the victim had been "physically harmed or tortured." The trial judge's response was "No, as to both victims, excluding the actual murdering of the two victims."

The Georgia Supreme Court affirmed the judgments of the trial court in all respects. . . .

In *Furman v. Georgia,* the Court held that the penalty of death may not be imposed under sentencing procedures that create a substantial risk that the punishment will be inflicted in an arbitrary and capricious manner. *Gregg v. Georgia* reaffirmed this holding. . . .

This means that if a State wishes to authorize capital punishment it has a constitutional responsibility to tailor and apply its law in a manner that avoids the arbitrary and capricious infliction of the death penalty. Part of a State's responsibility in this regard is to define the crimes for which death may be the sentence in a way that obviates "standardless [sentencing] discretion." . . . It must channel the sentencer's discretion by "clear and objective standards" that provide "specific and detailed guidance," and that "make rationally reviewable the process for imposing a sentence of death." As was made clear in *Gregg,* a death penalty "system could have standards so vague that they would fail adequately to channel the

"One question on the form asked whether or not the victim had been 'physically harmed or tortured.'"

sentencing decision patterns of juries with the result that a pattern of arbitrary and capricious sentencing like that found unconstitutional in *Furman* could occur."

In the case before us, the Georgia Supreme Court has affirmed a sentence of death based upon no more than a finding that the offense was "outrageously or wantonly vile, horrible and inhuman." There is nothing in these few words, standing alone, that implies any inherent restraint on the arbitrary and capricious infliction of the death sentence. A person of ordinary sensibility could fairly characterize almost every murder as "outrageously or wantonly vile, horrible and inhuman." . . .

Thus, the validity of the petitioner's death sentences turns on whether, in light of the facts and circumstances of the murders that he was convicted of committing, the Georgia Supreme Court can be said to have applied a constitutional construction of the phrase "outrageously or wantonly vile, horrible or inhuman in that [they] involved . . . depravity of mind. . . ." We conclude that the answer must be no.

Gardner v. Florida (1977) was another case dealing with transparency and reliability in death penalty cases, this time when a defendant was sentenced based on a presentence report that was not disclosed to him. In *Maynard v. Cartwright* (1988) the Court struck down an Oklahoma statute similar to the one at issue in *Godfrey* that defined as an aggravating factor that a murder was "especially heinous, atrocious, or cruel."

The petitioner's crimes cannot be said to have reflected a consciousness materially more "depraved" than that of any person guilty of murder. His victims were killed instantaneously. They were members of his family who were causing him extreme emotional trauma. Shortly after the killings, he acknowledged his responsibility and the heinous nature of his crimes. These factors certainly did not remove the criminality from the petitioner's acts. But, as was said in *Gardner v. Florida*, it "is of vital importance to the defendant and to the community that any decision to impose the death sentence be, and appear to be, based on reason rather than caprice or emotion."

That cannot be said here. There is no principled way to distinguish this case, in which the death penalty was imposed, from the many cases in which it was not. Accordingly, the judgment of the Georgia Supreme Court . . . is reversed, and the case is remanded to that court for further proceedings.

Justices Marshall and Brennan repeated their categorical rejection of capital punishment.

JUSTICE MARSHALL, with whom MR. JUSTICE BRENNAN joins, concurring in the judgment.

I continue to believe that the death penalty is in all circumstances cruel and unusual punishment forbidden by the

Eighth and Fourteenth Amendments. In addition, I agree with the plurality that the Georgia Supreme Court's construction of the provision at issue in this case is unconstitutionally vague under *Gregg v. Georgia.* . . .

CHIEF JUSTICE BURGER, dissenting.

. . . I am convinced that the course the plurality embarks on today is sadly mistaken—indeed confused. It is this Court's function to insure that the rights of a defendant are scrupulously respected; and in capital cases we must see to it that the jury has rendered its decision with meticulous care. But it is emphatically not our province to second-guess the jury's judgment or to tell the states which of their "hideous," intentional murderers may be given the ultimate penalty. Because the plurality does both, I dissent.

JUSTICE WHITE, with whom JUSTICE REHNQUIST joins, dissenting.

. . . The question [is] whether the facts of this case bear sufficient relation to [the statute] to conclude that the Georgia Supreme Court responsibly and constitutionally discharged its review function. I believe that they do. . . .

Our role is to correct genuine errors of constitutional significance resulting from the application of Georgia's capital sentencing procedures; our role is not to peer majestically over the lower court's shoulder so that we might second-guess its interpretation of facts that quite reasonably—perhaps even quite plainly—fit within the statutory language.

Who is to say that the murders of Mrs. Godfrey and Mrs. Wilkerson were not "vile," or "inhuman," or "horrible"? . . . [The] petitioner employed a weapon known for its disfiguring effects on targets, human or other, and he succeeded in creating a scene so macabre and revolting that, if anything, "vile," "horrible," and "inhuman" are descriptively inadequate. . . .

The point is not that, in my view, petitioner's crimes were definitively vile, horrible, or inhuman, or that, as I assay the evidence, they beyond any doubt involved torture, depravity of mind, or an aggravated battery to the victims. Rather, the lesson is a much more elementary one, an instruction that, I should have thought, this Court would have taken to heart long ago. Our mandate does not extend to interfering

Chief Justice Burger regarded Godfrey's crimes as "hideous." Justices White and Rehnquist deferred to state-level determinations that the crimes were "vile," "inhuman," and "horrible."

with factfinders in state criminal proceedings or with state courts that are responsibly and consistently interpreting state law, unless that interference is predicated on a violation of the Constitution. . . . Faithful adherence to this standard of review compels our affirmance of the judgment below.

Additional Mitigating Factors

Eddings v. Oklahoma

January 19, 1982

INTRODUCTION

Monty Lee Eddings, a juvenile in Oklahoma, was charged with first-degree murder. He was tried as an adult. The judge considered Eddings's age as a mitigating factor but refused to consider the defendant's turbulent family history and emotional disturbance as additional mitigating factors. The Supreme Court struck down the death sentence on the ground that relevant mitigating factors had been excluded from consideration by the sentencing judge. Justice Powell delivered the opinion of the Court. Justices Brennan and O'Connor wrote separate concurring opinions. Chief Justice Burger, joined by Justices White, Blackmun, and Rehnquist, dissented.

JUSTICE POWELL delivered the opinion of the Court.

Petitioner Monty Lee Eddings was convicted of first-degree murder and sentenced to death. Because this sentence was imposed without "the type of individualized consideration of mitigating factors . . . required by the Eighth and Fourteenth Amendments in capital cases," *Lockett v. Ohio,* we reverse.

On April 4, 1977, Eddings, a 16-year-old youth, and several younger companions ran away from their Missouri homes. They traveled in a car owned by Eddings' brother, and drove without destination or purpose in a southwesterly direction eventually reaching the Oklahoma Turnpike. Eddings had in the car a shotgun and several rifles he had taken from his father. After he momentarily lost control of the car, he was signaled to pull over by Officer Crabtree of the Oklahoma Highway Patrol. Eddings did so, and when the officer approached the car, Eddings stuck a loaded shotgun out of the window and fired, killing the officer.

Because Eddings was a juvenile, the State moved to have him certified to stand trial as an adult. Finding that . . . Eddings was not amenable to rehabilitation within the juvenile system, the trial court granted the motion. The ruling was affirmed on appeal. Eddings was then charged with murder in the first degree, and the District Court of Creek County found him guilty. . . .

The Oklahoma death penalty statute provides in pertinent part:

"Upon conviction . . . of guilt of a defendant of murder in the first degree, the court shall conduct a separate sentencing proceeding to determine whether the defendant should be sentenced to death or life imprisonment. . . . In the sentencing proceeding, evidence may be presented as to any mitigating circumstances or as to any of the aggravating circumstances enumerated in this act."

[The statute] lists seven separate aggravating circumstances; the statute nowhere defines what is meant by "any mitigating circumstances."

At the sentencing hearing, the State alleged three of the aggravating circumstances enumerated in the statute: that the murder was especially heinous, atrocious, or cruel, that the crime was committed for the purpose of avoiding or preventing a lawful arrest, and that there was a probability that the defendant would commit criminal acts of violence that would constitute a continuing threat to society.

In mitigation, Eddings presented substantial evidence at the hearing of his troubled youth. The testimony of his supervising Juvenile Officer indicated that Eddings had been raised without proper guidance. His parents were divorced when he was 5 years old, and until he was 14 Eddings lived with his mother without rules or supervision. There is the suggestion that Eddings' mother was an alcoholic and possibly a prostitute. By the time Eddings was 14 he no longer could be controlled, and his mother sent him to live with his father. But neither could the father control the boy. Attempts to reason and talk gave way to physical punishment. The Juvenile Officer testified that Eddings was frightened and bitter, that his father overreacted and used excessive physical punishment. . . .

"The Juvenile Officer testified that Eddings was frightened and bitter, that his father overreacted and used excessive physical punishment."

Testimony from other witnesses indicated that Eddings was emotionally disturbed in general and at the time of the crime, and that his mental and emotional development were at a level several years below his age. A state psychologist stated that Eddings had a sociopathic or antisocial personality and that approximately 30% of youths suffering from such a disorder grew out of it as they aged. A sociologist specializing in juvenile offenders testified that Eddings was treatable. A psychiatrist testified that Eddings could be rehabilitated by intensive therapy over a 15- to 20-year period. He testified further that Eddings "did pull the trigger, he did kill someone, but I don't even think he knew that he was doing it." The psychiatrist suggested that, if treated, Eddings would no longer pose a serious threat to society.

At the conclusion of all the evidence, the trial judge weighed the evidence of aggravating and mitigating circumstances. He found that the State had proved each of the three alleged aggravating circumstances beyond a reasonable doubt. Turning to the evidence of mitigating circumstances, the judge found that Eddings' youth was a mitigating factor of great weight. . . . But he would not consider in mitigation the circumstances of Eddings' unhappy upbringing and emotional disturbance: "[T]he Court cannot be persuaded entirely by the . . . fact that the youth was sixteen years old when this heinous crime was committed. Nor can the Court in following the law, in my opinion, consider the fact of this young man's violent background." Finding that the only mitigating circumstance was Eddings' youth and finding further that this circumstance could not outweigh the aggravating circumstances present, the judge sentenced Eddings to death.

"Finding that the only mitigating circumstance was Eddings' youth . . . the judge sentenced Eddings to death."

The Court of Criminal Appeals affirmed the sentence of death. . . .

In *Lockett v. Ohio,* CHIEF JUSTICE BURGER, writing for the plurality, stated the rule that we apply today: "[W]e conclude that the Eighth and Fourteenth Amendments require that the sentencer . . . not be precluded from considering, as a mitigating factor, any aspect of a defendant's character or record and any of the circumstances of the offense that the defendant proffers as a basis for a sentence less than death." . . .

We now apply the rule in *Lockett* to the circumstances of this case. The trial judge stated that "in following the law," he could not "consider the fact of this young man's violent background." There is no dispute that by "violent background" the trial judge was referring to the mitigating evidence of Eddings' family history. From this statement it is clear that the trial judge did not evaluate the evidence in mitigation and find it wanting as a matter of fact; rather he found that as a matter of law he was unable even to consider the evidence. The Court of Criminal Appeals took the same approach. . . .

The Supreme Court consistently treats mitigating factors more expansively than it does
aggravating factors. In *Hitchcock v. Dugger*
(1987) the Court unanimously held that the
jury had to consider whatever evidence it
believed to be mitigating, whether or not it fit
into the categories recognized by state statute. And in a pair of decisions, *Mills v. Maryland* (1988) and *McKoy v. North Carolina*
(1990), the Court held that a state could not
require a jury to find the presence of a mitigating factor by a unanimous vote.

We find that the limitations placed by these courts upon the mitigating evidence they would consider violated the rule in *Lockett*. Just as the State may not by statute preclude the sentencer from considering any mitigating factor, neither may the sentencer refuse to consider, as a matter of law, any relevant mitigating evidence.

. . . Eddings was a youth of 16 years at the time of the murder. Evidence of a difficult family history and of emotional disturbance is typically introduced by defendants in mitigation. See *McGautha v. California*. In some cases, such evidence properly may be given little weight.

Powell discussed juveniles' general lack of
maturity and impulse control in addition to
Eddings's particular emotional injuries.

But when the defendant was 16 years old at the time of the offense there can be no doubt that evidence of a turbulent family history, of beatings by a harsh father, and of severe emotional disturbance is particularly relevant. . . .

Even the normal 16-year-old customarily lacks the maturity of an adult. In this case, Eddings was not a normal 16-year-old; he had been deprived of the care, concern, and paternal attention that children deserve. On the contrary, it is not disputed that he was a juvenile with serious emotional problems, and had been raised in a neglectful, sometimes even violent, family background. . . . In addition, there was testimony that Eddings' mental and emotional development were at a level several years below his chronological age. All of this does not suggest an absence of responsibility for the crime of murder, deliberately committed in this case. Rather, it is to say that just as the chronological age of a minor is itself a relevant mitigating factor of great weight, so must the background and mental and emotional development of a youthful defendant be duly considered in sentencing.

We are not unaware of the extent to which minors engage increasingly in violent crime. Nor do we suggest an absence of legal responsibility where crime is committed by a minor. We are concerned here only with the manner of the imposition of the ultimate penalty: the death sentence imposed for the crime of murder upon an emotionally disturbed youth with a disturbed child's immaturity.

On remand, the state courts must consider all relevant mitigating evidence and weigh it against the evidence of the aggravating circumstances. We do not weight the evidence for them.

Accordingly, the judgment is reversed to the extent that it sustains the imposition of the death penalty, and the case is remanded for further proceedings not inconsistent with this opinion. . . .

Powell found Eddings's age relevant, but the Court did not settle the question of whether or not juveniles can be executed. Instead, the Court reaffirmed that all relevant mitigating evidence must be considered and weighed before a death sentence can be imposed.

JUSTICE BRENNAN, concurring.

I join the Court's opinion without, however, departing from my view that the death penalty is in all circumstances cruel and unusual punishment prohibited by the Eighth and Fourteenth Amendments, *Gregg v. Georgia* (dissenting opinion).

JUSTICE O'CONNOR, concurring. [Omitted]

CHIEF JUSTICE BURGER, with whom JUSTICE WHITE, JUSTICE BLACKMUN, and JUSTICE REHNQUIST join, dissenting. [Omitted]

Chapter 5

Proportionality, Culpability, and Fitting the Punishment to the Crime: 1982–1989

Limits on the Death Penalty for Accomplices

Enmund v. Florida

July 2, 1982

INTRODUCTION

The 1980s was a busy time for the Supreme Court as it began to answer questions on laws governing the administration of the death penalty. The Court provided mixed signals. In *Enmund v. Florida* (1982), the Court ruled that a death sentence for a felony-murder accomplice who did not kill or intend to kill the victim was excessive. In *Solem v. Helm* (1983), the Court returned to the issue of disproportionality, ruling that a repeat offender statute produced an excessive penalty. In *Ford v. Wainwright* (1986), the Court concluded that it is unconstitutional to execute a person who is legally insane. In *Thompson v. Oklahoma* (1988), the Court held that a death sentence cannot be imposed on someone who was only 15 years old at the time of the crime. All of these decisions were applauded by capital punishment opponents.

But the Court also announced several decisions that were less popular with abolitionists. In *Tison v. Arizona* (1987) the Court narrowed *Enmund*, upholding the death penalty for an accomplice if he participated in the crime in a major way and demonstrated "reckless indifference" to the fate of the victim. In *McCleskey v. Kemp* (1987), the Court found that general statistical patterns of racial disparities in the application of the death penalty were not sufficient to overturn death sentences. Defendants have to demonstrate that they have been discriminated against personally. In *Stanford v. Kentucky* (1989), the Court upheld the imposition of the death penalty for a person who was 16 years of age when he committed murder. In *Penry v. Linaugh* (1989), the Court held that it is constitutionally permissible to execute a mentally retarded person.

Whether or not the Court clarified the legal status of capital punishment is debatable.

JUSTICE WHITE delivered the opinion of the Court.

The facts of this case. . . are as follows. On April 1, 1975, at approximately 7:45 a.m., Thomas and Eunice Kersey, aged 86 and 74, were robbed and fatally shot at their farmhouse in central Florida. The evidence showed that Sampson and Jeanette Armstrong had gone to the back door of the Kersey house and asked for water for an overheated car. When Mr. Kersey came out of the house, Sampson Armstrong grabbed him, pointed a gun at him, and told Jeanette Armstrong to take his money. Mr. Kersey cried for help, and his wife came out of the house with a gun and shot Jeanette Armstrong, wounding her. Sampson Armstrong, and perhaps Jeanette Armstrong, then shot and killed both of the Kerseys, dragged them into the kitchen, and took their money and fled.

Two witnesses testified that they drove past the Kersey house between 7:30 and 7:40 a.m. and saw a large cream- or yellow-colored car parked beside the road about 200 yards from the house and that a man was sitting in the car. Another witness testified that at approximately 6:45 a.m. he saw Ida Jean Shaw, petitioner's common-law wife and Jeanette Armstrong's mother, driving a yellow Buick with a vinyl top which belonged to her and petitioner Earl Enmund. Enmund was a passenger in the car along with an unidentified woman. At about 8 a.m. the same witness saw the car return at a high rate of speed. Enmund was driving, Ida Jean Shaw was in the front seat, and one of the other two people in the car was lying down across the back seat.

Enmund, Sampson Armstrong, and Jeanette Armstrong were indicted for the first-degree murder and robbery of the Kerseys. Enmund and Sampson Armstrong were tried together. The prosecutor maintained in his closing argument that "Sampson Armstrong killed the old people." The judge instructed the jury that "[t]he killing of a human being while engaged in the perpetration of or in the attempt to perpetrate the offense of robbery is murder in the first degree even though there is no premeditated design or intent to kill." He went on to instruct them that

> [i]n order to sustain a conviction of first degree murder while engaging in . . . the crime of robbery, the evidence must establish beyond a reasonable doubt that the defendant was actually present and was actively aiding and abetting the robbery . . . , and that the unlawful killing occurred in the perpetration . . . of the robbery.

Justice White noted that the Court should focus on "[Enmund's] culpability, not on that of those who committed the robbery and shot the victims." Enmund neither killed nor intended to kill, so his culpability was plainly different from that of those who killed. As such, White concluded that a death sentence for Enmund's offense was excessive. Justice Brennan, repeating his unconditional rejection of the death penalty, concurred. Justice O'Connor, joined by Chief Justice Burger and Justices Powell and Rehnquist, dissented.

The jury found both Enmund and Sampson Armstrong guilty of two counts of first-degree murder and one count of robbery. A separate sentencing hearing was held and the jury recommended the death penalty for both defendants under the Florida procedure whereby the jury advises the trial judge whether to impose the death penalty. . . . The trial judge then sentenced Enmund to death on the two counts of first-degree murder. . . .

The Florida Supreme Court affirmed Enmund's conviction and sentences. . . .

We granted Enmund's petition for *certiorari*, presenting the question whether death is a valid penalty under the Eighth and Fourteenth Amendments for one who neither took life, attempted to take life, nor intended to take life.

. . . [T]he Florida Supreme Court held that the record supported no more than the inference that Enmund was the person in the car by the side of the road at the time of the killings, waiting to help the robbers escape. This was enough under Florida law to make Enmund a constructive aider and abettor and hence a principal in first-degree murder upon whom the death penalty could be imposed. It was thus irrelevant to Enmund's challenge to the death sentence that he did not himself kill and was not present at the killings; also beside the point was whether he intended that the Kerseys be killed or anticipated that lethal force would or might be used if necessary to effectuate the robbery or a safe escape. We have concluded that imposition of the death penalty in these circumstances is inconsistent with the Eighth and Fourteenth Amendments.

The Cruel and Unusual Punishments Clause of the Eighth Amendment is directed, in part, "'against all punishments which by their excessive length or severity are greatly disproportioned to the offenses charged.'" . . . This Court most recently held a punishment excessive in relation to the crime charged in *Coker v. Georgia.* There the plurality opinion concluded that the imposition of the death penalty for the rape of an adult woman "is grossly disproportionate and excessive punishment for the crime of rape and is therefore forbidden by the Eighth Amendment as cruel and unusual punishment." In reaching this conclusion, it was stressed that our judgment "should be informed by objective factors to the maximum possible extent." Accordingly, the Court looked to

Even states that make appellate review of other crimes optional have mandatory review of capital sentences, often directly in the highest court of the state. In addition to the usual tasks of checking for legal error, the state's highest court is charged with ensuring uniformity in the types of murders and murderers who receive the death penalty by comparing a particular verdict with all other death penalty cases.

But comparing culpability is also done by the jury in cases where there are multiple defendants. A clear example of this is the so-called Beltway Sniper case. In October 2002, John Allen Muhammad and Lee Boyd Malvo, then a 17-year-old, murdered at least 13 persons in Washington, D.C., and its suburbs. At Malvo's first trial, his attorneys presented the mitigating evidence that he had been recruited as a child soldier and brainwashed by Muhammad. The jury imposed a life sentence. Malvo testified for the prosecution at Muhammad's trial. Muhammed was convicted by a Virginia jury and sentenced to death. He was executed on November 10, 2009.

A troubling phenomenon from the comparison process is the "let's make a deal" negotiations that frequently result in the first defendant agreeing to testify against others and being spared the risk of the death penalty, regardless of culpability. This is not a consequence of any new Supreme Court ruling. While in earlier centuries an accomplice was incompetent to testify at all, in federal court and many states the uncorroborated word of an accomplice is enough to convict. This occasionally becomes a cause célèbre. In 1955, California executed Barbara Graham for the 1954 murder of Mabel Monaghan, based on the testimony of an alleged accomplice who himself may have committed the murder. The case was made into a 1958 movie, *I Want to Live,* that portrayed Graham as the victim of unscrupulous prosecutors and opportunistic codefendants.

the historical development of the punishment at issue, legislative judgments, international opinion, and the sentencing decisions juries have made before bringing its own judgment to bear on the matter. We proceed to analyze the punishment at issue in this case in a similar manner.

The *Coker* plurality observed that "[a]t no time in the last 50 years have a majority of the States authorized death as a punishment for rape." More importantly, in reenacting death penalty laws in order to satisfy the criteria established in *Furman v. Georgia,* only three States provided the death penalty for the rape of an adult woman in their revised statutes. The plurality therefore concluded that "[t]he current judgment with respect to the death penalty for rape . . . among state legislatures . . . weighs very heavily on the side of rejecting capital punishment as a suitable penalty for raping an adult woman."

Thirty-six state and federal jurisdictions presently authorize the death penalty. Of these, only eight jurisdictions authorize imposition of the death penalty solely for participation in a robbery in which another robber takes life. . . .

Thus only a small minority of jurisdictions—eight—allow the death penalty to be imposed solely because the defendant somehow participated in a robbery in the course of which a murder was committed. . . . Moreover, of the eight States which have enacted new death penalty statutes since 1978, none authorize capital punishment in such circumstances. . . . [T]he current legislative judgment . . . weighs on the side of rejecting capital punishment for the crime at issue.

Society's rejection of the death penalty for accomplice liability in felony murders is also indicated by the sentencing decisions that juries have made. As we have previously observed, "'[t]he jury . . . is a significant and reliable objective index of contemporary values because it is so directly involved.'" *Coker v Georgia.* **The evidence is overwhelming that American juries have repudiated imposition of the death penalty for crimes such as petitioner's. . . .**

That juries have rejected the death penalty in cases such as this one where the defendant did not commit the homicide, was not present when the killing took place, and did

Culpability presents a death penalty defendant with a dilemma at trial. On the one hand, failure to contest guilt in all but the most obvious cases gives up a chance for the defendant to avoid the death penalty entirely. On the other hand, because in almost every instance the same jury panel that decides guilt or innocence will decide whether death or a lesser sentence is appropriate, vigorously denying guilt might well be seen as inconsistent with later seeking a jury determination that a defendant is capable of rehabilitation, is remorseful, or has accepted responsibility. One study of 37 cases tried between 1988 and 1992 reported that juries imposed death sentences by a 2:1 ratio where the defendant contested guilt and imposed life sentences by a 3:2 ratio where the defendant admitted guilt at least to homicide and sought a lesser conviction than capital murder. For this reason, some defense attorneys will seek a trial before a judge alone, if the judge is known to be reluctant to impose a death sentence, in what is often referred to as a slow guilty plea. To counter this, the prosecutor in most jurisdictions has the option of asking for a jury trial even if the defendant does not.

not participate in a plot or scheme to murder is also shown by petitioner's survey of the Nation's death row population. As of October 1, 1981, there were 796 inmates under sentences of death for homicide. . . . [O]nly 3, including petitioner, . . . were sentenced to die absent a finding that they hired or solicited someone else to kill the victim or participated in a scheme designed to kill the victim. The figures for Florida are similar. . . . In only one case—Enmund's—there was no finding of an intent to kill and the defendant was not the triggerman. . . .

. . . The fact remains that we are not aware of a single person convicted of felony murder over the past quarter century who did not kill or attempt to kill, and did not intend the death of the victim, who has been executed, and that only three persons in that category are presently sentenced to die. . . . Petitioner's argument is that because he did not kill, attempt to kill, and he did not intend to kill, the death penalty is disproportionate as applied to him, and the statistics he cites are adequately tailored to demonstrate that juries—and perhaps prosecutors as well—consider death a disproportionate penalty for those who fall within his category.

Although the judgments of legislatures, juries, and prosecutors weigh heavily in the balance, it is for us ultimately to judge whether the Eighth Amendment permits imposition of the death penalty on one such as Enmund who aids and abets a felony in the course of which a murder is committed by others but who does not himself kill, attempt to kill, or intend that a killing take place or that lethal force will be employed. We have concluded, along with most legislatures and juries, that it does not.

We have no doubt that robbery is a serious crime deserving serious punishment. It is not, however, a crime "so grievous an affront to humanity that the only adequate response may be the penalty of death." *Gregg v. Georgia.* "[I]t does not compare with murder, which does involve the unjustified taking of human life." . . . As was said of the crime of rape in *Coker,* we have the abiding conviction that the death penalty, which is "unique in its severity and irrevocability," *Gregg v. Georgia,* is an excessive penalty for the robber who, as such, does not take human life.

"[W]e have an abiding conviction that the death penalty . . . is an excessive penalty for the robber who, as such, does not take human life."

Here the robbers did commit murder; but they were subjected to the death penalty only because they killed as well as robbed. The question before us is not the disproportionality of death as a penalty for murder, but rather the validity of capital punishment for Enmund's own conduct. The focus must be on his culpability, not on that of those who committed the robbery and shot the victims, for we insist on "individualized consideration as a constitutional requirement in imposing the death sentence," *Lockett v. Ohio,* which means that we must focus on "relevant facets of the character and record of the individual offender." *Woodson v. North Carolina.* Enmund himself did not kill or attempt to kill; and, as construed by the Florida Supreme Court, the record before us does not warrant a finding that Enmund had any intention of participating in or facilitating a murder. Yet under Florida law death was an authorized penalty because Enmund aided and abetted a robbery in the course of which murder was committed. It is fundamental that "causing harm intentionally must be punished more severely than causing the same harm unintentionally." Enmund did not kill or intend to kill and thus his culpability is plainly different from that of the robbers who killed; yet the State treated them alike and attributed to Enmund the culpability of those who killed the Kerseys. This was impermissible under the Eighth Amendment.

. . . In *Gregg v. Georgia* the opinion announcing the judgment observed that "[t]he death penalty is said to serve two principal social purposes: retribution and deterrence of capital crimes by prospective offenders." Unless the death penalty when applied to those in Enmund's position measurably contributes to one or both of these goals, it "is nothing more than the purposeless and needless imposition of pain and suffering," and hence an unconstitutional punishment. We are quite unconvinced, however, that the threat that the death penalty will be imposed for murder will measurably deter one who does not kill and has no intention or purpose that life will be taken. . . .

As for retribution as a justification for executing Enmund, we think this very much depends on the degree of Enmund's culpability—what Enmund's intentions, expectations, and actions were. . . . [T]he Court has found criminal penalties to be unconstitutionally excessive in the absence of intentional wrongdoing. . . .

Enmund of course had been convicted of intentional wrongdoing. What the Court meant was that simple participation in felony murder cannot be a constitutionally adequate aggravating circumstance. What remedy is appropriate when an aggravating circumstance is struck down? Should a reviewing court impose a life sentence, remand the case for a new sentencing hearing, or even consider whether the other aggravating circumstances were enough to support a death sentence?

For purposes of imposing the death penalty, Enmund's criminal culpability must be limited to his participation in the robbery, and his punishment must be tailored to his personal responsibility and moral guilt. Putting Enmund to death to

On remand, the Florida courts sentenced Enmund to life imprisonment with eligibility for parole after 25 years. In *Zant v. Stephens* (1983), the Supreme Court acknowledged that there can be "no perfect procedure" to decide eligibility for a death sentence. The Georgia Supreme Court was required by state law to review every death sentence for proportionality. In August 1974, Alpha Stephens escaped from jail and two days later kidnapped and executed a man who interrupted Stephens in the course of a home burglary. The jury found as aggravating circumstances that Stephens had a prior conviction for a capital felony or a substantial history of serious assault convictions and that he committed murder while being escaped from custody. While his case was on appeal, the Georgia Supreme Court decided in another case that "substantial history of serious assault convictions" was too vague to use as an aggravating factor. Stephens argued that since one of the aggravating circumstances was invalidated, so was the death sentence. The U.S. Supreme Court disagreed. As Justice Stevens wrote, with only Justices Marshall and Brennan dissenting, the Model Penal Code's instructions that aggravating and mitigating factors should be weighed against each other were not necessary. As long as the aggravating factors were permissible and narrowed the category of murderers eligible for the death penalty enough to guide the discretion of the jury, the sentence was constitutional. Since Stephens unquestionably was an escapee and had a capital felony record, there were sufficient aggravating factors to differentiate his case from those in which the death penalty could not be imposed. On December 12, 1984, Georgia electrocuted Stephens.

avenge two killings that he did not commit and had no intention of committing or causing does not measurably contribute to the retributive end of ensuring that the criminal gets his just deserts. This is the judgment of most of the legislatures that have recently addressed the matter, and we have no reason to disagree with that judgment for purposes of construing and applying the Eighth Amendment.

Because the Florida Supreme Court affirmed the death penalty in this case in the absence of proof that Enmund killed or attempted to kill, and regardless of whether Enmund intended or contemplated that life would be taken,

we reverse the judgment upholding the death penalty and remand for further proceedings not inconsistent with this opinion....

JUSTICE BRENNAN, concurring.

I join the Court's opinion. However, I adhere to my view that the death penalty is in all circumstances cruel and unusual punishment prohibited by the Eighth and Fourteenth Amendments. See *Gregg v. Georgia* (dissenting opinion).

JUSTICE O'CONNOR, with whom THE CHIEF JUSTICE, JUSTICE POWELL, and JUSTICE REHNQUIST join, dissenting.

Today the Court holds that the Eighth Amendment prohibits a State from executing a convicted felony murderer. I dissent from this holding.... Earl Enmund's claim in this Court is that the death sentence imposed by the Florida trial court, and affirmed by the Florida Supreme Court, is unconstitutionally disproportionate to the role he played in the robbery and murders of the Kerseys. In particular, he contends that because he had no actual intent to kill the victims—in effect, because his behavior and intent were no more blameworthy than that of any robber—capital punishment is too extreme a penalty....

Coker teaches... the magnitude of the punishment imposed must be related to the degree of the harm inflicted on the victim, as well as to the degree of the defendant's blameworthiness....

In sum, in considering the petitioner's challenge, the Court should decide not only whether the petitioner's sentence of death offends contemporary standards as reflected in the responses of legislatures and juries, but also whether it is disproportionate to the harm that the petitioner caused and to the petitioner's involvement in the crime. . . .

. . . I conclude that . . . the death penalty for felony murder does not fall short of our national "standards of decency."

Although the Court disingenuously seeks to characterize Enmund as only a "robber," it cannot be disputed that he is responsible, along with Sampson and Jeanette Armstrong, for the murders of the Kerseys. There is no dispute that their lives were unjustifiably taken, and that the petitioner, as one who aided and abetted the armed robbery, is legally liable for their deaths. Quite unlike the defendant in *Coker*, the petitioner cannot claim that the penalty imposed is "grossly out of proportion" to the harm for which he admittedly is at least partly responsible. . . .

The Court's holding today is especially disturbing because it makes intent a matter of federal constitutional law, requiring this Court both to review highly subjective definitional problems customarily left to state criminal law and to develop an Eighth Amendment meaning of intent. . . . Under the circumstances, the determination of the degree of blameworthiness is best left to the sentencer, who can sift through the facts unique to each case. . . .

In sum, the petitioner and the Court have failed to show that contemporary standards, as reflected in both jury determinations and legislative enactments, preclude imposition of the death penalty for accomplice felony murder. Moreover, examination of the qualitative factors underlying the concept of proportionality do [*sic*] not show that the death penalty is disproportionate as applied to Earl Enmund. In contrast to the crime in *Coker*, the petitioner's crime involves the very type of harm that this Court has held justifies the death penalty. Finally, because of the unique and complex mixture of facts involving a defendant's actions, knowledge, motives, and participation during the commission of a felony murder, I believe that the factfinder is best able to assess the defendant's blameworthiness. Accordingly, I conclude that the death penalty is not disproportionate to the crime of felony murder, even though the defendant did not actually kill or intend to kill his victims. . . .

Notice that the Court distinguishes between eligibility for death under Florida law and under the Eighth Amendment. Although the Supreme Court is the highest court in the land, its authority is limited to construing federal law. In *Michigan v. Long* (1983), the Court announced that it could not review a judgment of a state court that rested on an adequate and independent basis in state law. That is, if a state court makes a decision based on state law, unless that state law itself violates the U.S. Constitution, the Supreme Court has no power to change it. A state court can interpret its own state's constitution and laws to give a defendant more legal protection than the U.S. Constitution does, such as when California struck down the death penalty under its state constitution, not the Eighth Amendment. On the other hand, in *Kansas v. Marsh* (2006), the Supreme Court reversed the Kansas Supreme Court's holding that its death penalty statute was unconstitutional. Kansas law provided that a defendant should be subject to the death sentence if the state proved either that aggravating factors outweighed mitigating factors or that the two were evenly balanced. The Kansas Supreme Court held that this assigned the burden of proof to the defendant in violation of the Eighth Amendment. The U.S. Supreme Court held that this was an error, but the Kansas Supreme Court could easily have made the same decision as a matter of state law and not been subject to review by the U.S. Supreme Court.

The more common application of this independent state ground rule is when a state rule of procedure requires a defendant to make an objection or raise a defense at a particular time and the defendant fails to do so. If the state courts properly rely on that procedural rule to reject a defendant's defense, the federal court has no federal issue to review. For example, the Supreme Court has ruled that a state cannot force a defendant to stand trial in prison garb. Some defendants, however, may wish to wear prison garb to elicit sympathy from the jury. A trial judge may reasonably require an inmate to raise the issue before the jury is seated, even if the result is that a defendant who fails to make a timely request for civilian clothes may end up standing trial in prison clothes. The defendant, because he did not comply with the state's rules, would not be able to argue that the state violated the Constitution by forcing him to wear prison clothes.

This too can be a life or death matter. Codefendants Rebecca Machetti and John Eldon Smith were sentenced to death after separate trials for a 1974 double murder. Machetti, the mastermind of the murder, had her death sentence overturned on her claim of unconstitutional composition of the jury pool and was released after 36 years in prison. Smith was tried in the same county by a jury from the same discriminatorily composed pool. His lawyers failed to object, and on December 15, 1983, he was the first defendant electrocuted by Georgia after *Gregg*.

Repeat Offender Statutes

Solem v. Helm

June 28, 1983

INTRODUCTION

The Cruel and Unusual Punishment Clause in the Eighth Amendment is not the Cruel and Unusual Executions Clause; as *Weems v. United States* showed in 1910, it applies to sentences other than death and has repeatedly been held to prohibit excessive penalties, not just cruel or unusual ones. Jerry Helm was convicted in South Dakota of writing a bad check for $100 and sentenced to life imprisonment without possibility of parole. It was Helm's seventh nonviolent felony conviction.

In his majority opinion, Justice Powell wrote that "a criminal sentence must be proportionate to the crime for which the defendant has been convicted." Powell conceded that states can punish repeat offenders more severely, but in this case Helm's offenses were all "relatively minor." In fact, his sentence of life without parole was the most severe punishment authorized by South Dakota law for any crime. Powell concluded that sentences that are "significantly disproportionate" to the crime are constitutionally impermissible. Chief Justice Burger, joined by Justices White, Rehnquist, and O'Connor, dissented.

JUSTICE POWELL delivered the opinion of the Court.

By 1975 the State of South Dakota had convicted respondent Jerry Helm of six nonviolent felonies. In 1964, 1966, and 1969 Helm was convicted of third-degree burglary. In 1972 he was convicted of obtaining money under false pretenses. In 1973 he was convicted of grand larceny. And in 1975 he was convicted of third-offense driving while intoxicated. The record contains no details about the circumstances of any of these offenses, except that they were all nonviolent, none was a crime against a person, and alcohol was a contributing factor in each case.

In 1979 Helm was charged with uttering a "no account" check for $100. . . . Helm pleaded guilty.

Ordinarily the maximum punishment for uttering a "no account" check would have been five years' imprisonment in the state penitentiary and a $5,000 fine. . . . As a result of his criminal record, however, Helm was subject to South Dakota's recidivist statute:

"When a defendant has been convicted of at least three prior convictions [*sic*] in addition to the principal felony, the

95

sentence for the principal felony shall be enhanced to the sentence for a Class 1 felony." . . . The maximum penalty for a "Class 1 felony" was life imprisonment in the state penitentiary and a $25,000 fine. Moreover, South Dakota law explicitly provides that parole is unavailable: "A person sentenced to life imprisonment is not eligible for parole." . . . The Governor is authorized to pardon prisoners, or to commute their sentences, but no other relief from sentence is available even to a rehabilitated prisoner.

Immediately after accepting Helm's guilty plea, the South Dakota Circuit Court sentenced Helm to life imprisonment under [the statute]. . . .

The South Dakota Supreme Court, in a 3–2 decision, affirmed the sentence despite Helm's argument that it violated the Eighth Amendment.

After Helm had served two years in the state penitentiary, he requested the Governor to commute his sentence to a fixed term of years . . . making Helm eligible to be considered for parole. . . . The Governor denied Helm's request in May 1981. . . .

In November 1981, Helm sought *habeas* relief in the United States District Court for the District of South Dakota. . . . [T]he District Court . . . denied the writ.

The United States Court of Appeals for the Eighth Circuit reversed . . . conclud[ing] . . . that Helm's sentence was "grossly disproportionate to the nature of the offense." It therefore directed the District Court to issue the writ unless the State resentenced Helm.

We granted *certiorari* to consider the Eighth Amendment question presented by this case. We now affirm.

The Eighth Amendment declares: "Excessive bail shall not be required, nor excessive fines imposed, nor cruel and unusual punishments inflicted." The final clause prohibits not only barbaric punishments, but also sentences that are disproportionate to the crime committed.

The principle that a punishment should be proportionate to the crime is deeply rooted and frequently repeated in common-law jurisprudence. In 1215 three chapters of *Magna Carta* were devoted to the rule that "amercements"

Amercements are fines. The Magna Carta expressed the concern of the barons that King John was taxing them through arbitrary decision that they owed penalties for nonexistent or trivial offenses. This was a concern for the wallets of the barons, not for harsh sentences imposed on the common criminal. As Blackstone observed, theft of an amount above 12 pence remained a capital crime well into the 18th century in England. Historians sometimes complain about "law office history" in Supreme Court opinions, that is, the taking of a historical event or writing out of its context to justify a desired outcome. Justice Powell, usually a careful writer, may have been appealing to what lawyers have imagined the Magna Carta to be rather than what it was.

may not be excessive. And the principle was repeated and extended in the First Statute of Westminster (1275). These were not hollow guarantees, for the royal courts relied on them to invalidate disproportionate punishments. . . .

The English Bill of Rights, presented to William and Mary in 1689 as one of the conditions of their taking the throne, was aimed at cruel judges and did not constrain the legislature from passing harsh statutes. In the decades following the Bill of Rights, Parliament passed several acts increasing the number of death penalty offenses in England, particularly for poaching and other offenses against property. If there was a principle of proportionality in the English Bill of Rights, it was overlooked well into the 19th century.

The English Bill of Rights repeated the principle of proportionality in language that was later adopted in the Eighth Amendment. . . .

When the Framers of the Eighth Amendment adopted the language of the English Bill of Rights, they also adopted the English principle of proportionality. Indeed, one of the consistent themes of the era was that Americans had all the rights of English subjects. . . . Thus our Bill of Rights was designed in part to ensure that these rights were preserved. Although the Framers may have intended the Eighth Amendment to go beyond the scope of its English counterpart, their use of the language of the English Bill of Rights is convincing proof that they intended to provide at least the same protection—including the right to be free from excessive punishments.

The constitutional principle of proportionality has been recognized explicitly in this Court for almost a century. . . .

Most recently, the Court has applied the principle of proportionality to hold capital punishment excessive in certain circumstances. *Enmund v. Florida* (1982) (death penalty excessive for felony murder when defendant did not take life, attempt to take life, or intend that a life be taken or that lethal force be used); *Coker v. Georgia* (1977) ("sentence of death is grossly disproportionate and excessive punishment for the crime of rape"). . . . And the Court has continued to recognize that the Eighth Amendment proscribes grossly disproportionate punishments. . . .

The Court's excessive sentence jurisprudence, like its death penalty decisions, directly affects only the extreme cases. While the number of persons being held in state or federal prisons grew roughly in parallel with the population for the first three quarters of the 20th century, the *Solem* decision came at the beginning of three decades of dramatic growth in the prison population, from roughly 320,000 in 1980 to a crest of about 1.6 million in 2009. Jail populations and the number of persons on parole or probation increased dramatically as well before beginning to diminish slightly since 2010.

There is no basis for the State's assertion that the general principle of proportionality does not apply to felony prison sentences. . . .

In sum, we hold as a matter of principle that a criminal sentence must be proportionate to the crime for which the defendant has been convicted. Reviewing courts, of course, should grant substantial deference to the broad authority that legislatures necessarily possess

in determining the types and limits of punishments for crimes, as well as to the discretion that trial courts possess in sentencing convicted criminals. But no penalty is *per se* constitutional. . . .

When sentences are reviewed under the Eighth Amendment, courts should be guided by objective factors that our cases have recognized. First, we look to the gravity of the offense and the harshness of the penalty. . . .

Second, it may be helpful to compare the sentences imposed on other criminals in the same jurisdiction. If more serious crimes are subject to the same penalty, or to less serious penalties, that is some indication that the punishment at issue may be excessive. . . .

Third, courts may find it useful to compare the sentences imposed for commission of the same crime in other jurisdictions. . . .

In sum, a court's proportionality analysis under the Eighth Amendment should be guided by objective criteria. . . .

Helm's crime was "one of the most passive felonies a person could commit." It involved neither violence nor threat of violence to any person. The $100 face value of Helm's "no account" check was not trivial, but neither was it a large amount. One hundred dollars was less than half the amount South Dakota required for a felonious theft. It is easy to see why such a crime is viewed by society as among the less serious offenses. . . .

Helm, of course, was not charged simply with uttering a "no account" check, but also with being a habitual offender. And a State is justified in punishing a recidivist more severely than it punishes a first offender. Helm's status, however, cannot be considered in the abstract. His prior offenses, although classified as felonies, were all relatively minor. All were nonviolent and none was a crime against a person. . . .

Helm's present sentence is life imprisonment without possibility of parole. . . . Helm's sentence is the most severe punishment that the State could have imposed on any criminal for any crime. . . . Only capital punishment, a penalty

Although the Supreme Court found Helm's sentence unconstitutional because it was disproportionate for the type of crime committed, in *Pulley v. Harris* (1984) the Supreme Court said, with only Justices Brennan and Marshall dissenting, that scrutiny of every individual sentence for proportionality is not constitutionally required, even in capital cases. Robert Alton Harris and his brother stole a car from two teenage boys to use as a getaway vehicle in a bank robbery in 1978 and then murdered the boys when they attempted to escape. The California jury, finding special circumstances of multiple murders and that the murders were committed in the course of a robbery, sentenced Harris to death after it heard mitigating evidence about Harris but also heard evidence that Harris had a previous conviction for manslaughter and had committed rape while in prison. Harris contended, and the Ninth Circuit Court of Appeals agreed in reviewing Harris's habeas corpus petition, that the Eighth Amendment requires an appellate court to compare the death sentence in each case to the sentences imposed in similar cases to ensure that the punishment was not more severe than in similar cases. The Supreme Court disagreed. Although 30 states provided for proportionality review, California did not require it. California required the trial judge and the state's highest court to review the evidence that the jury used to support the finding of special circumstances. This review of previously specified aggravating circumstances adequately guided the discretion of the jury and adequately limited the death sentence to a "small sub-class of capital eligible cases."

not authorized in South Dakota when Helm was sentenced, exceeds it.

We next consider the sentences that could be imposed on other criminals in the same jurisdiction. . . .

[T]here were a handful of crimes that were necessarily punished by life imprisonment: murder, and, on a second or third offense, treason, first-degree manslaughter, first-degree arson, and kidnaping. . . .

Criminals committing [serious] offenses ordinarily would be thought more deserving of punishment than one uttering a "no account" check—even when the bad-check writer had already committed six minor felonies. Moreover, there is no indication in the record that any habitual offender other than Helm has ever been given the maximum sentence on the basis of comparable crimes. It is more likely that the possibility of life imprisonment under [the statute] generally is reserved for criminals such as fourth-time heroin dealers, while habitual bad-check writers receive more lenient treatment. In any event, Helm has been treated in the same manner as, or more severely than, criminals who have committed far more serious crimes.

Finally, we compare the sentences imposed for commission of the same crime in other jurisdictions. The Court of Appeals found that "Helm could have received a life sentence without parole for his offense in only one other state, Nevada," and we have no reason to doubt this finding. . . . At the very least, therefore, it is clear that Helm could not have received such a severe sentence in 48 of the 50 States. But even under Nevada law, a life sentence without possibility of parole is merely authorized in these circumstances. . . . We are not advised that any defendant such as Helm, whose prior offenses were so minor, actually has received the maximum penalty in Nevada. It appears that Helm was treated more severely than he would have been in any other State.

In *Rummel v. Estelle* (1980), the Court upheld a life sentence with the possibility of parole for felony fraud imposed under a Texas three-strikes law.

The State argues that the present case is essentially the same as *Rummel v. Estelle,* for the possibility of parole in that case is matched by the possibility of executive clemency here.

The State reasons that the Governor could commute Helm's sentence to a term of years. We conclude, however, that the

South Dakota commutation system is fundamentally different from the parole system that was before us in *Rummel.*

As a matter of law, parole and commutation are different concepts, despite some surface similarities. Parole is a regular part of the rehabilitative process. Assuming good behavior, it is the normal expectation in the vast majority of cases. . . . Thus it is possible to predict, at least to some extent, when parole might be granted. Commutation, on the other hand, is an *ad hoc* exercise of executive clemency. A Governor may commute a sentence at any time for any reason without reference to any standards. . . .

In South Dakota commutation is more difficult to obtain than parole. . . . In fact, no life sentence has been commuted in over eight years. . . . Furthermore, even if Helm's sentence were commuted, he merely would be eligible to be considered for parole. . . .

. . . We conclude that [Helm's] sentence is significantly disproportionate to his crime, and is therefore prohibited by the Eighth Amendment. The judgment of the Court of Appeals is accordingly [a]ffirmed.

CHIEF JUSTICE BURGER, with whom JUSTICE WHITE, JUSTICE REHNQUIST, and JUSTICE O'CONNOR join, dissenting.

The controlling law governing this case is crystal clear, but today the Court blithely discards any concept of *stare decisis,* trespasses gravely on the authority of the states, and distorts the concept of proportionality of punishment by tearing it from its moorings in capital cases. Only three Terms ago, we held in *Rummel v. Estelle,* that a life sentence imposed after only a third nonviolent felony conviction did not constitute cruel and unusual punishment under the Eighth Amendment. Today, the Court ignores its recent precedent and holds that a life sentence imposed after a seventh felony conviction constitutes cruel and unusual punishment under the Eighth Amendment. Moreover, I reject the fiction that all Helm's crimes were innocuous or nonviolent. Among his felonies were three burglaries and a third conviction for drunken driving. By comparison *Rummel* was a relatively "model citizen." Although today's holding cannot rationally be reconciled with *Rummel,* the Court does not purport to overrule *Rummel.*

I therefore dissent. . . .

Neither the majority nor the dissent gave any indication that they were considering the real-world effect of lengthy prison sentences on crowding and costs. In fact, the Supreme Court came late to the legal battle over prison conditions. American had at its founding been known for its relatively mild punishments and its experiments in more effective and humane conditions, including efforts to teach inmates trades and have them support their upkeep by prison industries, but opposition from skilled craftsmen and organized labor in the later 19th century caused prisons to devolve into more isolated worlds where long-term offenders lived at the mercy of wardens and their fellow inmates with only the hope of parole. Chain gangs were common particularly in the South, but conditions were stark almost everywhere. State governments, sometimes independently and sometimes due to suits filed in state and lower federal courts, began an era of active reform in the 1960s. For example, Justice Blackmun, a judge on the Eight Circuit Court of Appeals before joining the Supreme Court, held in *Jackson v. Bishop* (Eighth Circuit, 1968) that Arkansas's use of flogging with the strap for violating prison rules was barred by the Eighth Amendment.

In *Estelle v. Gamble* (1976), the Court held for the first time that the Eighth Amendment's ban on cruel and unusual punishments extended to conditions of confinement, such as improper medical treatment, even if those conditions were not intended as punishment. In *Hutto v. Finney* (1978), the Court approved another intervention of the lower federal courts into Arkansas's system of disciplinary confinement, which consisted of 4–11 inmates, both healthy and with infectious diseases, being confined in a windowless 8-by-10-foot cell with a faucet and a toilet flushable from the outside. Inmates, sometimes held for months in punitive isolation, were fed less than 1,000 calories per day.

This would embark the federal courts on decades of inmate litigation. Eventually the ridiculous lawsuits came to outweigh the meritorious ones so markedly that Congress passed the Prison Litigation Reform Act (PLRA) in 1996, requiring federal courts to screen complaints for merit before litigation commenced and restricting inmates who filed three or more meritless complaints from doing so unless they did so at their own expense. The PLRA also restricted the power of federal judges to issue injunctions to reduce prison overcrowding.

In *Brown v. Plata* (2011), one of the few post-PLRA prison condition cases to reach the Supreme Court, the justices affirmed an injunction requiring California to reduce overcrowding in its prisons from almost double capacity to 137.5 percent because inmates with serious mental disorders were not receiving necessary treatment. Around the country, other states had already begun slashing their prison populations due to the high cost of incarceration.

Execution of the Insane

Ford v. Wainwright

June 26, 1986

INTRODUCTION

Well before the founding of this country, it was generally understood that a person who was insane could not be convicted because he was not legally responsible for his actions. Since executions followed convictions more rapidly than at present, courts did not often confront the question of executing an inmate who became insane on death row. Mental illness was poorly understood and in most cases beyond treatment, so incarceration of the criminally insane was more a matter of safety than humanity. Because of the nearly universal recognition that executing an inmate who had become insane was barbaric, it was not until this case that the Supreme Court considered whether the U.S. Constitution prohibits the execution of a prisoner who becomes insane while awaiting execution. As the dissent pointed out, it was not the death penalty itself that the Court was changing but rather the procedure used to determine whether the inmate was insane. The divisions on the Court foreshadowed subsequent examinations of the execution of mentally retarded inmates and most recently the protocols used for lethal injection.

JUSTICE MARSHALL announced the judgment of the Court and delivered the opinion of the Court with respect to Parts I and II and an opinion with respect to Parts III, IV, and V, in which JUSTICE BRENNAN, JUSTICE BLACKMUN, and JUSTICE STEVENS join.

For centuries no jurisdiction has countenanced the execution of the insane, yet this Court has never decided whether the Constitution forbids the practice. Today we keep faith with our common-law heritage in holding that it does.

I

Alvin Bernard Ford was convicted of murder in 1974 and sentenced to death. There is no suggestion that he was incompetent at the time of his offense, at trial, or at sentencing. In early 1982, however, Ford began to manifest gradual changes in behavior. They began as an occasional peculiar idea or confused perception, but became more serious over time. After reading in the newspaper that the Ku Klux Klan had held a rally in nearby Jacksonville, Florida, Ford developed an obsession focused upon the Klan. His letters to various people reveal endless brooding about his

"Klan work," and an increasingly pervasive delusion that he had become the target of a complex conspiracy, involving the Klan and assorted others, designed to force him to commit suicide. He believed that the prison guards, part of the conspiracy, had been killing people and putting the bodies in the concrete enclosures used for beds. Later, he began to believe that his women relatives were being tortured and sexually abused somewhere in the prison. This notion developed into a delusion that the people who were tormenting him at the prison had taken members of Ford's family hostage. The hostage delusion took firm hold and expanded, until Ford was reporting that 135 of his friends and family were being held hostage in the prison, and that only he could help them. By "day 287" of the "hostage crisis," the list of hostages had expanded to include "senators, Senator Kennedy, and many other leaders." In a letter to the Attorney General of Florida, written in 1983, Ford appeared to assume authority for ending the "crisis," claiming to have fired a number of prison officials. He began to refer to himself as "Pope John Paul, III," and reported having appointed nine new justices to the Florida Supreme Court.

. . . Counsel for Ford invoked the procedures of Florida law governing the determination of competency of a condemned inmate. Following the procedures set forth in the statute, the Governor of Florida appointed a panel of three psychiatrists to evaluate whether, under [State law], Ford had "the mental capacity to understand the nature of the death penalty and the reasons why it was imposed upon him." At a single meeting, the three psychiatrists together interviewed Ford for approximately 30 minutes. Each doctor then filed a separate two- or three-page report with the Governor, to whom the statute delegates the final decision. One doctor concluded that Ford suffered from "psychosis with paranoia" but had "enough cognitive functioning to understand the nature and the effects of the death penalty, and why it is to be imposed on him." Another found that, although Ford was "psychotic," he did "know fully what can happen to him." The third concluded that Ford had a "severe adaptational disorder," but did "comprehend his total situation including being sentenced to death, and all of the implications of that penalty." He believed that Ford's disorder, "although severe, seem[ed] contrived and recently learned." Thus, the interview produced three different diagnoses, but accord on the question of sanity as defined by state law.

"He began to refer to himself as 'Pope John Paul, III,' and reported having appointed nine new justices to the Florida Supreme Court."

"The bar against executing a prisoner who has lost his sanity bears impressive historical credentials; the practice consistently has been branded 'savage and inhuman.'"

II

We begin, then, with the common law. The bar against executing a prisoner who has lost his sanity bears impressive historical credentials; the practice consistently has been branded "savage and inhuman." . . .

As is often true of common-law principles . . . the reasons for the rule are less sure and less uniform than the rule itself. One explanation is that the execution of an insane person simply offends humanity; another, that it provides no example to others and thus contributes nothing to whatever deterrence value is intended to be served by capital punishment. Other commentators postulate religious underpinnings. . . . It is also said that execution serves no purpose in these cases because madness is its own punishment. . . . More recent commentators opine that the community's quest for "retribution"—the need to offset a criminal act by a punishment of equivalent "moral quality"—is not served by execution of an insane person. . . . Unanimity of rationale, therefore, we do not find. "But whatever the reason of the law is, it is plain the law is so." We know of virtually no authority condoning the execution of the insane at English common law. . . .

This ancestral legacy has not outlived its time. Today, no State in the Union permits the execution of the insane. It is clear that the ancient and humane limitation upon the State's ability to execute its sentences has as firm a hold upon the jurisprudence of today as it had centuries ago in England. The various reasons put forth in support of the common-law restriction have no less logical, moral, and practical force than they did when first voiced. . . . Whether its aim be to protect the condemned from fear and pain without comfort of understanding, or to protect the dignity of society itself from the barbarity of exacting mindless vengeance, the restriction finds enforcement in the Eighth Amendment.

III

The Eighth Amendment prohibits the State from inflicting the penalty of death upon a prisoner who is insane. Petitioner's allegation of insanity in his *habeas corpus* petition, if proved, therefore, would bar his execution. The question before us is whether the District Court was under an obligation to hold an evidentiary hearing on the question of Ford's sanity. . . .

IV

The first deficiency in Florida's procedure lies in its failure to include the prisoner in the truth-seeking process. . . . [S]tate practice does not permit any material relevant to the ultimate decision to be submitted on behalf of the prisoner facing execution. . . .

A related flaw in the Florida procedure is the denial of any opportunity to challenge or impeach the state-appointed psychiatrists' opinions. . . . Cross-examination of the psychiatrists, or perhaps a less formal equivalent, would contribute markedly to the process of seeking truth in sanity disputes by bringing to light the bases for each expert's beliefs, the precise factors underlying those beliefs, any history of error or caprice of the examiner, any personal bias with respect to the issue of capital punishment, the expert's degree of certainty about his or her own conclusions, and the precise meaning of ambiguous words used in the report. Without some questioning of the experts concerning their technical conclusions, a factfinder simply cannot be expected to evaluate the various opinions, particularly when they are themselves inconsistent. . . . The failure of the Florida procedure to afford the prisoner's representative any opportunity to clarify or challenge the state experts' opinions or methods creates a significant possibility that the ultimate decision made in reliance on those experts will be distorted.

Perhaps the most striking defect in the procedures of [the Florida statute] . . . is the State's placement of the decision wholly within the executive branch. Under this procedure, the person who appoints the experts and ultimately decides whether the State will be able to carry out the sentence that it has long sought is the Governor, whose subordinates have been responsible for initiating every stage of the prosecution of the condemned from arrest through sentencing. The commander of the State's corps of prosecutors cannot be said to have the neutrality that is necessary for reliability in the factfinding proceeding. . . .

As both the majority and the dissent recognized, due process and the Eighth Amendment were intertwined. Since the 1960s, Justices Brennan and Marshall had been particularly active in developing the constitutional doctrine that the more important the legal interest at stake, the more like a trial the procedural protections needed to be. The 1980s saw the Court's high-water mark in elaborating on protections under the Due Process Clause and the Sixth Amendment's right to counsel. Since the first federal criminal statute in 1790, defendants in federal death penalty cases were to be appointed up to two attorneys "learned in the law." The Sixth Amendment's guarantee of representation by counsel has been applied to the states as well but with varying degrees of effectiveness. In *Powell v. Alabama* (1932), the Supreme Court reversed the convictions of the so-called Scottsboro Boys, several black teenagers sentenced to death for the alleged rape of two white women, on the grounds that counsel appointed literally the morning of trial could not have prepared an effective defense. The Court formally announced a test for the Sixth Amendment effective assistance of counsel in *Strickland v. Washington* (1984). David Washington committed three murders in Florida in September 1976 but argued that he had received the death penalty because his lawyer was ineffective. The Supreme Court held that to obtain a new trial or sentencing hearing, a defendant had to show that counsel did more than make a mistake and had fallen below prevailing professional standards. Furthermore, the deficiency had to have caused "prejudice" to the defendant, that is, the loss of a meritorious claim or defense. Washington could not show that on the evidence presented anything his lawyer could have done would have saved him. Florida executed Washington on July 13, 1984.

Subsequent cases indicate that unless the defendant forbids his counsel to put on a defense, an effective counsel almost always can say something to explain why the defendant does not deserve death. The American Bar Association promulgated guidelines in 1989 and 2003 that suggest that counsel can and must investigate at least the following: the defendant's complete prenatal, pediatric, and adult medical information, including exposure to harmful substances in utero and in the environment; mental health history, multigenerational family history, genetic disorders and vulnerabilities; educational, employment, military, criminal, and substance abuse histories; and the defendant's sexual orientation and socioeconomic, religious, racial, cultural, and political influences. Usually counsel need not look that deep. In *Wiggins v. Smith* (2003), the Court vacated a Maryland death sentence imposed on Kevin Wiggins for the murder of a 77-year-old woman during a 1988 burglary because counsel had not attempted to present evidence to the sentencing jury about their client's past. The evidence was that Wiggins, who had no prior record, was borderline retarded and had been alternately neglected and abused—starved, forced to eat paint chips and garbage, and beaten and burned by being forced against a hot stove burner—by his alcoholic mother and then was shuttled from foster home to foster home, including one where he was gang-raped. The Court held, 7–2, that the decision not to introduce this evidence of Wiggins's background was unreasonable. On remand, Wiggins and Maryland agreed that Wiggins would plead guilty to murder with a life sentence that gave him a chance at parole.

That counsel can always say something does not mean that counsel are ineffective if they do not say everything. The defendant must show that there is reasonable probability that the result would have been different. Consider *Smith v. Spisak* (2010). Frank Spisak murdered three people in 1982, and in an unsuccessful attempt to establish an insanity defense he testified at his trial that he committed the crimes as a follower of Adolf Hitler and would commit more murders if he had the chance. As Justice Stevens commented in his concurrence to the Court's rejection of the claim that Spisak's attorney was ineffective, even a closing argument befitting Clarence Darrow would not have made a difference. Ohio executed Spisak by lethal injection on February 17, 2011.

In *Panetti v. Quarterman* (2007), a majority of the Court finally settled on a definition of sanity first proposed by Justice Powell in *Ford v. Wainwright*: inmates must have a rational understanding of the punishment they are to suffer and why they are to suffer it. An inmate who sincerely holds the delusional belief that he is to be executed as a religious martyr or a political prisoner is one too insane to execute.

Another part of our common-law heritage examined by the Court in the 1980s was the traditional practice of allowing peremptory challenges (in addition to the challenges for cause already discussed in *Witherspoon*), challenges that attorneys could make to jurors without the need for an explanation. In *Batson v. Kentucky* (1986), the Court held that the prosecutor's use of peremptory challenges to strike all the black prospective jurors violated the Sixth Amendment's guarantee of a fair jury to Batson, a black man on trial for burglary.

Eventually the Court extended *Batson v. Kentucky*'s general principle to white criminal defendants who complained that the prosecutor was excluding black jurors on the basis of race in *Powers v. Ohio* (1991) and to peremptory challenges used to exclude jurors on the basis of sex. In *Georgia v. McCollum* (1992), the Court put the last brick in the wall: the government too can object to a defendant's improper use of peremptory challenges to exclude jurors on the basis of race or sex.

V

Having identified various failings of the Florida scheme, we must conclude that the State's procedures for determining sanity are inadequate. . . . We do not here suggest that only a full trial on the issue of sanity will suffice to protect the federal interests; we leave to the State the task of developing appropriate ways to enforce the constitutional restriction upon its execution of sentences. . . .

JUSTICE POWELL, concurring in part and concurring in the judgment. [Omitted]

JUSTICE O'CONNOR, with whom JUSTICE WHITE joins, concurring in the result in part and dissenting in part. [Omitted]

JUSTICE REHNQUIST, with whom THE CHIEF JUSTICE joins, dissenting.

The Court today holds that the Eighth Amendment prohibits a State from carrying out a lawfully imposed sentence of death upon a person who is currently insane. This holding is based almost entirely on two unremarkable observations. First, the Court states that it "know[s] of virtually no authority condoning the execution of the insane at English common law." Second, it notes that "[t]oday, no State in the Union permits the execution of the insane." Armed with these facts, and shielded by the claim that it is simply "keep[ing] faith with our common-law heritage," the Court proceeds to cast aside settled precedent and to significantly alter both the common-law and current practice of not executing the insane. It manages this feat by carefully ignoring the fact that the Florida scheme it finds unconstitutional, in which the Governor is assigned the ultimate responsibility of deciding whether a condemned prisoner is currently insane, is fully consistent with the "common-law heritage" and current practice on which the Court purports to rely.

The Court places great weight on the "impressive historical credentials" of the common-law bar against executing a prisoner who has lost his sanity. What it fails to mention, however, is the equally important and unchallenged fact that at common law it was the executive who passed upon the sanity of the condemned. . . . So when the Court

today creates a constitutional right to a determination of sanity outside of the executive branch, it does so not in keeping with but at the expense of "our common-law heritage." . . .

What is a satisfactory nondiscriminatory explanation of an attorney's hunch that leads to a peremptory challenge? The Court gave no guidance to the lower courts for almost 20 years after *Batson v. Kentucky*. In *Johnson v. California* (2005), the Court held that a defendant need not prove that discrimination was likely in order to require an explanation, only that discrimination was possible. That settled the question about what evidence the trial court should use, but what about the Court's decision that discrimination had not occurred? How willing would the Court be to review that? In *Miller-El v. Dretke* (2005), the Court seemed willing to use statistics to prove discrimination but only statistics from the case under review. Thomas Miller-El, a black man, robbed a hotel in Texas in 1985, killing 1 bound and gagged employee and wounding another. The prosecutor used 10 of its 15 peremptory challenges to remove 10 of the 11 black jury panelists. The jury convicted Miller-El and recommended the death penalty. Justice Souter wrote for the majority (3 justices dissented) that it "blinks reality" to deny that prosecutors were striking jurors on the basis of race. On remand for a new sentencing hearing, Miller-El and the prosecutor agreed in 2008 that Miller-El would serve a life sentence with no right to appeal.

Allowing the Death Penalty for Accomplices

Tison v. Arizona

April 21, 1987

INTRODUCTION

In *Tison v. Arizona,* the Supreme Court upheld the death penalty for accomplices to murder if their participation in the crime was "major" and if they displayed "reckless indifference to human life." Justice O'Connor, who had been a member of the Arizona legislature and was the only member of the Court who had held elective office, consistently advocated deference to elected officials' legal choices in criminal matters.

JUSTICE O'CONNOR delivered the opinion of the Court.

The question presented is whether the petitioners' participation in the events leading up to and following the murder of four members of a family makes the sentences of death imposed by the Arizona courts constitutionally permissible although neither petitioner specifically intended to kill the victims and neither inflicted the fatal gunshot wounds. . . .

Gary Tison was sentenced to life imprisonment as the result of a prison escape during the course of which he had killed a guard. After he had been in prison a number of years, Gary Tison's wife, their three sons Donald, Ricky, and Raymond, Gary's brother Joseph, and other relatives made plans to help Gary Tison escape again. . . . The Tison family assembled a large arsenal of weapons for this purpose. Plans for escape were discussed with Gary Tison, who insisted that his cellmate, Randy Greenawalt, also a convicted murderer, be included in the prison break. . . .

On July 30, 1978, the three Tison brothers entered the Arizona State Prison at Florence carrying a large ice chest filled with guns. The Tisons armed Greenawalt and their father, and the group, brandishing their weapons, locked the prison guards and visitors present in a storage closet. The five men fled the prison grounds in the Tisons' Ford Galaxy automobile. No shots were fired at the prison.

After leaving the prison, the men abandoned the Ford automobile and proceeded on to an isolated house in a white

Lincoln automobile that the brothers had parked at a hospital near the prison. At the house, the Lincoln automobile had a flat tire; the only spare tire was pressed into service. After two nights at the house, the group drove toward Flagstaff. As the group traveled on back roads and secondary highways through the desert, another tire blew out. The group decided to flag down a passing motorist and steal a car. Raymond stood out in front of the Lincoln; the other four armed themselves and lay in wait by the side of the road. . . . [A] Mazda occupied by John Lyons, his wife, Donnelda, his 2-year-old son, Christopher, and his 15-year-old niece, Theresa Tyson, pulled over to render aid.

As Raymond showed John Lyons the flat tire on the Lincoln, the other Tisons and Greenawalt emerged. The Lyons family was forced into the backseat of the Lincoln. Raymond and Donald drove the Lincoln down a dirt road off the highway and then down a gas line service road farther into the desert; Gary Tison, Ricky Tison, and Randy Greenawalt followed in the Lyons' Mazda. The two cars were parked trunk to trunk and the Lyons family was ordered to stand in front of the Lincoln's headlights. The Tisons transferred their belongings from the Lincoln into the Mazda. They discovered guns and money in the Mazda which they kept, and they put the rest of the Lyons' possessions in the Lincoln.

Gary Tison then told Raymond to drive the Lincoln still farther into the desert. Raymond did so, and, while the others guarded the Lyons and Theresa Tyson, Gary fired his shotgun into the radiator, presumably to completely disable the vehicle. The Lyons and Theresa Tyson were then escorted to the Lincoln and again ordered to stand in its headlights. Ricky Tison reported that John Lyons begged, in comments "more or less directed at everybody," "Jesus, don't kill me." Gary Tison said he was "thinking about it." John Lyons asked the Tisons and Greenawalt to "[g]ive us some water . . . just leave us out here, and you all go home." Gary Tison then told his sons to go back to the Mazda and get some water. Raymond later explained that his father "was like in conflict with himself. . . . What it was, I think it was the baby being there and all this, and he wasn't sure about what to do."

The petitioners . . . went back towards the Mazda, along with Donald, while Randy Greenawalt and Gary Tison stayed at the Lincoln guarding the victims. . . . [P]etitioners agree they

"The group decided to flag down a passing motorist and steal a car. Raymond stood out in front of the Lincoln; the other four armed themselves and lay in wait by the side of the road."

saw Greenawalt and their father brutally murder their four captives with repeated blasts from their shotguns. Neither made an effort to help the victims, though both later stated they were surprised by the shooting. The Tisons got into the Mazda and drove away, continuing their flight. . . .

Several days later the Tisons and Greenawalt were apprehended after a shootout at a police roadblock. Donald Tison was killed. Gary Tison escaped into the desert where he subsequently died of exposure. Raymond and Ricky Tison and Randy Greenawalt were captured and tried jointly for the crimes associated with the prison break itself and the shootout at the roadblock; each was convicted and sentenced.

Consider the dilemmas posed by the prosecution of several defendants who have varying degrees of culpability in a crime that ends in a murder. This would multiply the expense and make the time for trial of some crimes impractically long if each defendant had to be tried separately, even if the witnesses could be reassembled again and again to give the same testimony. But the standard practice of trying all defendants together risks guilt by association in unique ways in death penalty cases. The defendants facing the death penalty can expect the jury to assume that they are more guilty than the other defendants because the prosecutor is seeking the death penalty only against them, while the noncapital defendants face a jury that is death-qualified and may not hesitate to find any defendant tried with a capital defendant guilty of something because the noncapital defendants, at least, are only facing prison and not execution.

The State then individually tried each of the petitioners for capital murder of the four victims as well as for the associated crimes of armed robbery, kidnaping, and car theft. The capital murder charges were based on Arizona felony-murder law providing that a killing occurring during the perpetration of robbery or kidnaping is capital murder and that each participant in the kidnaping or robbery is legally responsible for the acts of his accomplices. Each of the petitioners was convicted of the four murders under these accomplice liability and felony-murder statutes.

Arizona law also provided for a capital sentencing proceeding . . . to determine whether the crime was sufficiently aggravated to warrant the death sentence. The statute set out six aggravating and four mitigating factors. The judge found three statutory aggravating factors:

1. the Tisons had created a grave risk of death to others (not the victims);
2. the murders had been committed for pecuniary gain;
3. the murders were especially heinous.

The judge found no statutory mitigating factor. Importantly, the judge specifically found that the crime was not mitigated by the fact that each of the petitioners' "participation was relatively minor." Rather, he found that the "participation of each [petitioner] in the crimes giving rise to the application of the felony-murder rule in this case was very substantial." The trial judge also specifically found that each "could reasonably have foreseen that his conduct . . . would cause or create a grave risk of . . . death." He did find, however, three nonstatutory mitigating factors:

1. the petitioners' youth—Ricky was 20 and Raymond was 19;
2. neither had prior felony records;
3. each had been convicted of the murders under the felony-murder rule.

Nevertheless, the judge sentenced both petitioners to death.

On direct appeal, the Arizona Supreme Court affirmed.

. . . Petitioners argue strenuously that they did not "intend to kill" as that concept has been generally understood in the common law. We accept this as true. . . . [T]here is no evidence that either Ricky or Raymond Tison took any act which he desired to, or was substantially certain would, cause death.

"Petitioners argue strenuously that they did not 'intend to kill' as that concept has been generally understood in the common law."

. . . [T]he Tison brothers' participation in the crime was anything but minor. . . . [T]hey both subjectively appreciated that their acts were likely to result in the taking of innocent life. The issue raised by this case is whether the Eighth Amendment prohibits the death penalty in the intermediate case of the defendant whose participation is major and whose mental state is one of reckless indifference to the value of human life. *Enmund* does not specifically address this point. We now take up the task of determining whether the Eighth Amendment proportionality requirement bars the death penalty under these circumstances.

Like the *Enmund* Court, we find the state legislatures' judgment as to proportionality in these circumstances relevant to this constitutional inquiry. The largest number of States still fall into the two intermediate categories discussed in *Enmund*. Four States authorize the death penalty in felony-murder cases upon a showing of culpable mental state such as recklessness or extreme indifference to human life. Two jurisdictions require that the defendant's participation be substantial and the statutes of at least six more, including Arizona, take minor participation in the felony expressly into account in mitigation of the murder. . . . [T]he greater the defendant's participation in the felony murder, the more likely that he acted with reckless indifference to human life. At a minimum, however, it can be said that all these jurisdictions . . . specifically authorize the death penalty in a felony-murder case where, though the defendant's mental state fell short of intent to kill, the defendant was a major actor in a felony in which he knew death was highly likely to occur. . . . [S]ubstantial and recent legislative authorization of the death penalty for the crime of felony murder regardless of the absence of a finding of an intent to kill powerfully suggests that our society does not reject the death penalty as grossly excessive under these circumstances. . . .

A critical facet of the individualized determination of culpability required in capital cases is the mental state with which the defendant commits the crime. Deeply ingrained in our legal tradition is the idea that the more purposeful is the criminal conduct, the more serious is the offense, and, therefore, the more severely it ought to be punished. . . .

A narrow focus on the question of whether or not a given defendant "intended to kill," however, is a highly unsatisfactory means of definitively distinguishing the most culpable and dangerous of murderers. Many who intend to, and do, kill are not criminally liable at all—those who act in self-defense or with other justification or excuse. Other intentional homicides, though criminal, are often felt undeserving of the death penalty—those that are the result of provocation. On the other hand, some nonintentional murderers may be among the most dangerous and inhumane of all—the person who tortures another not caring whether the victim lives or dies, or the robber who shoots someone in the course of the robbery, utterly indifferent to the fact that the desire to rob may have the unintended consequence of killing the victim as well as taking the victim's property. This reckless indifference to the value of human life may be every bit as shocking to the moral sense as an "intent to kill." Indeed it is for this very reason that the common-law and modern criminal codes alike have classified behavior such as occurred in this case along with intentional murders. . . . *Enmund* held that when "intent to kill" results in its logical though not inevitable consequence—the taking of human life—the Eighth Amendment permits the State to exact the death penalty after a careful weighing of the aggravating and mitigating circumstances. Similarly, we hold that the reckless disregard for human life implicit in knowingly engaging in criminal activities known to carry a grave risk of death represents a highly culpable mental state, a mental state that may be taken into account in making a capital sentencing judgment when that conduct causes its natural, though also not inevitable, lethal result.

"This reckless indifference to the value of human life may be every bit as shocking to the moral sense as an 'intent to kill.'"

. . . [W]e . . . hold that major participation in the felony committed, combined with reckless indifference to human life, is sufficient to satisfy the *Enmund* culpability requirement. The Arizona courts have clearly found that the former exists; we now vacate the judgments below and remand for determination of the latter in further proceedings not inconsistent with this opinion. . . .

JUSTICE BRENNAN, with whom JUSTICE MARSHALL joins, and with whom JUSTICE BLACKMUN and JUSTICE STEVENS join as to Parts I through IV-A, dissenting. [Omitted]

The Tisons ultimately had their sentences reduced to life imprisonment. Greenawalt was executed by Arizona in 1997.

Would the defendant's dilemma of having to choose between arguing to the jury (or here to the judge) at the guilt phase that he is innocent and arguing at the penalty phase that it is a mitigating factor that he feels remorse be cured by empaneling two juries? If so, is that a proper thing to do, and if it is proper, is it required by the Eighth Amendment? In the first decade of the 21st century, some lower federal court judges attempted to experiment with empaneling two juries in death penalty cases under the Federal Death Penalty Act, a non–death-qualified one to find guilt and a death-qualified one to decide on the penalty in the case of guilt. Interpreting the federal statute to prohibit that option, courts of appeal have prevented the lower courts from enacting procedures not authorized by Congress. Another option that remains untried is to empanel a jury with a large number of alternate jurors and only death-qualifying 12 jurors at the penalty stage if the penalty phase jury found guilt.

Due to cost and prosecution opposition, these are likely never to be tried unless the Supreme Court requires them.

Use of Statistics Showing Racial Bias

McCleskey v. Kemp

April 22, 1987

INTRODUCTION

Citing a study by Professor David Baldus, Warren McCleskey claimed that Georgia's death penalty system reflected racial bias. The Baldus study revealed that the combination of black defendant and white murder victims was the most likely to result in a sentence of death. The Supreme Court rejected McCleskey's argument, holding that the general patterns contained in the Baldus study were not sufficient to sustain a claim of bias. Instead, the Court found that it would have been necessary for McCleskey to have shown that decision makers in this particular case acted with a racially discriminatory intent. Justice Powell's majority opinion concluded that "the Baldus study does not demonstrate a constitutionally significant risk of racial bias affecting the Georgia capital sentencing process" and that McCleskey's arguments would be "best presented to the legislative bodies." Justices Brennan, Marshall, Blackmun, and Stevens dissented.

After retiring in 1987, Justice Powell changed his mind about the death penalty. In a 1991 conversation with his former law clerk John Jeffries, Powell said that if he could, he would change his vote and find the death penalty unconstitutional: "I would vote the other way in any capital case. . . . I've come to think that capital punishment should be abolished."[1]

JUSTICE POWELL delivered the opinion of the Court.

This case presents the question whether a complex statistical study that indicates a risk that racial considerations enter into capital sentencing determinations proves that petitioner McCleskey's capital sentence is unconstitutional under the Eighth or Fourteenth Amendment.

McCleskey, a black man, was convicted of two counts of armed robbery and one count of murder in the Superior Court of Fulton County, Georgia. . . . McCleskey's convictions arose out of the robbery of a furniture store and the killing of a white police officer during the course of the robbery. The evidence at trial indicated that McCleskey and three accomplices planned and carried out the robbery. All four were armed. McCleskey entered the front of the store while the other three entered the rear. McCleskey secured the front of the store by rounding up the customers and forcing them to lie face down on the floor. The other three rounded up the employees in the rear and tied them up with tape. The manager was forced at gunpoint to turn over the store receipts, his watch, and \$6. During the course of the robbery, a police officer, answering a silent alarm, entered the store through the front door. As he was walking down the center aisle of the store, two shots were fired. Both struck the officer. One hit him in the face and killed him.

. . . Under Georgia law, the jury could not consider imposing the death penalty unless it found beyond a reasonable doubt that the murder was accompanied by one of the statutory aggravating circumstances. The jury in this case found two aggravating circumstances to exist beyond a reasonable doubt: the murder was committed during the course of an armed robbery; and the murder was committed upon a peace officer engaged in the performance of his duties. . . . McCleskey offered no mitigating evidence. The jury recommended that he be sentenced to death on the murder charge and to consecutive life sentences on the armed robbery charges. The court followed the jury's recommendation and sentenced McCleskey to death.

On appeal, the Supreme Court of Georgia affirmed the convictions and the sentences. . . .

McCleskey . . . filed a petition for a *writ of habeas corpus* in the Federal District Court for the Northern District of Georgia. His petition raised 18 claims, one of which was that the Georgia capital sentencing process is administered in a racially discriminatory manner in violation of the Eighth and Fourteenth Amendments to the United States Constitution. In support of his claim, McCleskey proffered a statistical study performed by Professors David C. Baldus, Charles Pulaski, and George Woodworth (the Baldus study) that purports to show a disparity in the imposition of the death sentence in Georgia based on the race of the murder victim and, to a lesser extent, the race of the defendant. The Baldus study is actually two sophisticated statistical studies that examine over 2,000 murder cases that occurred in Georgia during the 1970s. The raw numbers collected by Professor Baldus indicate that defendants charged with killing white persons received the death penalty in 11% of the cases, but defendants charged with killing blacks received the death penalty in only 1% of the cases. . . .

Baldus also divided the cases according to the combination of the race of the defendant and the race of the victim. He found that the death penalty was assessed in 22% of the cases involving black defendants and white victims; 8% of

"The raw numbers collected by Professor Baldus indicate that defendants charged with killing white persons received the death penalty in 11% of the cases, but defendants charged with killing blacks received the death penalty in only 1% of the cases."

the cases involving white defendants and white victims; 1% of the cases involving black defendants and black victims; and 3% of the cases involving white defendants and black victims. . . .

Baldus subjected his data to an extensive analysis, taking account of 230 variables that could have explained the disparities on nonracial grounds. One of his models concludes that, even after taking account of 39 nonracial variables, defendants charged with killing white victims were 4.3 times as likely to receive a death sentence as defendants charged with killing blacks. . . . Thus, the Baldus study indicates that black defendants, such as McCleskey, who kill white victims have the greatest likelihood of receiving the death penalty.

The District Court . . . concluded that McCleskey's "statistics do not demonstrate a *prima facie* case in support of the contention that the death penalty was imposed upon him because of his race, because of the race of the victim, or because of any Eighth Amendment concern." . . .

The Court of Appeals for the Eleventh Circuit, sitting *en banc,* carefully reviewed the District Court's decision on McCleskey's claim. It assumed the validity of the study itself and addressed the merits of McCleskey's Eighth and Fourteenth Amendment claims. That is, the court assumed that the study "showed that systematic and substantial disparities existed in the penalties imposed upon homicide defendants in Georgia based on race of the homicide victim, that the disparities existed at a less substantial rate in death sentencing based on race of defendants, and that the factors of race of the victim and defendant were at work in Fulton County." Even assuming the study's validity, the Court of Appeals found the statistics "insufficient to demonstrate discriminatory intent or unconstitutional discrimination in the Fourteenth Amendment context, [and] insufficient to show irrationality, arbitrariness and capriciousness under any kind of Eighth Amendment analysis." . . .

The Court of Appeals affirmed the denial by the District Court of McCleskey's petition for a *writ of habeas corpus.* . . . We granted *certiorari* and now affirm.

McCleskey's first claim is that the Georgia capital punishment statute violates the Equal Protection Clause of the Fourteenth Amendment. He argues that race has infected the administration of Georgia's statute. . . . As a black defendant who killed a white victim, McCleskey claims that the Baldus study demonstrates that he was discriminated against because of his race and because of the race of his victim. . . . We agree with the Court of Appeals, and every other court that has considered such a challenge, that this claim must fail.

Our analysis begins with the basic principle that a defendant who alleges an equal protection violation has the burden of proving "the existence of purposeful discrimination." A corollary to this principle is that a criminal defendant must prove that the purposeful discrimination "had a discriminatory effect" on him. Thus, to prevail under the Equal Protection Clause, McCleskey must prove that the decisionmakers in his case acted with discriminatory purpose. He offers no evidence specific to his own case that would support an inference that racial considerations played a part in his sentence. Instead, he relies solely on the Baldus study. McCleskey argues that the Baldus study compels an inference that his sentence rests on purposeful discrimination. . . . [T]he Baldus study is clearly insufficient to support an inference that any of the decisionmakers in McCleskey's case acted with discriminatory purpose. . . .

McCleskey also argues that the Baldus study demonstrates that the Georgia capital sentencing system violates the Eighth Amendment. . . .

. . . To evaluate McCleskey's challenge, we must examine exactly what the Baldus study may show. Even Professor Baldus does not contend that his statistics prove that race enters into any capital sentencing decisions or that race was a factor in McCleskey's particular case. Statistics at most may show only a likelihood that a particular factor entered into some decisions. There is, of course, some risk of racial prejudice influencing a jury's decision in a criminal case. There are similar risks that other kinds of prejudice will influence other criminal trials. . . . McCleskey asks us to accept the likelihood allegedly shown by the Baldus study as the constitutional measure of an unacceptable risk of racial prejudice influencing capital sentencing decisions. This we decline to do. . . .

The Court has consistently rejected statistical studies on the grounds that they do not prove anything about the verdict in the specific death penalty case before it. Even if members of the Court have opinions about the meanings of the Baldus study or the Ehrlich study on deterrence cited in *Gregg,* as an institution the Court has been skeptical. First, even when the Court has before it a defendant who alleges some convincing statistical disparity in the administration of the death penalty, such as *Maxwell v. Bishop* (1970) where the black defendant had been sentenced to death for rape, the Court has granted relief without relying on mathematical evidence. This is reasonable, because all statistical studies are retrospective examinations of aggregates of data that can show correlation but not prove causation in any individual case. Second, there would be no stopping point if statistics could be used to prove that juries are biased. It is even more likely that in nonhomicide offenses, there are statistical disparities: Why should a burglar not be able to attack his conviction using the same method as McCleskey? And since the last witch was hanged at Salem in 1692, men have received the death penalty at about 20 times the rate that women do. If the rather subtle results in the Baldus study were accepted as proving that juries discriminate on the basis of race, every man on death row could use the same logic as proof that they were condemned due to rather unsubtle sex discrimination. Third, because of the relatively small number of executions, a statistical oddity called Simpson's Paradox (in which combined data can show misleading results due to hidden variables) can result in two states, both with absolutely unbiased rates of execution, giving a combined execution rate that looks biased. Statisticians can handle these concepts, but attorneys are ethically required to present the best case for their clients, not conduct seminars in mathematics. If the Court opened the door to the social scientists, are judges capable of sorting out the evidence that would be presented?

"Where the discretion that is fundamental to our criminal process is involved, we decline to assume that what is unexplained is invidious."

At most, the Baldus study indicates a discrepancy that appears to correlate with race. Apparent disparities in sentencing are an inevitable part of our criminal justice system. The discrepancy indicated by the Baldus study is "a far cry from the major systemic defects identified in *Furman*." As this Court has recognized, any mode for determining guilt or punishment "has its weaknesses and the potential for misuse." . . . Specifically, "there can be 'no perfect procedure for deciding in which cases governmental authority should be used to impose death.'" Despite these imperfections, our consistent rule has been that constitutional guarantees are met when "the mode [for determining guilt or punishment] itself has been surrounded with safeguards to make it as fair as possible." Where the discretion that is fundamental to our criminal process is involved, we decline to assume that what is unexplained is invidious. In light of the safeguards designed to minimize racial bias in the process, the fundamental value of jury trial in our criminal justice system, and the benefits that discretion provides to criminal defendants, we hold that the Baldus study does not demonstrate a constitutionally significant risk of racial bias affecting the Georgia capital sentencing process.

Two additional concerns inform our decision in this case. First, McCleskey's claim, taken to its logical conclusion, throws into serious question the principles that underlie our entire criminal justice system. The Eighth Amendment is not limited in application to capital punishment, but applies to all penalties. Thus, if we accepted McCleskey's claim that racial bias has impermissibly tainted the capital sentencing decision, we could soon be faced with similar claims as to other types of penalty. Moreover, the claim that his sentence rests on the irrelevant factor of race easily could be extended to apply to claims based on unexplained discrepancies that correlate to membership in other minority groups, and even to gender. Similarly, since McCleskey's claim relates to the race of his victim, other claims could apply with equally logical force to statistical disparities that correlate with the race or sex of other actors in the criminal justice system, such as defense attorneys or judges. Also, there is no logical reason that such a claim need be limited to racial or sexual bias. If arbitrary and capricious punishment is the touchstone under the Eighth Amendment, such a claim could—at least in theory—be based upon any arbitrary variable, such as the defendant's facial characteristics, or the physical attractiveness of the defendant or the victim, that some statistical study indicates may be influential in jury decisionmaking.

As these examples illustrate, there is no limiting principle to the type of challenge brought by McCleskey. The Constitution does not require that a State eliminate any demonstrable disparity that correlates with a potentially irrelevant factor in order to operate a criminal justice system that includes capital punishment. As we have stated specifically in the context of capital punishment, the Constitution does not "plac[e] totally unrealistic conditions on its use."

Second, McCleskey's arguments are best presented to the legislative bodies. It is not the responsibility—or indeed even the right—of this Court to determine the appropriate punishment for particular crimes. . . . Legislatures also are better qualified to weigh and "evaluate the results of statistical studies in terms of their own local conditions and with a flexibility of approach that is not available to the courts."

Capital punishment is now the law in more than two-thirds of our States. It is the ultimate duty of courts to determine on a case-by-case basis whether these laws are applied consistently with the Constitution.

Despite McCleskey's wide-ranging arguments that basically challenge the validity of capital punishment in our multiracial society, the only question before us is whether in his case, the law of Georgia was properly applied. We agree with the District Court and the Court of Appeals for the Eleventh Circuit that this was carefully and correctly done in this case.

Accordingly, we affirm the judgment of the Court of Appeals. . . .

JUSTICE BRENNAN, with whom JUSTICE MARSHALL joins, and with whom JUSTICE BLACKMUN and JUSTICE STEVENS join in all but Part I, dissenting.

. . . The Court . . . maintains that accepting McCleskey's claim would pose a threat to all sentencing because of the prospect that a correlation might be demonstrated between sentencing outcomes and other personal characteristics. . . . Race is a consideration whose influence is expressly constitutionally proscribed. . . . That a decision to impose the

Powell's suggestion that the matter be dealt with by legislation was taken up only by North Carolina. The Racial Justice Act, enacted in 2009, permitted capital defendants in that state to block executions by using simple numerical imbalances as proof of bias. Almost every inmate on death row, regardless of race, claimed that he was a victim of bias. The statute was repealed in 2013.

The corollary to the Court's rejection of statistics because they say nothing about the individual jury verdict is that there should be a careful scrutiny of the actual jury itself. Voir dire, the phase of the trial in which the jury is selected, means "to speak the truth." Individual voir dire is the norm in murder trials. In *Turner v. Murray* (1986), the Court considered whether individual prospective jurors could be questioned about racial attitudes. Willie Lloyd Turner, a black man, robbed a Virginia jewelry store in 1978 and shot the white store owner in anger for triggering a silent alarm. The Virginia Supreme Court and the lower federal courts held that the simple fact that the two were of different race did not give Turner the legal right to ask jurors about prejudice. This was true: the Supreme Court had since *Aldridge v. United States* (1931) permitted such questioning in federal trials as a matter of its supervisory authority. As a matter of constitutional law binding on the states, however, hitherto the Court had held that only when racial issues were "inextricably bound up" with the trial, for instance, when the defendant claimed that he was being framed because of his civil rights work or when the killing was racially motivated. The Court changed that rule in *Turner* on the basis that "death is different." The Court vacated the death sentence and returned the matter for a new penalty hearing. The dissent criticized this as illogical, but the majority felt that guilt required a straightforward objective finding, while the decision that the jurors had to make at sentencing was far more subjective and therefore too susceptible to improper influence.

Part I of the dissent was Justices Brennan and Marshall's position that all death penalties were unconstitutional. Four Justices agreed in Part IV, as follows.

death penalty could be influenced by race is . . . a particularly repugnant prospect, and evidence that race may play even a modest role in levying a death sentence should be enough to characterize that sentence as "cruel and unusual."

Certainly, a factor that we would regard as morally irrelevant, such as hair color, at least theoretically could be associated with sentencing results to such an extent that we would regard as arbitrary a system in which that factor played a significant role. . . . [H]owever, the evaluation of evidence suggesting such a correlation must be informed not merely by statistics, but by history and experience. One could hardly contend that this Nation has on the basis of hair color inflicted upon persons deprivation comparable to that imposed on the basis of race. Recognition of this fact would necessarily influence the evaluation of data suggesting the influence of hair color on sentencing, and would require evidence of statistical correlation even more powerful than that presented by the Baldus study.

Furthermore, the Court's fear of the expansive ramifications of a holding for McCleskey in this case is unfounded because it fails to recognize the uniquely sophisticated nature of the Baldus study. . . .

The Court's projection of apocalyptic consequences for criminal sentencing is thus greatly exaggerated. . . .

Finally, the Court justifies its rejection of McCleskey's claim by cautioning against usurpation of the legislatures' role in devising and monitoring criminal punishment. . . . The judiciary's role in this society counts for little if the use of governmental power to extinguish life does not elicit close scrutiny. . . . Those whom we would banish from society or from the human community itself often speak in too faint a voice to be heard above society's demand for punishment. It is the particular role of courts to hear these voices, for the Constitution declares that the majoritarian chorus may not alone dictate the conditions of social life. The Court thus fulfills, rather than disrupts, the scheme of separation of powers by closely scrutinizing the imposition of the death penalty, for no decision of a society is more deserving of "sober second thought." . . .

JUSTICE BLACKMUN, with whom JUSTICE MARSHALL and JUSTICE STEVENS join, and with whom JUSTICE BRENNAN joins in all but Part IV-B, dissenting.

"Those whom we would banish from society or from the human community itself often speak in too faint a voice to be heard above society's demand for punishment."

The Court today sanctions the execution of a man despite his presentation of evidence that establishes a constitutionally intolerable level of racially based discrimination leading to the imposition of his death sentence. I am disappointed with the Court's action not only because of its denial of constitutional guarantees to petitioner McCleskey individually, but also because of its departure from what seems to me to be well-developed constitutional jurisprudence.

The Court's jurisprudence on racial discrimination was well developed but did not extend to acceptance of general statistical evidence. Consider the Court's decision the previous year in *Lockhart v. McCree* (1986). Ardia McCree was convicted of murdering the owner of a gas station during a 1978 robbery. McCree claimed that excluding *Witherspoon*-ineligible jurors (those who said they would not impose the death penalty under any circumstances) made the jury unconstitutionally biased. He also relied on a number of statistical studies, all of which claimed that death-qualifying a jury made it more prone to convict. Even assuming this to be true, the Court said that it did not violate the Eighth Amendment because it was not wholesale exclusion of a group based on group characteristics such as gender or race unrelated to their ability to sit as jurors but instead was selection of individual jurors on the basis of their ability to be impartial and follow the judge's instructions.

McCleskey's case raises concerns that are central not only to the principles underlying the Eighth Amendment, but also to the principles underlying the Fourteenth Amendment. Analysis of his case in terms of the Fourteenth Amendment is consistent with this Court's recognition that racial discrimination is fundamentally at odds with our constitutional guarantee of equal protection. The protections afforded by the Fourteenth Amendment are not left at the courtroom door. Nor is equal protection denied to persons convicted of crimes. The Court in the past has found that racial discrimination within the criminal justice system is particularly abhorrent. . . .

JUSTICE STEVENS, with whom JUSTICE BLACK-MUN joins, dissenting.

. . . The Court's decision appears to be based on a fear that the acceptance of McCleskey's claim would sound the death knell for capital punishment in Georgia. If society were indeed forced to choose between a racially discriminatory death penalty (one that provides heightened protection against murder "for whites only") and no death penalty at all, the choice mandated by the Constitution would be plain. But the Court's fear is unfounded. One of the lessons of the Baldus study is that there exist certain categories of extremely serious crimes for which prosecutors consistently seek, and juries consistently impose, the death penalty without regard to the race of the victim or the race of the offender. If Georgia were to narrow the class of death-eligible defendants to those categories, the danger of arbitrary and discriminatory imposition of the death penalty would be significantly decreased, if not eradicated. . . . [S]uch a restructuring of the sentencing scheme is surely not too high a price to pay. . . .

Note

1. John C. Jeffries Jr., *Justice Lewis F. Powell, Jr.: A Biography* (New York: Scribner, 1994), 451.

Death Penalty for Those under Age 16

Thompson v. Oklahoma

June 29, 1988

INTRODUCTION

William Wayne Thompson participated in a murder when he was 15 years old. The Supreme Court ruled that a defendant cannot be executed for a crime committed when he was below the age of 16. Justice Stevens, joined by Justices Brennan, Marshall, and Blackmun, wrote that executing such a young offender "would offend civilized standards of decency." Punishment should be "directly related to the personal culpability of the criminal defendant," and most agree that adolescents are "less mature and responsible than adults." As such, "less culpability [attaches] to a crime committed by a juvenile than to a comparable crime committed by an adult." Teenagers are "less able to evaluate the consequences" of their actions and are "more apt to be motivated by mere emotion or peer pressure" than are adults. Given the lesser culpability of juvenile offenders and their capacity for rehabilitation, the execution of offenders as young as Thompson does not serve retributive and deterrent objectives. Execution of such juvenile offenders is constitutionally impermissible. Justice O'Connor concurred. Justice Kennedy did not participate. Justice Scalia, joined by Chief Justice Rehnquist and Justice White, dissented.

Here the Court began an ongoing examination of the suitability of the death penalty for juvenile offenders.

JUSTICE STEVENS announced the judgment of the Court and delivered an opinion in which JUSTICE BRENNAN, JUSTICE MARSHALL, and JUSTICE BLACKMUN join.

Petitioner was convicted of first-degree murder and sentenced to death. The principal question presented is whether the execution of that sentence would violate the constitutional prohibition against the infliction of "cruel and unusual punishments" because petitioner was only 15 years old at the time of his offense.

. . . In concert with three older persons, petitioner actively participated in the brutal murder of his former brother-in-law in the early morning hours of January 23, 1983. The evidence disclosed that the victim had been shot twice, and that his throat, chest, and abdomen had been cut. He also had multiple bruises and a broken leg. His body had been chained to a concrete block and thrown into a river where it remained for almost four weeks. Each of the four participants was tried separately and each was sentenced to death.

Because petitioner was a "child" as a matter of Oklahoma law, the District Attorney filed a statutory petition seeking an order finding "that said child is competent and had the mental capacity to know and appreciate the wrongfulness of his [conduct]." After a hearing, the trial court concluded "that there are virtually no reasonable prospects for rehabilitation of William Wayne Thompson within the juvenile system and that William Wayne Thompson should be held accountable for his acts as if he were an adult and should be certified to stand trial as an adult." . . .

At the penalty phase of the trial, the prosecutor asked the jury to find two aggravating circumstances: that the murder was especially heinous, atrocious, or cruel; and that there was a probability that the defendant would commit criminal acts of violence that would constitute a continuing threat to society. The jury found the first, but not the second, and fixed petitioner's punishment at death.

. . . [I]n confronting the question whether the youth of the defendant—more specifically, the fact that he was less than 16 years old at the time of his offense—is a sufficient reason for denying the State the power to sentence him to death, we first review relevant legislative enactments, then refer to jury determinations, and finally explain why these indicators of contemporary standards of decency confirm our judgment that such a young person is not capable of acting with the degree of culpability that can justify the ultimate penalty.

. . . The line between childhood and adulthood is drawn in different ways by various States. There is, however, complete or near unanimity among all 50 States and the District of Columbia in treating a person under 16 as a minor for several important purposes. In no State may a 15-year-old vote or serve on a jury. Further, in all but one State a 15-year-old may not drive without parental consent, and in all but four States a 15-year-old may not marry without parental consent. Additionally, in those States that have legislated on the subject, no one under age 16 may purchase pornographic materials (50 States), and in most States that have some form of legalized gambling, minors are not permitted to participate without parental consent (42 States). Most relevant, however, is the fact that all States have enacted legislation designating the maximum age for juvenile court jurisdiction at no less than 16. All of this legislation is consistent with

The Supreme Court reviews state criminal law in two ways: by direct review, and by review of habeas corpus proceedings. Every case is controversial, but habeas corpus proceedings evoke additional arguments about federalism. Cases such as *Thompson v. Oklahoma* arise on direct review: the Supreme Court grants certiorari as the highest criminal court in the land, a function that it has assumed since John Marshall's days as chief justice. Cases titled like *Fay v. Noia* are habeas corpus cases. Habeas corpus began in medieval England as an inquiry into whether a court had proper jurisdiction to hold a defendant, but in the second half of the 20th century habeas corpus evolved into a second layer of appeals after direct review. When this resulted in a federal district court overturning a sentence of a state court, it drew protests not just from prosecutors but also from state court judges who had already heard the case. There was increasing friction between state and federal courts, as the actual trial was often considered as a first act to the main event in federal court. Beginning with the tenure of Chief Justice William Rehnquist, the Supreme Court began cutting back on the freedom with which state court judgments could be challenged in federal court. In *Teague v. Lane* (1989), the Supreme Court took the significant step of announcing that habeas corpus relief could not be granted on the basis of new rules of federal law that had not been announced until after a state conviction became final. This means that unless the principle is one of watershed significance, such as the holding in *Gideon v. Wainwright* (1963) that valid convictions cannot be obtained unless counsel is made available to an indigent defendant, the principle cannot justify overturning a criminal conviction. This limited the lower federal courts from announcing new constitutional law in habeas corpus proceedings and overturning verdicts years after a criminal trial, something that had been a particular sore point with state courts. This made the Supreme Court, in theory at least, the only court that could announce new rules of constitutional law.

In 1996, the Antiterrorism and Effective Death Penalty Amendments Act (AEDPA) expressly made *Teague v. Lane* part of statutory law and thereby limited the Court's ability to back-pedal from it. Federal courts are now limited to habeas relief based on rules of law that are clearly established by the holdings of the Supreme Court, not lower courts, at the time the state conviction became final.

The labyrinth of habeas corpus practice continues to cause state and federal conflict over where responsibility for constitutional law enforcement rests. The death penalty adds conflicts between the branches of government as well.

For instance, one of the sore points that the AEDPA addressed was the veto that federal courts could exercise over the death penalty simply by delay. A federal habeas petition is inevitably accompanied by a motion to stay any execution until the petition is decided: a federal district or appellate court judge could hold a decision, sometimes for years, until the district attorney litigating in support of the conviction and penalty had been replaced by one willing to deal or until the governor signing the execution warrant left office. Some of the 32 inmates who died of old age, suicide, or illness while on California's death row had at the time of their deaths habeas corpus petitions pending for more than a decade. The AEDPA required any federal habeas corpus petition to be filed within 180 days of the final review of a conviction by the state court, required federal district courts to conclude their handling of the petition within 450 days, and gave courts of appeal 120 days to deliberate any appeal if a state was certified to have an effective procedure for appointing competent counsel to represent indigent defendants on death row. No federal court certified any state to have an adequate system by 2001, when the USA PATRIOT Act moved the responsibility to the executive branch to certify that a state had an effective procedure. By December 2008, Attorney General Michael Mukasey had promulgated regulations for certifying that a state had competent counsel, but a district judge in California issued an injunction on January 20, 2009, preventing those regulations going into effect. Attorney General Eric Holder withdrew the regulations in November 2010 pending further review.

the experience of mankind, as well as the long history of our law, that the normal 15-year-old is not prepared to assume the full responsibilities of an adult.

Most state legislatures have not expressly confronted the question of establishing a minimum age for imposition of the death penalty. In 14 States, capital punishment is not authorized at all, and in 19 others capital punishment is authorized but no minimum age is expressly stated in the death penalty statute. One might argue on the basis of this body of legislation that there is no chronological age at which the imposition of the death penalty is unconstitutional and that our current standards of decency would still tolerate the execution of 10-year-old children. We think it self-evident that such an argument is unacceptable; indeed, no such argument has been advanced in this case. If, therefore, we accept the premise that some offenders are simply too young to be put to death, it is reasonable to put this group of statutes to one side because they do not focus on the question of where the chronological age line should be drawn. When we confine our attention to the 18 States that have expressly established a minimum age in their death penalty statutes, we find that all of them require that the defendant have attained at least the age of 16 at the time of the capital offense.

The conclusion that it would offend civilized standards of decency to execute a person who was less than 16 years old at the time of his or her offense is consistent with the views that have been expressed by respected professional organizations, by other nations that share our Anglo-American heritage, and by the leading members of the Western European community. . . .

The second societal factor the Court has examined in determining the acceptability of capital punishment to the American sensibility is the behavior of juries. . . .

While it is not known precisely how many persons have been executed during the 20th century for crimes committed under the age of 16, a scholar has recently compiled a table revealing this number to be between 18 and 20. All of these occurred during the first half of the century, with the last such execution taking place apparently in 1948. . . . The road we have traveled during the past four decades—in which thousands of juries have tried murder cases—leads to the unambiguous conclusion that the imposition of the death penalty on a 15-year-old offender is now generally abhorrent to the conscience of the community. . . .

It is generally agreed "that punishment should be directly related to the personal culpability of the criminal defendant." There is also broad agreement on the proposition that adolescents as a class are less mature and responsible than adults. . . .

. . . [T]he Court has already endorsed the proposition that less culpability should attach to a crime committed by a juvenile than to a comparable crime committed by an adult. . . . Inexperience, less education, and less intelligence make the teenager less able to evaluate the consequences of his or her conduct while at the same time he or she is much more apt to be motivated by mere emotion or peer pressure than is an adult. The reasons why juveniles are not trusted with the privileges and responsibilities of an adult also explain why their irresponsible conduct is not as morally reprehensible as that of an adult.

"The death penalty is said to serve two principal social purposes: retribution and deterrence of capital crimes by prospective offenders." In *Gregg* we concluded that as "an expression of society's moral outrage at particularly offensive conduct," retribution was not "inconsistent with our respect for the dignity of men." Given the lesser culpability of the juvenile offender, the teenager's capacity for growth, and society's fiduciary obligations to its children, this conclusion is simply inapplicable to the execution of a 15-year-old offender.

For such a young offender, the deterrence rationale is equally unacceptable. The Department of Justice statistics indicate that about 98% of the arrests for willful homicide involved persons who were over 16 at the time of the offense. Thus, excluding younger persons from the class that is eligible for the death penalty will not diminish the deterrent value of capital punishment for the vast majority of potential offenders. And even with respect to those under 16 years of age, it is obvious that the potential deterrent value of the death sentence is insignificant for two reasons. The likelihood that the teenage offender has made the kind of cost-benefit analysis that attaches any weight to the possibility of execution is so remote as to be virtually nonexistent. And, even if one posits such a cold-blooded calculation by a 15-year-old, it is fanciful to believe that he would be deterred by the knowledge that a small number of persons his age have been executed during the 20th century. In short, we are not persuaded that the imposition of the death penalty for offenses committed by persons under 16 years of age has made, or can be expected to make, any measurable contribution to the goals that capital punishment is intended to achieve. It is, therefore, "nothing more than the purposeless and needless imposition of pain and suffering," and thus an unconstitutional punishment.

The Court would go on to consider the culpability of juvenile offenders in several subsequent cases.

The judgment of the Court of Criminal Appeals is vacated, and the case is remanded with instructions to enter an appropriate order vacating petitioner's death sentence....

JUSTICE KENNEDY took no part in the consideration or decision of this case.

JUSTICE O'CONNOR, concurring in the judgment. [Omitted]

The dissenters maintained that at least some juvenile offenders deserved to die.

JUSTICE SCALIA, with whom THE CHIEF JUSTICE and JUSTICE WHITE join, dissenting.

... William Wayne Thompson is not a juvenile caught up in a legislative scheme that unthinkingly lumped him together with adults for purposes of determining that death was an appropriate penalty for him and for his crime. To the contrary, Oklahoma first gave careful consideration to whether, in light of his young age, he should be subjected to the normal criminal system at all. That question having been answered affirmatively, a jury then considered whether, despite his young age, his maturity and moral responsibility were sufficiently developed to justify the sentence of death. In upsetting this particularized judgment on the basis of a constitutional absolute, the plurality pronounces it to be a fundamental principle of our society that no one who is as little as one day short of his 16th birthday can have sufficient maturity and moral responsibility to be subjected to capital punishment for any crime. As a sociological and moral conclusion that is implausible; and it is doubly implausible as an interpretation of the United States Constitution. . . .

. . . [T]he statistics of executions demonstrate nothing except the fact that our society has always agreed that executions of 15-year-old criminals should be rare. . . . There is no rational basis for discerning in that a societal judgment that no one so much as a day under 16 can ever be mature and morally responsible enough to deserve that penalty; and there is no justification except our own predilection for converting a statistical rarity of occurrence into an absolute constitutional ban. . . .

. . . I respectfully dissent from the judgment of the Court.

Death Penalty for Those under Age 18

Stanford v. Kentucky

June 26, 1989

INTRODUCTION

In *Thompson,* a divided Court held that it is constitutionally impermissible to execute a 15-year-old convicted murderer. What about a murderer who committed the crime at age 16 or 17? Kevin Stanford was 17 when he committed a murder in Kentucky. Heath Wilkins was 16 when he committed a murder in Missouri. Unlike *Thompson,* involving a 15-year-old murderer, here the Court upheld death sentences that had been imposed on both juvenile defendants. Justice Scalia delivered the Court's opinion. Chief Justice Rehnquist and Justices White and O'Connor, who switched sides from *Thompson,* and Justice Kennedy, who did not vote in *Thompson,* also voted to uphold the capital sentences. Scalia stated that "a majority of the States that permit capital punishment authorize it for crimes committed at age 16 or above." In her concurring opinion, O'Connor declined to set aside the sentences imposed on Wilkins and Stanford because "no national consensus forbids the imposition of capital punishment on 16- or 17-year-old capital murderers." Justice Brennan, joined by Justices Marshall, Blackmun, and Stevens, dissented. In discerning "contemporary standards of decency," Brennan also looked to international sources and noted that "[w]ithin the world community, the imposition of the death penalty for juvenile crimes appears to be overwhelmingly disapproved."

JUSTICE SCALIA announced the judgment of the Court and delivered the opinion of the Court with respect to Parts I, II, III, and IV-A, and an opinion with respect to Parts IV-B and V, in which THE CHIEF JUSTICE, JUSTICE WHITE, and JUSTICE KENNEDY join.

These two consolidated cases require us to decide whether the imposition of capital punishment on an individual for a crime committed at 16 or 17 years of age constitutes cruel and unusual punishment under the Eighth Amendment.

I

The first case involves the shooting death of 20-year-old Barbel Poore in Jefferson County, Kentucky. Petitioner Kevin Stanford committed the murder on January 7, 1981, when he was approximately 17 years and 4 months of age. Stanford and his accomplice repeatedly raped and sodomized Poore during and after their commission of a robbery at a gas station where she worked as an attendant. They then drove her to a secluded area near the station, where Stanford shot her point blank in the face and then in the back of her head. The proceeds from the robbery were roughly 300 cartons of cigarettes, two gallons of fuel, and a small amount of cash. A corrections officer testified that petitioner explained the murder as follows: "'[H]e said, I had to shoot her, [she] lived next door to me and she would recognize me. . . . I guess we could have tied her up or something or beat [her up] . . . and tell her if she tells, we would kill her. . . . Then after he said that he started laughing.'"

After Stanford's arrest, a Kentucky juvenile court conducted hearings to determine whether he should be transferred for trial as an adult under [Kentucky law]. . . . Stressing the seriousness of petitioner's offenses and the unsuccessful attempts of the juvenile system to treat him for numerous instances of past delinquency, the juvenile court found certification for trial as an adult to be in the best interest of petitioner and the community.

Stanford was convicted of murder, first-degree sodomy, first-degree robbery, and receiving stolen property, and was sentenced to death and 45 years in prison. The Kentucky Supreme Court affirmed the death sentence. . . .

The second case before us today involves the stabbing death of Nancy Allen, a 26-year-old mother of two who was working behind the sales counter of the convenience store she and David Allen owned and operated in Avondale, Missouri. Petitioner Heath Wilkins committed the murder on July 27, 1985, when he was approximately 16 years and 6 months of age. The record reflects that Wilkins' plan was to rob the store and murder "whoever was behind the counter" because "a dead person can't talk." While Wilkins' accomplice, Patrick Stevens, held Allen, Wilkins stabbed her, causing her to fall to the floor. When Stevens had trouble operating the cash register, Allen spoke up to assist him, leading Wilkins to stab her three more times in her chest. Two of these wounds penetrated the victim's heart. When Allen began to beg for her life, Wilkins stabbed her four more times in the neck, opening her carotid artery. After helping themselves to liquor, cigarettes, rolling papers, and approximately $450 in cash and checks, Wilkins and Stevens left Allen to die on the floor.

Because he was roughly six months short of the age of majority for purposes of criminal prosecution [under Missouri

"The record reflects that Wilkins' plan was to rob the store and murder 'whoever was behind the counter' because 'a dead person can't talk.'"

law], Wilkins could not automatically be tried as an adult under Missouri law. Before that could happen, the juvenile court was required to terminate juvenile court jurisdiction and certify Wilkins for trial as an adult. . . . Relying on the "viciousness, force and violence" of the alleged crime, petitioner's maturity, and the failure of the juvenile justice system to rehabilitate him after previous delinquent acts, the juvenile court made the necessary certification.

Wilkins was charged with first-degree murder, armed criminal action, and carrying a concealed weapon. After the court found him competent, petitioner entered guilty pleas to all charges. A punishment hearing was held, at which both the State and petitioner himself urged imposition of the death sentence. Evidence at the hearing revealed that petitioner had been in and out of juvenile facilities since the age of eight for various acts of burglary, theft, and arson, had attempted to kill his mother by putting insecticide into Tylenol capsules, and had killed several animals in his neighborhood. Although psychiatric testimony indicated that Wilkins had "personality disorders," the witnesses agreed that Wilkins was aware of his actions and could distinguish right from wrong.

Determining that the death penalty was appropriate, the trial court entered the following order:

> [T]he court finds beyond reasonable doubt that the following aggravating circumstances exist:
>
> 1. The murder in the first degree was committed while the defendant was engaged in the perpetration of the felony of robbery, and
> 2. The murder in the first degree involved depravity of mind and that as a result thereof, it was outrageously or wantonly vile, horrible or inhuman.

. . . [T]he Supreme Court of Missouri affirmed. . . .

We granted *certiorari* in these cases to decide whether the Eighth Amendment precludes the death penalty for individuals who commit crimes at 16 or 17 years of age.

The thrust of both Wilkins' and Stanford's arguments is that imposition of the death penalty on those who were juveniles when they committed their crimes falls within the Eighth Amendment's prohibition against "cruel and unusual punishments." Wilkins would have us define juveniles as individuals 16 years of age and under; Stanford would draw the line at 17. . . .

"Although psychiatric testimony indicated that Wilkins had 'personality disorders,' the witnesses agreed that Wilkins was aware of his actions and could distinguish right from wrong."

Note that whether the U.S. Supreme Court is permitted to look to its own conceptions of decency is the most controversial modern divide among the justices. At this point, Justice Kennedy adhered to the position that the justices could not consider their own opinions. In subsequent decisions, he changed his mind. The switch is important, because in the last two decades Kennedy has been the deciding vote in more 5–4 decisions than any other justice. Experienced Supreme Court advocates candidly describe their arguments at the Court as aimed only at swaying the swing votes: with the retirements of O'Connor in 2006 and Stevens in 2010, Kennedy became for most purposes the deciding vote on socially divisive issues.

[P]etitioners . . . argue that their punishment is contrary to the "evolving standards of decency that mark the progress of a maturing society." . . . In determining what standards have "evolved," . . . we have looked not to our own conceptions of decency, but to those of modern American society as a whole. As we have said, "Eighth Amendment judgments should not be, or appear to be, merely the subjective views of individual Justices; judgment should be informed by objective factors to the maximum possible extent." . . .

Of the 37 States whose laws permit capital punishment, 15 decline to impose it upon 16-year-old offenders and 12 decline to impose it on 17-year-old offenders. This does not establish the degree of national consensus this Court has previously thought sufficient to label a particular punishment cruel and unusual. In invalidating the death penalty for rape of an adult woman, we stressed that Georgia was the sole jurisdiction that authorized such a punishment. In striking down capital punishment for participation in a robbery in which an accomplice takes a life, we emphasized that only eight jurisdictions authorized similar punishment. In finding that the Eighth Amendment precludes execution of the insane and thus requires an adequate hearing on the issue of sanity, we relied upon (in addition to the common-law rule) the fact that "no State in the Union" permitted such punishment. And in striking down a life sentence without parole under a recidivist statute, we stressed that "[i]t appears that [petitioner] was treated more severely than he would have been in any other State."

Since a majority of the States that permit capital punishment authorize it for crimes committed at age 16 or above, petitioners' cases are more analogous to *Tison v. Arizona* than *Coker, Enmund, Ford,* and *Solem.* In *Tison,* which upheld Arizona's imposition of the death penalty for major participation in a felony with reckless indifference to human life, we noted that only 11 of those jurisdictions imposing capital punishment rejected its use in such circumstances. . . . We think the same conclusion as in *Tison* is required in these cases. . . .

IV A

Wilkins and Stanford argue, however, that even if the laws themselves do not establish a settled consensus, the application of the laws does. That contemporary society views capital punishment of 16- and 17-year-old offenders as inappropriate is demonstrated, they say, by the reluctance of juries to impose, and prosecutors to seek, such sentences. Petitioners are quite correct that a far smaller number of offenders under 18 than over 18 have been sentenced to death in this country. . . . And it appears that actual executions for crimes committed under age 18 accounted for only about 2 percent of the total number of executions that occurred between 1642 and 1986. . . . These statistics, however, carry little significance. Given the undisputed fact that a far smaller percentage of capital crimes are committed by persons under 18 than over 18, the discrepancy in treatment is much less than might seem. Granted, however, that a substantial discrepancy exists, that does not establish the requisite proposition that the death sentence for offenders under 18 is categorically unacceptable to prosecutors and juries. To the contrary, it is not only possible, but overwhelmingly probable, that the very considerations which induce petitioners and their supporters to believe that death should never be imposed on offenders under 18 cause prosecutors and juries to believe that it should rarely be imposed.

B

This last point suggests why there is also no relevance to the laws cited by petitioners and their *amici* which set 18 or more as the legal age for engaging in various activities, ranging from driving to drinking alcoholic beverages to voting. It is, to begin with, absurd to think that one must be mature enough to drive carefully, to drink responsibly, or to vote intelligently, in order to be mature enough to understand that murdering another human being is profoundly wrong, and to conform one's conduct to that most minimal of all civilized standards. But even if the requisite degrees of maturity were comparable, the age statutes in question would still not be relevant. They do not represent a social judgment that all persons under the designated ages are not responsible enough to drive, to drink, or to vote, but at most a judgment that the vast majority are not. These laws set the appropriate ages for the operation of a system that makes its determinations in gross, and that does not conduct individualized maturity tests for each driver, drinker, or voter. The criminal justice system, however, does provide individualized testing. In the realm of capital punishment in particular, "individualized consideration [is] a constitutional requirement" and one of the individualized mitigating factors that sentencers

"It is, to begin with, absurd to think that one must be mature enough to drive carefully, to drink responsibly, or to vote intelligently, in order to be mature enough to understand that murdering another human being is profoundly wrong, . . ."

must be permitted to consider is the defendant's age. . . . The application of this particularized system to the petitioners can be declared constitutionally inadequate only if there is a consensus, not that 17 or 18 is the age at which most persons, or even almost all persons, achieve sufficient maturity to be held fully responsible for murder; but that 17 or 18 is the age before which no one can reasonably be held fully responsible. . . .

JUSTICE O'CONNOR, concurring in part and concurring in the judgment.

In *Thompson* I noted that ". . . every single American legislature that has expressly set a minimum age for capital punishment has set that age at 16 or above." It is this difference between *Thompson* and these cases, more than any other, that convinces me there is no national consensus forbidding the imposition of capital punishment for crimes committed at the age of 16 and older. As the Court indicates, "a majority of the States that permit capital punishment authorize it for crimes committed at age 16 or above." . . .

JUSTICE BRENNAN, with whom JUSTICE MARSHALL, JUSTICE BLACKMUN, and JUSTICE STEVENS join, dissenting.

. . . The fact that juries have on occasion sentenced a minor to death shows, the Court says, that the death penalty for adolescents is not categorically unacceptable to juries. This, of course, is true; but it is not a conclusion that takes Eighth Amendment analysis very far. . . . [W]e have never adopted the extraordinary view that a punishment is beyond Eighth Amendment challenge if it is sometimes handed down by a jury. . . .

Both in absolute and in relative terms, imposition of the death penalty on adolescents is distinctly unusual. . . .

The Court speculates that this very small number of capital sentences imposed on adolescents indicates that juries have considered the youth of the offender when determining sentence, and have reserved the punishment for rare cases in which it is nevertheless appropriate. . . . It is certainly true that in the vast majority of cases, juries have not sentenced juveniles to death, and it seems to me perfectly proper to conclude that a sentence so rarely imposed is "unusual."

Further indicators of contemporary standards of decency that should inform our consideration of the Eighth Amendment question are the opinions of respected organizations . . . that the state-sanctioned killing of minors is unjustified. A number, indeed, have filed briefs *amicus curiae* in these cases, in support of petitioners. The American Bar Association[,] . . . the National Council of Juvenile and Family Court Judges, [t]he American Law Institute's Model Penal Code, . . . [a]nd the National Commission on Reform of the Federal Criminal Laws . . . recommended that 18 be the minimum age.

Our cases recognize that objective indicators of contemporary standards of decency in the form of legislation in other countries is [*sic*] also of relevance to Eighth Amendment analysis. Many countries, of course—over 50, including nearly all in Western Europe—have formally abolished the death penalty, or have limited its use to exceptional crimes such as treason. Twenty-seven others do not in practice impose the penalty. Of the nations that retain capital punishment, a majority—65—prohibit the execution of juveniles. Sixty-one countries retain capital punishment and have no statutory provision exempting juveniles, though some of these nations are ratifiers of international treaties that do prohibit the execution of juveniles. . . . In addition to national laws, three leading human rights treaties ratified or signed by the United States explicitly prohibit juvenile death penalties. Within the world community, the imposition of the death penalty for juvenile crimes appears to be overwhelmingly disapproved.

. . . [Furthermore,] the execution of juveniles fails to satisfy two well-established and independent Eighth Amendment requirements—that a punishment not be disproportionate, and that it make a contribution to acceptable goals of punishment.

"In addition to national laws, three leading human rights treaties ratified or signed by the United States explicitly prohibit juvenile death penalties."

Execution of the Mentally Retarded

Penry v. Lynaugh

June 26, 1989

INTRODUCTION

The Court held that mentally retarded individuals who are convicted of capital crimes can sometimes be executed but vacated Johnny Paul Penry's death sentence on the ground that the jury had not been properly instructed about how to account for his mental retardation and other mitigating factors. After several appeals within the Texas courts and another trip to the Supreme Court, prosecutors and Penry's counsel agreed in February 2008 that Penry would serve three consecutive life sentences. The plea agreement required Penry to stipulate that he was not mentally retarded.

JUSTICE O'CONNOR delivered the opinion of the Court.

On the morning of October 25, 1979, Pamela Carpenter was brutally raped, beaten, and stabbed with a pair of scissors in her home in Livingston, Texas. She died a few hours later in the course of emergency treatment. Before she died, she described her assailant. Her description led two local sheriff's deputies to suspect Penry, who had recently been released on parole after conviction on another rape charge. Penry subsequently gave two statements confessing to the crime and was charged with capital murder.

At a competency hearing held before trial, a clinical psychologist, Dr. Jerome Brown, testified that Penry was mentally retarded. As a child, Penry was diagnosed as having organic brain damage, which was probably caused by trauma to the brain at birth. Penry was tested over the years as having an IQ between 50 and 63, which indicates mild to moderate retardation. Dr. Brown's own testing before the trial indicated that Penry had an IQ of 54. Dr. Brown's evaluation also revealed that Penry, who was 22 years old at the time of the crime, had the mental age of a 6½-year-old. . . . Penry's social maturity, or ability to function in the world, was that of a 9- or 10-year-old. Dr. Brown testified that "there's a point at which anyone with [Penry's] IQ is always incompetent, but, you know, this man is more in the borderline range."

The jury found Penry competent to stand trial. . . . The trial court determined that Penry's confessions were voluntary, and they were introduced into evidence. At trial, Penry raised an insanity defense and presented the testimony of a psychiatrist, Dr. Jose Garcia. Dr. Garcia testified that Penry suffered from organic brain damage and moderate retardation, which resulted in poor impulse control and an inability to learn from experience. . . . In Dr. Garcia's judgment, Penry was suffering from an organic brain disorder at the time of the offense which made it impossible for him to appreciate the wrongfulness of his conduct or to conform his conduct to the law.

The State introduced the testimony of two psychiatrists to rebut the testimony of Dr. Garcia. Dr. Kenneth Vogtsberger testified that although Penry was a person of limited mental ability, he was not suffering from any mental illness or defect at the time of the crime, and that he knew the difference between right and wrong and had the potential to honor the law. . . .

Dr. Felix Peebles also testified for the State that Penry was legally sane at the time of the offense and had a "full-blown anti-social personality." . . . Although they disagreed with the defense psychiatrist over the extent and cause of Penry's mental limitations, both psychiatrists for the State acknowledged that Penry was a person of extremely limited mental ability, and that he seemed unable to learn from his mistakes.

The jury rejected Penry's insanity defense and found him guilty of capital murder. The following day, at the close of the penalty hearing, the jury decided the sentence to be imposed on Penry by answering three "special issues":

1. "whether the conduct of the defendant that caused the death of the deceased was committed deliberately and with the reasonable expectation that the death of the deceased or another would result;
2. "whether there is a probability that the defendant would commit criminal acts of violence that would constitute a continuing threat to society; and
3. "if raised by the evidence, whether the conduct of the defendant in killing the deceased was unreasonable in response to the provocation, if any, by the deceased."

If the jury unanimously answers "yes" to each issue submitted, the trial court must sentence the defendant to death. Otherwise, the defendant is sentenced to life imprisonment. . . .

The jury answered "yes" to all three special issues, and Penry was sentenced to death. The Texas Court of Criminal Appeals affirmed his conviction and sentence on direct appeal. . . .

". . . [B]oth psychiatrists for the State acknowledge that Perry was a person of extremely limited mental ability, . . ."

... Although Penry offered mitigating evidence of his mental retardation and abused childhood as the basis for a sentence of life imprisonment rather than death, the jury that sentenced him was only able to express its views on the appropriate sentence by answering three questions: Did Penry act deliberately when he murdered Pamela Carpenter? Is there a probability that he will be dangerous in the future? Did he act unreasonably in response to provocation? The jury was never instructed that it could consider the evidence offered by Penry as mitigating evidence and that it could give mitigating effect to that evidence in imposing sentence. ...

The Court had already overturned death sentences in *Lockett v. Ohio* (1978) and *Eddings v. Oklahoma* (1982) because all of the potential mitigating circumstances were not considered.

Penry argues that his mitigating evidence of mental retardation and childhood abuse has relevance to his moral culpability beyond the scope of the special issues, and that the jury was unable to express its "reasoned moral response" to that evidence in determining whether death was the appropriate punishment. We agree. Thus, we reject the State's contrary argument that the jury was able to consider and give effect to all of Penry's mitigating evidence in answering the special issues without any jury instructions on mitigating evidence. ...

In this case, in the absence of instructions informing the jury that it could consider and give effect to the mitigating evidence of Penry's mental retardation and abused background by declining to impose the death penalty, we conclude that the jury was not provided with a vehicle for expressing its "reasoned moral response" to that evidence in rendering its sentencing decision. Our reasoning in *Lockett* and *Eddings* thus compels a remand for resentencing so that we do not "risk that the death penalty will be imposed in spite of factors which may call for a less severe penalty." ...

Penry's second claim is that it would be cruel and unusual punishment, prohibited by the Eighth Amendment, to execute a mentally retarded person like himself with the reasoning capacity of a 7-year-old. He argues that because of their mental disabilities, mentally retarded people do not possess the level of moral culpability to justify imposing the death sentence. He also argues that there is an emerging national consensus against executing the mentally retarded.

The Eighth Amendment categorically prohibits the infliction of cruel and unusual punishments. At a minimum, the Eighth

Amendment prohibits punishment considered cruel and unusual at the time the Bill of Rights was adopted. The prohibitions of the Eighth Amendment are not limited, however, to those practices condemned by the common law in 1789.

The prohibition against cruel and unusual punishments also recognizes the "evolving standards of decency that mark the progress of a maturing society." In discerning those "evolving standards," we have looked to objective evidence of how our society views a particular punishment today.

The Court began to recognize "evolving standards" with *Trop v. Dulles* (1958).

The clearest and most reliable objective evidence of contemporary values is the legislation enacted by the country's legislatures. We have also looked to data concerning the actions of sentencing juries. . . .

The common-law prohibition against punishing "idiots" for their crimes suggests that it may indeed be "cruel and unusual" punishment to execute persons who are profoundly or severely retarded and wholly lacking the capacity to appreciate the wrongfulness of their actions. Because of the protections afforded by the insanity defense today, such a person is not likely to be convicted or face the prospect of punishment. Moreover, under *Ford v. Wainwright,* someone who is "unaware of the punishment they are about to suffer and why they are to suffer it" cannot be executed.

Such a case is not before us today. Penry was found competent to stand trial. In other words, he was found to have the ability to consult with his lawyer with a reasonable degree of rational understanding, and was found to have a rational as well as factual understanding of the proceedings against him. In addition, the jury rejected his insanity defense, which reflected their conclusion that Penry knew that his conduct was wrong and was capable of conforming his conduct to the requirements of the law.

Penry argues, however, that there is objective evidence today of an emerging national consensus against execution of the mentally retarded, reflecting the "evolving standards of decency that mark the progress of a maturing society." Only one State [Georgia], however, currently bans execution of retarded persons who have been found guilty of a capital offense. Maryland has enacted a similar statute which will take effect on July 1, 1989.

In contrast, in *Ford v. Wainwright,* which held that the Eighth Amendment prohibits execution of the insane, considerably more evidence of a national consensus was available. No State permitted the execution of the insane, and 26 States had statutes explicitly requiring suspension of the execution of a capital defendant who became insane. . . . In our view, the two state statutes prohibiting execution of the mentally retarded, even when added to the 14 States that have rejected capital punishment completely, do not provide sufficient evidence at present of a national consensus. . . .

> *". . . [T]here is insufficient evidence of a national consensus against executing mentally retarded people convicted of capital offenses for us to conclude that it is categorically prohibited by the Eighth Amendment."*

. . . [A]t present, there is insufficient evidence of a national consensus against executing mentally retarded people convicted of capital offenses for us to conclude that it is categorically prohibited by the Eighth Amendment. . . .

On the record before the Court today . . . I cannot conclude that all mentally retarded people of Penry's ability—by virtue of their mental retardation alone, and apart from any individualized consideration of their personal responsibility—inevitably lack the cognitive, volitional, and moral capacity to act with the degree of culpability associated with the death penalty. Mentally retarded persons are individuals whose abilities and experiences can vary greatly. . . .

Not surprisingly, courts have long been reluctant to rely on the concept of mental age as a basis for exculpating a defendant from criminal responsibility. Moreover, reliance on mental age to measure the capabilities of a retarded person for purposes of the Eighth Amendment could have a disempowering effect if applied in other areas of the law. Thus, on that premise, a mildly mentally retarded person could be denied the opportunity to enter into contracts or to marry by virtue of the fact that he had a "mental age" of a young child. In light of the inherent problems with the mental age concept, and in the absence of better evidence of a national consensus against execution of the retarded, mental age should not be adopted as a line-drawing principle in our Eighth Amendment jurisprudence.

In sum, mental retardation is a factor that may well lessen a defendant's culpability for a capital offense. But we cannot conclude today that the Eighth Amendment precludes the execution of any mentally retarded person of Penry's ability convicted of a capital offense simply by virtue of his or her mental retardation alone. So long as sentencers can consider and give effect to mitigating evidence of mental retardation in imposing sentence, an individualized determination whether "death is the appropriate punishment" can be made in each particular case. While a national consensus against execution of the mentally retarded may someday emerge reflecting the "evolving standards of decency that mark the progress of a maturing society," there is insufficient evidence of such a consensus today.

Accordingly, the judgment below is affirmed in part and reversed in part, and the case is remanded for further proceedings consistent with this opinion. . . .

JUSTICE BRENNAN, joined by JUSTICE MARSHALL, filed an opinion concurring in part and dissenting in part. [Omitted]

JUSTICE STEVENS, joined by JUSTICE BLACKMUN, filed an opinion concurring in part and dissenting in part. [Omitted]

JUSTICE SCALIA, joined by CHIEF JUSTICE REHNQUIST and JUSTICES WHITE and KENNEDY, filed an opinion concurring in part and dissenting in part. [Omitted]

Chapter 6

From *Harmelin* to *Ring*: 1991–2002

Life Sentences for Drug Possession

Harmelin v. Michigan

June 27, 1991

INTRODUCTION

The administrations of George H. W. Bush, William Clinton, and George W. Bush were years of relative stability in the Supreme Court's personnel, with only six justices appointed in 20 years and no turnover at all from 1994 to 2005. Nevertheless, these years featured continuing ambivalence and dissonance in thinking about the death penalty and about the concept of cruel and unusual punishment in sentences under three-strikes and zero-tolerance laws. For example, in *Harmelin v. Michigan* (1991), the Supreme Court appeared to retreat from its position in *Solem v. Helm* that disproportionate sentences are prohibited by the Eighth Amendment. In *Harmelin,* the Court upheld a life sentence against the claim that it was disproportionate to the crime of cocaine possession.

The Supreme Court had long since moved away from the era of *Fay v. Noia* and in the early 1990s moved to limit repetitive and last-minute habeas corpus petitions. In *Gomez v. United States District Court* (1992), a majority held that a judge could take the last-minute nature of even a meritorious second or subsequent petition into account in deciding whether to stay an execution. After an all-night exchange of judicial opinions by fax machine between California and Washington, D.C., the Supreme Court vacated four separate stays of execution issued by lower federal courts and finally ordered that despite the claim that California's gas chamber inflicted cruel and unusual punishment, no further stays could be issued. The next morning, April 21, 1992, California carried out its first execution in 25 years. Robert Alton Harris, after 13 years on death row, died for kidnapping and murdering two teenage boys because he wanted their car to use in a robbery. The Supreme Court went still further in *Herrera v. Collins* (1993), holding that habeas corpus was

(continued)

not for the purpose of correcting errors of fact: a last-minute confession by the death row inmate's brother or a recantation by a prosecution witness, in the absence of a claim that some other federal constitutional provision was violated, should not result in a stay of execution. How to handle genuine claims of actual innocence would trouble state legislatures, the Court, and Congress for years.

In *Kansas v. Hendricks* (1997), the Court upheld a Kansas statute that permitted a sex offender who was scheduled to be released to be retained in custody in order to prevent him from committing additional future crimes. The Court's decisions sometimes favored defendants. In *Atkins v. Virginia* (2002), the Court reversed *Penry v. Lynaugh* and prohibited the execution of mentally retarded individuals. In *Ring v. Arizona,* also decided in 2002, the Court held that juries, not judges, must decide whether or not to impose a capital sentence.

Political developments reflected similar ambivalence. For example, in 1992, Governor Bill Clinton found it politically advantageous to interrupt his presidential campaign to return to Arkansas for the execution of Ricky Ray Rector. In 1994, Kansas reenacted a death penalty statute and Congress passed the Violent Crime Control Act, providing the option of the death penalty for numerous federal crimes. The same year, Illinois executed the high-profile serial killer John Wayne Gacy. In 1995, New York governor George Pataki signed a measure reinstating the death penalty in the state. In 1996, Congress passed the Antiterrorism and Effective Death Penalty Act, restricting federal and state inmates in most cases to one habeas corpus petition, imposing a one-year statute of limitations on the filing of petitions, and commanding federal courts to defer to state court rejection of inmate claims unless the state court's findings were not just wrong but "unreasonable." The Supreme Court upheld the act against a constitutional challenge in *Felker v. Turpin* (1996). In 1997, Timothy McVeigh was convicted and sentenced to death for the 1995 bombing of a federal building in Oklahoma City. He was executed in 2001.

But not all developments during these years signaled the advance and expansion of the death penalty. For example, in 1999, Nebraska funded a study of the fairness of the application of the death penalty in the state. In 2000, Illinois governor George Ryan announced a moratorium on executions in the state, following several exonerations and reversals of death sentences. In 2002, Maryland governor Parris Glendening imposed a moratorium on executions in the state and announced a study to determine whether or not there were racial biases in Maryland's application of the death penalty. The Death Penalty Information Center reported that nationwide, 53 death row inmates had been exonerated between 1991 and 2002, following the presentation of new evidence.[1]

Public opinion was also mixed. Public support for the death penalty reached 80 percent in 1994 Gallup Polls—an all-time high. In May 2001, Gallup showed public support for the death penalty to be at 65 percent—the lowest level in 20 years. In May 2002, approximately eight months after the terrorist attacks of September 11, 2001, public support for the death penalty was back up to 72 percent.

In *Solem v. Helm,* the Court held that the Eighth Amendment prohibits sentences that are disproportionate to the crime. In *Harmelin,* five members of the Court upheld a sentence of life imprisonment without possibility of parole for possession of 672 grams of cocaine. Justice Scalia, joined by Chief Justice Rehnquist, wanted to overturn *Solem*'s proportionality rule in noncapital cases. Justice Kennedy, joined by Justices O'Connor and Souter, distinguished *Harmelin* from *Solem.* These justices found that Harmelin's crime—possession of a large amount of cocaine—was "far more grave" than the crime at issue in *Solem*: writing a bad check. As such, unlike Solem, Harmelin's sentence was not "grossly disproportionate" to the crime. Justices White, Blackmun, Stevens, and Marshall dissented.

JUSTICE SCALIA announced the judgment of the Court and delivered the opinion of the Court with respect to Part IV, and an opinion with respect to Parts I, II, and III, in which THE CHIEF JUSTICE joins.

Petitioner was convicted of possessing 672 grams of cocaine and sentenced to a mandatory term of life in prison without possibility of parole. . . . [W]e granted *certiorari.*

Petitioner claims that his sentence is unconstitutionally "cruel and unusual" for two reasons: first, because it is "significantly disproportionate" to the crime he committed; second, because the sentencing judge was statutorily required to impose it, without taking into account the particularized circumstances of the crime and of the criminal.

I

The Eighth Amendment, which applies against the States by virtue of the Fourteenth Amendment, provides: "Excessive bail shall not be required, nor excessive fines imposed, nor cruel and unusual punishments inflicted." In *Rummel v. Estelle,* we held that it did not constitute "cruel and unusual punishment" to impose a life sentence, under a recidivist statute, upon a defendant who had been convicted, successively, of fraudulent use of a credit card to obtain $80 worth of goods or services, passing a forged check in the amount of $28.36, and obtaining $120.75 by false pretenses. . . .

Two years later, in *Hutto v. Davis,* we similarly rejected an Eighth Amendment challenge to a prison term of 40 years and fine of $20,000 for possession and distribution of approximately nine ounces of marijuana. . . .

A year and a half after *Davis* we uttered what has been our last word on this subject to date. *Solem v. Helm* set aside under the Eighth Amendment, because it was disproportionate, a sentence of life imprisonment without possibility of parole, imposed under a South Dakota recidivist statute for successive offenses that included three convictions of third-degree burglary, one of obtaining money by false pretenses, one of grand larceny, one of third-offense driving while intoxicated, and one of writing a "no account" check with intent to defraud. . . . Having decreed that a general principle of disproportionality exists, the Court used as the criterion for its application the three-factor test that had been explicitly rejected in both *Rummel* and *Davis.* . . .

... [O]ur 5-to-4 decision ... in *Solem* was scarcely the expression of clear and well-accepted constitutional law. We have long recognized, of course, that the doctrine of *stare decisis* is less rigid in its application to constitutional precedents, and we think that to be especially true of a constitutional precedent that is both recent and in apparent tension with other decisions. Accordingly, we have addressed anew, and in greater detail, the question whether the Eighth Amendment contains a proportionality guarantee—with particular attention to the background of the Eighth Amendment . . . and to the understanding of the Eighth Amendment before the end of the 19th century. . . .

We conclude from this examination that *Solem* was simply wrong; the Eighth Amendment contains no proportionality guarantee.

Scalia, with Rehnquist agreeing, claimed that the framers of the U.S. Constitution did not require proportionality in sentencing. He laid the foundation for arguments that the original intent of the Eighth Amendment does not prohibit disproportionate punishment.

Solem based its conclusion principally upon the proposition that a right to be free from disproportionate punishments was embodied within the "cruell and unusuall Punishments" provision of the English Declaration of Rights of 1689, and was incorporated, with that language, in the Eighth Amendment. . . .

As *Solem* observed, the principle of proportionality was familiar to English law at the time the Declaration of Rights was drafted. . . . Despite this familiarity, the drafters of the Declaration of Rights did not explicitly prohibit "disproportionate" or "excessive" punishments. Instead, they prohibited punishments that were "cruell and unusuall." The *Solem* Court simply assumed, with no analysis, that the one included the other. As a textual matter, of course, it does not: a disproportionate punishment can perhaps always be considered "cruel," but it will not always be (as the text also requires) "unusual." . . .

Most historians agree that the "cruell and unusuall Punishments" provision of the English Declaration of Rights was prompted by the abuses attributed to the infamous Lord Chief Justice Jeffreys of the King's Bench during the Stuart reign of James II. . . .

But the vicious punishments for treason decreed in the Bloody Assizes (drawing and quartering, burning of women felons, beheading, disemboweling, etc.) were common in that period—indeed, they were specifically authorized by law and remained so for many years afterwards. . . .

"... [T]he ultimate question is not what 'cruell and unusuall punishments' meant in the Declaration of Rights, but what its meaning was to the Americans who adopted the Eighth Amendment."

In sum, we think it most unlikely that the English Cruell and Unusuall Punishments Clause was meant to forbid "disproportionate" punishments. There is even less likelihood that proportionality of punishment was one of the traditional "rights and privileges of Englishmen" apart from the Declaration of Rights, which happened to be included in the Eighth Amendment. . . .

. . . [H]owever, the ultimate question is not what "cruel and unusuall punishments" meant in the Declaration of Rights, but what its meaning was to the Americans who adopted the Eighth Amendment. . . .

. . . According to its terms . . . , the Clause disables the Legislature from authorizing particular forms or "modes" of punishment—specifically, cruel methods of punishment that are not regularly or customarily employed. . . .

The early commentary on the Clause contains no reference to disproportionate or excessive sentences, and again indicates that it was designed to outlaw particular modes of punishment. . . .

Perhaps the most persuasive evidence of what "cruel and unusual" meant, however, is found in early judicial constructions of the Eighth Amendment and its state counterparts. . . .

Throughout the 19th century, state courts interpreting state constitutional provisions with identical or more expansive wording (i.e., "cruel or unusual") concluded that these provisions did not proscribe disproportionality but only certain modes of punishment. . . .

II

We think it enough that those who framed and approved the Federal Constitution chose, for whatever reason, not to include within it the guarantee against disproportionate sentences that some State Constitutions contained. . . . While there are relatively clear historical guidelines and accepted practices that enable judges to determine which modes of punishment are "cruel and unusual," proportionality does not lend itself to such analysis. . . . The real function of a constitutional proportionality principle, if it exists, is to enable judges to evaluate a penalty that some assemblage of men and women has considered proportionate—and to say that it is not. For that real-world enterprise, the standards seem so inadequate that the proportionality principle becomes an invitation to imposition of subjective values.

This becomes clear, we think, from a consideration of the three factors that *Solem* found relevant to the proportionality determination: (1) the inherent gravity of the offense, (2) the sentences imposed for similarly grave offenses in the same jurisdiction, and (3) sentences imposed for the same crime in other jurisdictions. As to the first factor: of course some offenses, involving violent harm to human beings, will always and everywhere be regarded as serious, but that is only half the equation. The issue is what else should be regarded to be as serious as these offenses, or even to be more serious than some of them. On that point, judging by the statutes that Americans have enacted, there is enormous variation—even within a given age, not to mention across the many generations ruled by the Bill of Rights. . . .

The second factor suggested in *Solem* fails for the same reason. One cannot compare the sentences imposed by the jurisdiction for "similarly grave" offenses if there is no objective standard of gravity. . . .

As for the third factor mentioned by *Solem*—the character of the sentences imposed by other States for the same crime—it must be acknowledged that that can be applied with clarity and ease. The only difficulty is that it has no conceivable relevance to the Eighth Amendment. . . . [A] State is entitled to treat with stern disapproval an act that other States punish with the mildest of sanctions . . . [or] that other States do not criminalize at all. . . . Diversity not only in policy, but in the means of implementing policy, is the very *raison d'etre* of our federal system. . . .

IV

Petitioner claims that his sentence violates the Eighth Amendment for a reason in addition to its alleged disproportionality. He argues that it is "cruel and unusual" to impose a mandatory sentence of such severity, without any consideration of so-called mitigating factors such as, in his case, the fact that he had no prior felony convictions. . . .

. . . [T]his claim has no support in the text and history of the Eighth Amendment. Severe, mandatory penalties may be cruel, but they are not unusual in the constitutional sense, having been employed in various forms throughout our

"Severe, mandatory penalties may be cruel, but they are not unusual in the constitutional sense, having been employed in various forms throughout our nation's history."

Nation's history. . . . [M]andatory death sentences abounded in our first Penal Code. They were also common in the several States—both at the time of the founding and throughout the 19th century. There can be no serious contention, then, that a sentence which is not otherwise cruel and unusual becomes so simply because it is "mandatory." . . .

It is true that petitioner's sentence is unique in that it is the second most severe known to the law; but life imprisonment with possibility of parole is also unique in that it is the third most severe. And if petitioner's sentence forecloses some "flexible techniques" for later reducing his sentence, it does not foreclose all of them, since there remain the possibilities of retroactive legislative reduction and executive clemency. . . . We have drawn the line of required individualized sentencing at capital cases, and see no basis for extending it further.

The judgment of the Michigan Court of Appeals is Affirmed.

JUSTICE KENNEDY, with whom JUSTICE O'CONNOR and JUSTICE SOUTER join, concurring in part and concurring in the judgment.

I concur in Part IV of the Court's opinion and in the judgment. I write this separate opinion because my approach to the Eighth Amendment proportionality analysis differs from JUSTICE SCALIA's. . . . *Stare decisis* counsels our adherence to the narrow proportionality principle that has existed in our Eighth Amendment jurisprudence for 80 years. Although our proportionality decisions have not been clear or consistent in all respects, they can be reconciled, and they require us to uphold petitioner's sentence.

Our decisions recognize that the Cruel and Unusual Punishments Clause encompasses a narrow proportionality principle. . . .

Though our decisions recognize a proportionality principle, its precise contours are unclear. This is so in part because we have applied the rule in few cases and even then to sentences of different types. Our most recent pronouncement on the subject in *Solem*, furthermore, appeared to apply a different analysis than in *Rummel* and *Davis*. *Solem* twice stated, however, that its decision was consistent with *Rummel* and thus did not overrule it. Despite these tensions, close analysis of

The concurring justices insisted that extreme sentences that are disproportionate to a crime are forbidden (e.g., life imprisonment for overtime parking). A narrow proportionality principle has been recognized. In the present case, however, the sentence was not grossly disproportionate.

our decisions yields some common principles that give content to the uses and limits of proportionality review.

The first of these principles is that the fixing of prison terms for specific crimes involves a substantive penological judgment that, as a general matter, is "properly within the province of legislatures, not courts.". . .

The second principle is that the Eighth Amendment does not mandate adoption of any one penological theory. . . . The federal and state criminal systems have accorded different weights at different times to the penological goals of retribution, deterrence, incapacitation, and rehabilitation. . . .

Third, marked divergences both in underlying theories of sentencing and in the length of prescribed prison terms are the inevitable, often beneficial, result of the federal structure. . . . State sentencing schemes may embody different penological assumptions, making interstate comparison of sentences a difficult and imperfect enterprise. . . . Thus, the circumstance that a State has the most severe punishment for a particular crime does not by itself render the punishment grossly disproportionate. . . .

. . . [F]ourth[,] . . . proportionality review by federal courts should be informed by "'objective factors to the maximum possible extent.'" The most prominent objective factor is the type of punishment imposed. . . . [O]ur decisions recognize that we lack clear objective standards to distinguish between sentences for different terms of years. Although "no penalty is *per se* constitutional," the relative lack of objective standards concerning terms of imprisonment has meant that "'[o]utside the context of capital punishment, successful challenges to the proportionality of particular sentences [are] exceedingly rare.'"

All of these principles—the primacy of the legislature, the variety of legitimate penological schemes, the nature of our federal system, and the requirement that proportionality review be guided by objective factors—inform the final one: The Eighth Amendment does not require strict proportionality between crime and sentence. Rather, it forbids only extreme sentences that are "grossly disproportionate" to the crime.

With these considerations stated, it is necessary to examine the challenged aspects of petitioner's sentence: its severe length and its mandatory operation.

"The Eighth Amendment does not require strict proportionality between crime and sentence. Rather, it forbids only extreme sentences that are 'grossly disproportionate' to the crime."

"Petitioner's suggestion that his crime was nonviolent and victimless, echoed by the dissent, is false to the point of absurdity."

Petitioner's life sentence without parole is the second most severe penalty permitted by law. It is the same sentence received by the petitioner in *Solem.* Petitioner's crime, however, was far more grave than the crime at issue in *Solem.*

The crime of uttering a no account check at issue in *Solem* was "'one of the most passive felonies a person could commit.'" It "involved neither violence nor threat of violence to any person," and was "viewed by society as among the less serious offenses." . . .

Petitioner was convicted of possession of more than 650 grams (over 1.5 pounds) of cocaine. This amount of pure cocaine has a potential yield of between 32,500 and 65,000 doses. . . . From any standpoint, this crime falls in a different category from the relatively minor, nonviolent crime at issue in *Solem.* Possession, use, and distribution of illegal drugs represent "one of the greatest problems affecting the health and welfare of our population." Petitioner's suggestion that his crime was nonviolent and victimless, echoed by the dissent, is false to the point of absurdity. To the contrary, petitioner's crime threatened to cause grave harm to society. . . .

. . . [R]eports detailing the pernicious effects of the drug epidemic in this country . . . demonstrate that the Michigan Legislature could with reason conclude that the threat posed to the individual and society by possession of this large an amount of cocaine—in terms of violence, crime, and social displacement—is momentous enough to warrant the deterrence and retribution of a life sentence without parole. . . .

. . . *Solem* is best understood as holding that comparative analysis within and between jurisdictions is not always relevant to proportionality review. The Court stated that "it may be helpful to compare sentences imposed on other criminals in the same jurisdiction," and that "courts may find it useful to compare the sentences imposed for commission of the same crime in other jurisdictions." It did not mandate such inquiries.

A better reading of our cases leads to the conclusion that intrajurisdictional and interjurisdictional analyses are appropriate only in the rare case in which a threshold comparison of the crime committed and the sentence imposed leads to an inference of gross disproportionality. . . .

The proper role for comparative analysis of sentences, then, is to validate an initial judgment that a sentence is grossly disproportionate to a crime. . . . In light of the gravity of petitioner's offense, a comparison of his crime with his sentence does not give rise to an inference of gross disproportionality, and comparative analysis of his sentence with others in Michigan and across the Nation need not be performed.

Petitioner also attacks his sentence because of its mandatory nature. Petitioner would have us hold that any severe penalty scheme requires individualized sentencing so that a judicial official may consider mitigating circumstances. Our precedents do not support this proposition, and petitioner presents no convincing reason to fashion an exception or adopt a new rule in the case before us. The Court demonstrates that our Eighth Amendment capital decisions reject any requirement of individualized sentencing in noncapital cases. . . .

In asserting the constitutionality of this mandatory sentence, I offer no judgment on its wisdom. Mandatory sentencing schemes can be criticized for depriving judges of the power to exercise individual discretion when remorse and acknowledgment of guilt, or other extenuating facts, present what might seem a compelling case for departure from the maximum. On the other hand, broad and unreviewed discretion exercised by sentencing judges leads to the perception that no clear standards are being applied, and that the rule of law is imperiled by sentences imposed for no discernible reason other than the subjective reactions of the sentencing judge. The debate illustrates that . . . arguments for and against particular sentencing schemes are for legislatures to resolve. . . .

. . . Reasonable minds may differ about the efficacy of Michigan's sentencing scheme, and it is far from certain that Michigan's bold experiment will succeed. The accounts of pickpockets at Tyburn hangings are a reminder of the limits of the law's deterrent force, but we cannot say the law before us has no chance of success and is on that account so disproportionate as to be cruel and unusual punishment. . . . I conclude that petitioner's sentence of life imprisonment without parole for his crime of possession of more than 650 grams of cocaine does not violate the Eighth Amendment.

JUSTICE WHITE, with whom JUSTICE BLACKMUN and JUSTICE STEVENS join, dissenting.

"The accounts of pickpockets at Tyburn hangings are a reminder of the limits of the law's deterrent force, . . ."

"Nor would it be unreasonable to conclude that it would be both cruel and unusual to punish overtime parking by life imprisonment, . . ."

The Eighth Amendment provides that "[e]xcessive bail shall not be required, nor excessive fines imposed, nor cruel and unusual punishments inflicted." JUSTICE SCALIA concludes that "the Eighth Amendment contains no proportionality guarantee." Accordingly, he says *Solem v. Helm* "was simply wrong" in holding otherwise, as would be the Court's other cases interpreting the Amendment to contain a proportionality principle. JUSTICE KENNEDY, on the other hand, asserts that the Eighth Amendment's proportionality principle is so "narrow" that *Solem*'s analysis should be reduced from three factors to one. With all due respect, I dissent.

The language of the Amendment does not refer to proportionality in so many words, but it does forbid "excessive" fines, a restraint that suggests that a determination of excessiveness should be based at least in part on whether the fine imposed is disproportionate to the crime committed. Nor would it be unreasonable to conclude that it would be both cruel and unusual to punish overtime parking by life imprisonment, or, more generally, to impose any punishment that is grossly disproportionate to the offense for which the defendant has been convicted. . . .

. . . [T]he [Eighth] Amendment as ratified contained the words "cruel and unusual," and there can be no doubt that prior decisions of this Court have construed these words to include a proportionality principle. . . .

. . . Indeed, *Rummel v. Estelle,* the holding of which JUSTICE SCALIA does not question, itself recognized that the Eighth Amendment contains a proportionality requirement, for it did not question *Coker* and indicated that the proportionality principle would come into play in some extreme, nonfelony cases.

. . . JUSTICE SCALIA . . . appears to accept that the Amendment does indeed insist on proportional punishments in . . . cases . . . that involve sentences of death. His fallback position is that outside the capital cases, proportionality review is not required by the Amendment. With the exception of capital cases, the severity of the sentence for any crime is a matter that the Amendment leaves to the discretion of legislators. Any prison sentence, however severe, for any crime, however petty, will be beyond review under the Eighth Amendment. This position . . . ignores the generality of the Court's several pronouncements about the Eighth Amendment's proportionality component. And it fails to explain why the

words "cruel and unusual" include a proportionality requirement in some cases but not in others. . . . The Court's capital
punishment cases requiring proportionality reject JUSTICE
SCALIA's notion that the Amendment bars only cruel and
unusual modes or methods of punishment. Under that view,
capital punishment—a mode of punishment—would either
be completely barred or left to the discretion of the legislature. Yet neither is true. The death penalty is appropriate
in some cases and not in others. The same should be true of
punishment by imprisonment. . . .

The Court . . . has recognized that a punishment may violate the Eighth Amendment if it is contrary to the "evolving
standards of decency that mark the progress of a maturing
society." In evaluating a punishment under this test, "we
have looked not to our own conceptions of decency, but to
those of modern American society as a whole" in determining what standards have "evolved," and thus have focused
not on "the subjective views of individual Justices," but on
"objective factors to the maximum possible extent." It is this
type of objective factor which forms the basis for the tripar-
tite proportionality analysis set forth in *Solem.*

Contrary to JUSTICE SCALIA's suggestion, the *Solem* analysis has worked well in practice. Courts appear to have had
little difficulty applying the analysis to a given sentence, and
application of the test by numerous state and federal appellate courts has resulted in a mere handful of sentences being
declared unconstitutional. Thus, it is clear that reviewing
courts have not baldly substituted their own subjective moral
values for those of the legislature. . . . *Solem* is wholly consistent with this approach, and when properly applied, its
analysis affords "substantial deference to the broad authority that legislatures necessarily possess in determining the
types and limits of punishments for crimes, as well as to the
discretion that trial courts possess in sentencing convicted
criminals" and will only rarely result in a sentence failing
constitutional muster. The fact that this is one of those rare
instances is no reason to abandon the analysis. . . .

Two dangers lurk in JUSTICE SCALIA's analysis. First,
he provides no mechanism for addressing a situation such
as that proposed in *Rummel,* in which a legislature makes
overtime parking a felony punishable by life imprisonment.
He concedes that "one can imagine extreme examples"—
perhaps such as the one described in *Rummel*—"that no rational person, in no time or place, could accept," but attempts

*"The death penalty is
appropriate in some cases
and not in others. The same
should be true of punishment by
imprisonment."*

to offer reassurance by claiming that "for the same reason these examples are easy to decide, they are certain never to occur." This is cold comfort indeed, for absent a proportionality guarantee, there would be no basis for deciding such cases should they arise.

Second, . . . JUSTICE SCALIA's position that the Eighth Amendment addresses only modes or methods of punishment is quite inconsistent with our capital punishment cases, which do not outlaw death as a mode or method of punishment, but instead put limits on its application. If the concept of proportionality is downgraded in the Eighth Amendment calculus, much of this Court's capital penalty jurisprudence will rest on quicksand.

While JUSTICE SCALIA seeks to deliver a swift death sentence to *Solem,* JUSTICE KENNEDY prefers to eviscerate it, leaving only an empty shell. The analysis JUSTICE KENNEDY proffers is contradicted by the language of *Solem* itself and by our other cases interpreting the Eighth Amendment. . . .

Because there is no justification for overruling or limiting *Solem,* it remains to apply that case's proportionality analysis to the sentence imposed on petitioner. Application of the *Solem* factors to the statutorily mandated punishment at issue here reveals that the punishment fails muster under *Solem* and, consequently, under the Eighth Amendment to the Constitution. . . .

. . . [T]he Michigan statute at issue fails constitutional muster. The statutorily mandated penalty of life without possibility of parole for possession of narcotics is unconstitutionally disproportionate in that it violates the Eighth Amendment's prohibition against cruel and unusual punishment. Consequently, I would reverse the decision of the Michigan Court of Appeals.

Marshall reiterated his categorical rejection of the death penalty.

JUSTICE MARSHALL, dissenting.

I agree with JUSTICE WHITE's dissenting opinion, except insofar as it asserts that the Eighth Amendment's Cruel and Unusual Punishments Clause does not proscribe the death penalty. I adhere to my view that capital punishment is in all instances unconstitutional. . . . However, my view that capital punishment is especially proscribed . . . is not inconsistent with JUSTICE WHITE's central conclusion that the Eighth

Amendment also imposes a general proportionality requirement. As JUSTICE WHITE notes, this Court has recognized and applied that requirement in both capital and noncapital cases, and had it done so properly here it would have concluded that Michigan's law mandating life sentences with no possibility of parole even for first-time drug possession offenders is unconstitutional.

JUSTICE STEVENS, with whom JUSTICE BLACKMUN joins, dissenting.

While I agree wholeheartedly with JUSTICE WHITE's dissenting opinion, I believe an additional comment is appropriate.

The severity of the sentence that Michigan has mandated for the crime of possession of more than 650 grams of cocaine, whether diluted or undiluted, does not place the sentence in the same category as capital punishment. I remain convinced that Justice Stewart correctly characterized the penalty of death as "unique" because of "its absolute renunciation of all that is embodied in our concept of humanity." Nevertheless, a mandatory sentence of life imprisonment without the possibility of parole does share one important characteristic of a death sentence: The offender will never regain his freedom. Because such a sentence does not even purport to serve a rehabilitative function, the sentence must rest on a rational determination that the punished "criminal conduct is so atrocious that society's interest in deterrence and retribution wholly outweighs any considerations of reform or rehabilitation of the perpetrator." Serious as this defendant's crime was, I believe it is irrational to conclude that every similar offender is wholly incorrigible. . . .

". . . [A] mandatory sentence of life imprisonment without the possibility of parole does share one important characteristic of a death sentence: The offender will never regain his freedom."

Note

1. See "Innocence: List of Those Freed from Death Row," Death Penalty Information Center, http://www.deathpenaltyinfo .org/innocence-list-those-freed-death-row.

Justice Blackmun Reconsiders the Death Penalty

Callins v. Collins

February 22, 1994

INTRODUCTION

This Texas case involved an appeal by Bruce Edwin Callins, a murderer awaiting execution for his 1980 killing of a man during a robbery. The Court denied his petition for a writ of certiorari without a written opinion. Nevertheless, Justice Blackmun, who had voted to uphold the death penalty in *Gregg* and on other occasions earlier in his career, issued a dissenting opinion expressing his personal frustration with the death penalty itself and with attempts to devise rules to make capital punishment fair and constitutionally workable. Here, just two months before announcing his retirement, Blackmun concluded in no uncertain terms that the "death penalty experiment has failed." He announced that he would "no longer tinker with the machinery of death." Like Justices Brennan and Marshall (and, based on his 1991 interview, Powell) before him, Blackmun joined the ranks of those who regarded the death penalty as categorically prohibited by the Constitution. Justice Scalia took issue with Blackmun in a strongly worded opinion of his own. Excerpts from Scalia's concurring opinion appear first, followed by excerpts from Blackmun's dissent.

The petition for a *writ of certiorari* is denied.

JUSTICE SCALIA, concurring.

. . . The Fifth Amendment provides that "[n]o person shall be held to answer for a capital . . . crime, unless on a presentment or indictment of a Grand Jury . . . nor be deprived of life . . . without due process of law." This clearly permits the death penalty to be imposed, and establishes beyond doubt that the death penalty is not one of the "cruel and unusual punishments" prohibited by the Eighth Amendment.

. . . [H]owever, over the years since 1972 this Court has attached to the imposition of the death penalty two quite incompatible sets of commands: the sentencer's discretion to impose death must be closely confined, but the sentencer's discretion *not* to impose death (to extend mercy) must be unlimited. These commands were invented without benefit of any textual or historical support; they are the product of just such "intellectual, moral, and personal" perceptions as JUSTICE BLACKMUN expresses today, some of which . . . have been made part of what is called "the Court's Eighth Amendment jurisprudence." . . .

Convictions in opposition to the death penalty are often passionate and deeply held. That would be no excuse for reading them into a Constitution that does not contain them, even if they represented the convictions of a majority of Americans. Much less is there any excuse for using that course to thrust a minority's views upon the people. JUSTICE BLACKMUN begins his statement by describing with poignancy the death of a convicted murderer by lethal injection. He chooses, as the case in which to make that statement, one of the less brutal of the murders that regularly come before us—the murder of a man ripped by a bullet suddenly and unexpectedly, with no opportunity to prepare himself and his affairs, and left to bleed to death on the floor of a tavern. The death by injection which JUSTICE BLACKMUN describes looks pretty desirable next to that. It looks even better next to some of the other cases currently before us which Justice Blackmun did not select as the vehicle for his announcement that the death penalty is always unconstitutional—for example, the case of the 11-year-old girl raped by four men and then killed by stuffing her panties down her throat. . . . How enviable a quiet death by lethal injection compared with that! If the people conclude that such more brutal deaths may be deterred by capital punishment; indeed, if they merely conclude that justice requires such brutal deaths to be avenged by capital punishment; the creation of false, untextual and unhistorical contradictions within "the Court's Eighth Amendment jurisprudence" should not prevent them.

JUSTICE BLACKMUN, dissenting.

On February 23, 1994, at approximately 1:00 a.m., Bruce Edwin Callins will be executed by the State of Texas. Intravenous tubes attached to his arms will carry the instrument of death, a toxic fluid designed specifically for the purpose of killing human beings. The witnesses, standing a few feet away, will behold Callins, no longer a defendant, an appellant, or a petitioner, but a man, strapped to a gurney, and seconds away from extinction.

Within days, or perhaps hours, the memory of Callins will begin to fade. The wheels of justice will churn again, and somewhere, another jury or another judge will have the unenviable task of determining whether some human being is to live or die. We hope, of course, that the defendant whose life is at risk will be represented by competent counsel. . . . [W]e hope that the prosecution, in urging the penalty of death, will have exercised its discretion wisely, free from bias, prejudice, or political motive, and will be humbled, rather than emboldened, by the awesome authority conferred by the State.

But even if we can feel confident that these actors will fulfill their roles to the best of their human ability, our collective conscience will remain uneasy. Twenty years have passed since this Court declared that the death penalty must be imposed fairly, and with reasonable consistency, or not at all, and, despite the effort of the States and courts to devise legal formulas and procedural rules to meet this daunting challenge, the death penalty remains fraught with arbitrariness, discrimination, caprice, and mistake. . . .

From this day forward, I no longer shall tinker with the machinery of death. For more than 20 years I have endeavored—indeed, I have struggled—along with a majority of this Court, to develop procedural and substantive rules that would lend more than the mere appearance of fairness to the death penalty endeavor. Rather than continue to coddle the Court's delusion that the desired level of fairness has been achieved and the need for regulation eviscerated, I feel morally and intellectually obligated simply to concede that the death penalty experiment has failed. It is virtually self-evident to me now that no combination of procedural rules or substantive regulations ever can save the death penalty from its inherent constitutional deficiencies. . . . The problem is that the inevitability of factual, legal, and moral error gives us a system that we know must wrongly kill some defendants, a system that fails to deliver the fair, consistent, and reliable sentences of death required by the Constitution. . . .

> *"Rather than continue to coddle the Court's delusion that the desired level of fairness has been achieved and the need for regulation eviscerated, I feel morally and intellectually obligated simply to concede that the death penalty experiment has failed."*

Perhaps one day this Court will develop procedural rules or verbal formulas that actually will provide consistency, fairness, and reliability in a capital sentencing scheme. I am not optimistic that such a day will come. I am more optimistic, though, that this Court eventually will conclude that the effort to eliminate arbitrariness while preserving fairness "in the infliction of [death] is so plainly doomed to failure that it—and the death penalty—must be abandoned altogether."

Callins was executed by lethal injection.

I may not live to see that day, but I have faith that eventually it will arrive. . . .

Continuing Incarceration of Sex Offenders

Kansas v. Hendricks

June 23, 1997

INTRODUCTION

Responding to horrific crimes committed by persons released from prison, Kansas's Sexually Violent Predator Act (1994) provided for the civil commitment of persons who were likely to engage in predatory sexual violence. Leroy Hendricks was a convicted pedophile. He was scheduled for release from prison, but he admitted that he continued to harbor sexual desires for children. Under the Kansas act, he was committed to a mental institution prior to his release from prison in order to prevent him from endangering others if he were set free. This was the first time that the state applied this statute. The Supreme Court upheld this "pre-commitment." Justice Thomas wrote for the Court and stressed that states "may take measures to restrict the freedom of the dangerously mentally ill. This is a legitimate nonpunitive governmental objective and has been historically so regarded." Justice Kennedy wrote a concurring opinion. Justices Breyer, Stevens, Souter, and Ginsburg dissented.

JUSTICE THOMAS delivered the opinion of the Court.

In 1994, Kansas enacted the Sexually Violent Predator Act, which establishes procedures for the civil commitment of persons who, due to a "mental abnormality" or a "personality disorder," are likely to engage in "predatory acts of sexual violence." The State invoked the Act for the first time to commit Leroy Hendricks, an inmate who had a long history of sexually molesting children, and who was scheduled for release from prison shortly after the Act became law.

Hendricks challenged his commitment on . . . "substantive" due process, double jeopardy, and *ex post-facto* grounds.

Substantive due process prohibits the government from arbitrarily enforcing laws that deprive people of life, liberty, or property. This right is included in the due process guarantees of the Fifth and Fourteenth Amendments. Article 1, Section 9, of the U.S. Constitution prohibits Congress from passing ex post facto, or retroactive, laws.

The Kansas Supreme Court invalidated the Act, holding that its pre-commitment condition of a "mental abnormality" did not satisfy . . . the "substantive" due process requirement that involuntary civil commitment must be predicated on a finding of "mental illness." . . . We granted *certiorari* . . . and now reverse the judgment below.

The Kansas Legislature enacted the Sexually Violent Predator Act (Act) in 1994 to grapple with the problem of managing repeat sexual offenders. Although Kansas already had a statute addressing the involuntary commitment of those defined as "mentally ill," the legislature determined that existing civil commitment procedures were inadequate to confront the risks presented by "sexually violent predators." In the Act's preamble, the legislature explained:

> [A] small but extremely dangerous group of sexually violent predators exist who . . . have anti-social personality features which are unamenable to existing mental illness treatment modalities and those features render them likely to engage in sexually violent behavior. The legislature further finds that sexually violent predators' likelihood of engaging in repeat acts of predatory sexual violence is high. The existing involuntary commitment procedure . . . is inadequate to address the risk these sexually violent predators pose to society. The legislature further finds that the prognosis for rehabilitating sexually violent predators in a prison setting is poor, the treatment needs of this population are very long term and the treatment modalities for this population are very different than the traditional treatment modalities for people appropriate for commitment under the [general involuntary civil commitment statute].

As a result, the Legislature found it necessary to establish "a civil commitment procedure for the long-term care and treatment of the sexually violent predator." The Act defined a "sexually violent predator" as:

> any person who has been convicted of or charged with a sexually violent offense and who suffers from a mental abnormality or personality disorder which makes the person likely to engage in the predatory acts of sexual violence.

A "mental abnormality" was defined, in turn, as a "congenital or acquired condition . . . which predisposes the person to commit sexually violent offenses in a degree constituting such person a menace to the health and safety of others." . . .

In addition to placing the burden of proof upon the State, the Act afforded the individual a number of other procedural safeguards. . . .

Prisoners convicted of sexual offenses were to be screened for dangerousness before being released from prison. The state could next use a civil commitment proceeding, including a jury trial, to determine if the prisoner should be placed in a mental institution after being released from prison.

Once an individual was confined, the Act required that "[t]he involuntary detention or commitment . . . shall conform to constitutional requirements for care and treatment." Confined persons were afforded three different avenues of review: First, the committing court was obligated to conduct an annual review to determine

whether continued detention was warranted. Second, the Secretary [of Social and Rehabilitative Services] was permitted, at any time, to decide that the confined individual's condition had so changed that release was appropriate. . . . Finally, even without the Secretary's permission, the confined person could at any time file a release petition. If the court found that the State could no longer satisfy its burden under the initial commitment standard, the individual would be freed from confinement.

In 1984, Hendricks was convicted of taking "indecent liberties" with two 13-year-old boys. After serving nearly 10 years of his sentence, he was slated for release to a halfway house. Shortly before his scheduled release, however, the State filed a petition in state court seeking Hendricks' civil confinement as a sexually violent predator. . . . [T]he court . . . concluded that there was probable cause to support a finding that Hendricks was a sexually violent predator, and therefore ordered that he be evaluated at the Larned State Security Hospital.

Hendricks subsequently requested a jury trial to determine whether he qualified as a sexually violent predator. During that trial, Hendricks' own testimony revealed a chilling history of repeated child sexual molestation and abuse. . . .

Hendricks admitted that he had repeatedly abused children whenever he was not confined. He explained that when he "get[s] stressed out," he "can't control the urge" to molest children. Although Hendricks recognized that his behavior harms children, and he hoped he would not sexually molest children again, he stated that the only sure way he could keep from sexually abusing children in the future was "to die." Hendricks readily agreed with the state physician's diagnosis that he suffers from pedophilia and that he is not cured of the condition; indeed, he told the physician that "treatment is bull—." The jury unanimously found beyond a reasonable doubt that Hendricks was a sexually violent predator. The trial court subsequently determined, as a matter of state law, that pedophilia qualifies as a "mental abnormality" as defined by the Act, and thus ordered Hendricks committed to the Secretary's custody.

Hendricks appealed, claiming, among other things, that application of the Act to him violated the Federal Constitution's

Due Process, Double Jeopardy, and *ExPost-Facto* Clauses. The Kansas Supreme Court accepted Hendricks' due process claim. . . .

Kansas argues that the Act's definition of "mental abnormality" satisfies "substantive" due process requirements. We agree. Although freedom from physical restraint "has always been at the core of the liberty protected by the Due Process Clause from arbitrary governmental action," that liberty interest is not absolute. The Court has recognized that an individual's constitutionally protected interest in avoiding physical restraint may be overridden even in the civil context. . . .

Accordingly, States have in certain narrow circumstances provided for the forcible civil detainment of people who are unable to control their behavior and who thereby pose a danger to the public health and safety. We have consistently upheld such involuntary commitment statutes provided the confinement takes place pursuant to proper procedures and evidentiary standards. It thus cannot be said that the involuntary civil confinement of a limited subclass of dangerous persons is contrary to our understanding of ordered liberty.

The challenged Act unambiguously requires a finding of dangerousness either to one's self or to others as a prerequisite to involuntary confinement. Commitment proceedings can be initiated only when a person "has been convicted of or charged with a sexually violent offense," and "suffers from a mental abnormality or personality disorder which makes the person likely to engage in the predatory acts of sexual violence." The statute thus requires proof of more than a mere predisposition to violence; rather, it requires evidence of past sexually violent behavior and a present mental condition that creates a likelihood of such conduct in the future if the person is not incapacitated. . . .

Thomas concluded that the Kansas Sexually Violent Predator Act contained such necessary procedural safeguards.

A finding of dangerousness, standing alone, is ordinarily not a sufficient ground upon which to justify indefinite involuntary commitment. We have sustained civil commitment statutes when they have coupled proof of dangerousness with the proof of some additional factor, such as a "mental illness" or "mental abnormality." These added statutory requirements serve to limit involuntary civil confinement to those who suffer from a volitional impairment rendering them dangerous beyond their control. . . .

To the extent that the civil commitment statutes we have considered set forth criteria relating to an individual's inability to control his dangerousness, the Kansas Act sets forth comparable criteria and Hendricks' condition doubtless satisfies those criteria. The mental health professionals who evaluated Hendricks diagnosed him as suffering from pedophilia, a condition the psychiatric profession itself classifies as a serious mental disorder. . . . Hendricks' diagnosis as a pedophile, which qualifies as a "mental abnormality" under the Act, thus plainly suffices for due process purposes.

. . . The thrust of Hendricks' argument is that the Act establishes criminal proceedings; hence confinement under it necessarily constitutes punishment. He contends that where, as here, newly enacted "punishment" is predicated upon past conduct for which he has already been convicted and forced to serve a prison sentence, the Constitution's Double Jeopardy and *Ex Post-Facto* Clauses are violated. We are unpersuaded by Hendricks' argument that Kansas has established criminal proceedings.

. . . Nothing on the face of the statute suggests that the legislature sought to create anything other than a civil commitment scheme designed to protect the public from harm. . . .

As a threshold matter, commitment under the Act does not implicate either of the two primary objectives of criminal punishment: retribution or deterrence. The Act's purpose is not retributive because it does not affix culpability for prior criminal conduct. Instead, such conduct is used solely for evidentiary purposes, either to demonstrate that a "mental abnormality" exists or to support a finding of future dangerousness. . . . In addition, the Kansas Act does not make a criminal conviction a prerequisite for commitment—persons absolved of criminal responsibility may nonetheless be subject to confinement under the Act. An absence of the necessary criminal responsibility suggests that the State is not seeking retribution for a past misdeed. Thus, the fact that the Act may be "tied to criminal activity" is "insufficient to render the statut[e] punitive." . . .

Nor can it be said that the legislature intended the Act to function as a deterrent. Those persons committed under the Act are, by definition, suffering from a "mental abnormality" or a "personality disorder" that prevents them from exercising adequate control over their behavior. Such persons are therefore unlikely to be deterred by the threat of confinement. . . .

"Those persons committed under the Act are, by definition, suffering from a 'mental abnormality' or a 'personality disorder' that prevents them from exercising adequate control over their behavior."

. . . The State may take measures to restrict the freedom of the dangerously mentally ill. This is a legitimate nonpunitive governmental objective and has been historically so regarded. . . .

Hendricks focuses on his confinement's potentially indefinite duration as evidence of the State's punitive intent. That focus, however, is misplaced. Far from any punitive objective, the confinement's duration is instead linked to the stated purposes of the commitment, namely, to hold the person until his mental abnormality no longer causes him to be a threat to others. If, at any time, the confined person is adjudged "safe to be at large," he is statutorily entitled to immediate release. . . .

Hendricks next contends that the State's use of procedural safeguards traditionally found in criminal trials makes the proceedings here criminal rather than civil. . . . That Kansas chose to afford such procedural protections does not transform a civil commitment proceeding into a criminal prosecution.

Finally, Hendricks argues that the Act is necessarily punitive because it fails to offer any legitimate "treatment." Without such treatment, Hendricks asserts, confinement under the Act amounts to little more than disguised punishment. . . .

. . . We have already observed that, under the appropriate circumstances and when accompanied by proper procedures, incapacitation may be a legitimate end of the civil law. Accordingly, the Kansas [Supreme C]ourt's determination that the Act's "overriding concern" was the continued "segregation of sexually violent offenders" is consistent with our conclusion that the Act establishes civil proceedings, especially when that concern is coupled with the State's ancillary goal of providing treatment to those offenders, if such is possible. While we have upheld state civil commitment statutes that aim both to incapacitate and to treat, we have never held that the Constitution prevents a State from civilly detaining those for whom no treatment is available, but who nevertheless pose a danger to others. . . . [I]t would be of little value to require treatment as a precondition for civil confinement of the dangerously insane when no acceptable treatment existed. To conclude otherwise would obligate a State to release certain confined individuals who were both mentally ill and dangerous simply because they could not be successfully treated for their afflictions. . . .

"[I]t would be of little value to require treatment as a precondition for civil confinement of the dangerously insane when no acceptable treatment existed."

Where the State has "disavowed any punitive intent" limited confinement to a small segment of particularly dangerous individuals; provided strict procedural safeguards; directed that confined persons be segregated from the general prison population and afforded the same status as others who have been civilly committed; recommended treatment if such is possible; and permitted immediate release upon a showing that the individual is no longer dangerous or mentally impaired, we cannot say that it acted with punitive intent. We therefore hold that the Act does not establish criminal proceedings and that involuntary confinement pursuant to the Act is not punitive. Our conclusion that the Act is non-punitive thus removes an essential prerequisite for both Hendricks' double jeopardy and *ex post-facto* claims. . . .

We hold that the Kansas Sexually Violent Predator Act comports with due process requirements and neither runs afoul of double jeopardy principles nor constitutes an exercise in impermissible *ex post-facto* lawmaking. Accordingly, the judgment of the Kansas Supreme Court is reversed. . . .

JUSTICE KENNEDY, concurring. [Omitted]

JUSTICE BREYER, with whom JUSTICES STEVENS and SOUTER join, and with whom Justice GINSBURG joins as to Parts II and III, dissenting.

Was this really a mental health law? Was the state trying to provide meaningful treatment? Justice Breyer was unconvinced. The state showed little regard for treatment. To Breyer, the Kansas Sexually Violent Predator Act was primarily punitive.

I agree with the majority that the Kansas Act's "definition of 'mental abnormality'" satisfies the "substantive" requirements of the Due Process Clause. Kansas, however, concedes that Hendricks' condition is treatable; yet the Act did not provide Hendricks (or others like him) with any treatment until after his release date from prison and only inadequate treatment thereafter. These, and certain other, special features of the Act convince me that it was not simply an effort to commit Hendricks civilly, but rather an effort to inflict further punishment upon him. The *Ex Post-Facto* Clause therefore prohibits the Act's application to Hendricks, who committed his crimes prior to its enactment. . . .

Prohibiting the Execution of the Mentally Retarded

Atkins v. Virginia

June 20, 2002

INTRODUCTION

Should the death penalty ever be imposed on a mentally retarded criminal? In *Atkins,* the Supreme Court reversed its position from *Penry v. Lynaugh* and ruled that execution of mentally retarded individuals constitutes cruel and unusual punishment. Justice Stevens, joined by Justices O'Connor, Kennedy, Souter, Ginsburg, and Breyer, delivered the opinion of the Court. Stevens noted that mentally retarded persons have "disabilities in areas of reasoning, judgment, and control of their impulses." As such, they "do not act with the level of moral culpability that characterizes the most serious adult criminal conduct." Pointing to an increase in the number of states that banned such executions since *Penry* was decided in 1989, the Court concluded that a national consensus had developed that capital punishment is "excessive" for mentally retarded offenders.

JUSTICE STEVENS, joined by JUSTICES O'CONNOR, KENNEDY, SOUTER, GINSBURG, and BREYER, delivered the opinion of the Court.

hose mentally retarded persons who meet the law's requirements for criminal responsibility should be tried and punished when they commit crimes. Because of their disabilities in areas of reasoning, judgment, and control of their impulses, however, they do not act with the level of moral culpability that characterizes the most serious adult criminal conduct. Moreover, their impairments can jeopardize the reliability and fairness of capital proceedings against mentally retarded defendants. Presumably for these reasons, in the 13 years since we decided *Penry v. Lynaugh,* the American public, legislators, scholars, and judges have deliberated over the question whether the death penalty should ever be imposed on a mentally retarded criminal. The consensus reflected in those deliberations informs our answer to the question presented by this case: whether such executions are cruel and unusual punishments prohibited by the Eighth Amendment to the Federal Constitution.

Petitioner, Daryl Renard Atkins, was convicted of abduction, armed robbery, and capital murder, and sentenced to death. At approximately midnight on August 16, 1996,

Atkins and William Jones, armed with a semiautomatic handgun, abducted Eric Nesbitt, robbed him of the money on his person, drove him to an automated teller machine in his pickup truck where cameras recorded their withdrawal of additional cash, then took him to an isolated location where he was shot eight times and killed. . . .

The prosecution offered Jones a plea bargain in exchange for his testimony against Atkins. Both Jones and Atkins testified in the guilt phase of Atkins's trial. Each blamed the other for the murder. Jones's testimony was "more coherent and credible" than Atkins's and was credited by the jury in establishing Atkins's guilt. Atkins's testimony contradicted statements that he made to the police when he was arrested. Jones had remained silent, refusing to make an initial statement to the police.

In the penalty phase, the defense relied on one witness, Dr. Evan Nelson, a forensic psychologist who had evaluated Atkins before trial and concluded that he was mildly mentally retarded. His conclusion was based on interviews with people who knew Atkins, a review of school and court records, and the administration of a standard intelligence test which indicated that Atkins had a full scale IQ of 59.5. . . .

IQs lower than 70 are generally considered in the mildly mentally retarded range. An IQ of 59 placed Atkins in the lowest one percentile in intelligence. The state presented Dr. Stanton Same as a rebuttal witness. He testified that Atkins was "of average intelligence, at least." The jury sentenced Atkins to death.

The Supreme Court of Virginia affirmed the imposition of the death penalty. Atkins . . . contend[ed] that he is mentally retarded and thus cannot be sentenced to death. The majority of the state court rejected this contention, relying on our holding in *Penry.* The Court was not willing to commute Atkins' sentence of death to life imprisonment merely because of his IQ score.

Justice Hassell and Justice Koontz dissented. They . . . concluded that the imposition of the sentence of death upon a criminal defendant who has the mental age of a child between the ages of 9 and 12 is excessive. In their opinion, it is indefensible to conclude that individuals who are mentally retarded are not to some degree less culpable for their criminal acts. By definition, such individuals have substantial limitations not shared by the general population. A moral and civilized society diminishes itself if its system of justice does not afford recognition and consideration of those limitations in a meaningful way.

Because of the gravity of the concerns expressed by the dissenters, and in light of the dramatic shift in the state legislative landscape that has occurred in the past 13 years, we granted *certiorari* to revisit the issue that we first addressed in the *Penry* case.

The Eighth Amendment succinctly prohibits excessive sanctions. . . . In *Weems v. United States,* we held that a punishment of 12 years jailed in irons at hard and painful labor for the crime of falsifying records was excessive. We explained that it is a precept of justice that punishment for crime should be graduated and proportioned to the offense. We have repeatedly applied this proportionality precept in later cases interpreting the Eighth Amendment. . . .

> *"A claim that punishment is excessive is judged not by the standards that prevailed . . . when the Bill of Rights was adopted, but rather by those that currently prevail."*

A claim that punishment is excessive is judged not by the standards that prevailed . . . when the Bill of Rights was adopted, but rather by those that currently prevail. As Chief Justice Warren explained in . . . *Trop v. Dulles*: The basic concept underlying the Eighth Amendment is nothing less than the dignity of man. The Amendment must draw its meaning from the evolving standards of decency that mark the progress of a maturing society.

Proportionality review under those evolving standards should be informed by objective factors to the maximum possible extent. . . . [T]he clearest and most reliable objective evidence of contemporary values is the legislation enacted by the country's legislatures. Relying in part on such legislative evidence, we have held that death is an impermissibly excessive punishment for the rape of an adult woman, *Coker v. Georgia,* or for a defendant who neither took life, attempted to take life, nor intended to take life, *Enmund v. Florida.* . . .

We also acknowledged in *Coker* that the objective evidence, though of great importance, did not wholly determine the controversy, for the Constitution contemplates that in the end our own judgment will be brought to bear on the question of the acceptability of the death penalty under the Eighth Amendment. . . .

Thus, in cases involving a consensus, our own judgment is brought to bear by asking whether there is reason to disagree with the judgment reached by the citizenry and its legislators.

Guided by our approach in these cases, we shall first review the judgment of legislatures that have addressed the suitability of imposing the death penalty on the mentally retarded and then consider reasons for agreeing or disagreeing with their judgment.

. . . In [1986], the public reaction to the execution of a mentally retarded murderer in Georgia apparently led to the enactment of the first state statute prohibiting such executions. In 1988, when Congress enacted legislation reinstating the federal death penalty, it expressly provided that a sentence of death shall not be carried out upon a person who is mentally retarded. In 1989, Maryland enacted a similar prohibition. It was in that year that we decided *Penry,* and concluded that those two state enactments, even when added to the 14 States that have rejected capital punishment completely, do not provide sufficient evidence at present of a national consensus.

Much has changed since then. Responding to . . . our decision in *Penry,* state legislatures across the country began to address the issue. In 1990 Kentucky and Tennessee enacted statutes similar to those in Georgia and Maryland, as did New Mexico in 1991, and Arkansas, Colorado, Washington, Indiana, and Kansas in 1993 and 1994. In 1995, when New York reinstated its death penalty, it emulated the Federal Government by expressly exempting the mentally retarded. Nebraska followed suit in 1998. There appear to have been no similar enactments during the next two years, but in 2000 and 2001 six more States—South Dakota, Arizona, Connecticut, Florida, Missouri, and North Carolina—joined the procession. The Texas Legislature unanimously adopted a similar bill, and bills have passed at least one house in other States, including Virginia and Nevada.

It is not so much the number of these States that is significant, but the consistency of the direction of change. Given the well-known fact that anti-crime legislation is far more popular than legislation providing protections for persons guilty of violent crime, the large number of States prohibiting the execution of mentally retarded persons (and the complete absence of States passing legislation reinstating the power to conduct such executions) provides powerful evidence that today our society views mentally retarded offenders as categorically less culpable than the average criminal. . . .

Moreover, even in those States that allow the execution of mentally retarded offenders, the practice is uncommon. . . . The practice, therefore, has become truly unusual, and it is fair to say that a national consensus has developed against it.

A consensus against executing the mentally retarded may have developed, but disagreements remained about how mental retardation would be recognized and defined. The Court left such matters to states. Not surprisingly, states have differed.

To the extent there is serious disagreement about the execution of mentally retarded offenders, it is in determining which offenders are in fact retarded. . . . As was our approach in *Ford v. Wainwright,* with regard to insanity, we leave to the State[s] the task of developing appropriate ways to enforce the constitutional restriction upon its execution of sentences.

". . . [S]ome characteristics of mental retardation undermine the strength of the procedural protections that our capital jurisprudence steadfastly guards."

This consensus unquestionably reflects widespread judgment about the relative culpability of mentally retarded offenders, and the relationship between mental retardation and the penological purposes served by the death penalty. Additionally, it suggests that some characteristics of mental retardation undermine the strength of the procedural protections that our capital jurisprudence steadfastly guards.

. . . Mentally retarded persons frequently know the difference between right and wrong and are competent to stand trial. Because of their impairments, however, . . . they have diminished capacities to understand and process information, to communicate, to abstract from mistakes and learn from experience, to engage in logical reasoning, to control impulses, and to understand the reactions of others. There is no evidence that they are more likely to engage in criminal conduct than others, but there is abundant evidence that they often act on impulse rather than pursuant to a premeditated plan, and that in group settings they are followers rather than leaders. Their deficiencies do not warrant an exemption from criminal sanctions, but they do diminish their personal culpability.

In light of these deficiencies, our death penalty jurisprudence provides two reasons consistent with the legislative consensus that the mentally retarded should be categorically excluded from execution. First . . . *Gregg v. Georgia* identified retribution and deterrence of capital crimes . . . [as] the social purposes served by the death penalty. Unless the imposition of the death penalty on a mentally retarded person measurably contributes to one or both of these goals, it is nothing more than the purposeless and needless imposition of pain and suffering, and hence an unconstitutional punishment.

With respect to retribution . . . the severity of the appropriate punishment necessarily depends on the culpability of the offender. . . . Thus, pursuant to our narrowing jurisprudence, which seeks to ensure that only the most deserving of execution are put to death, an exclusion for the mentally retarded is appropriate.

With respect to deterrence . . . it seems likely that capital punishment can serve as a deterrent only when murder is the result of premeditation and deliberation. Exempting the mentally retarded from that punishment will not affect the cold calculus that precedes the decision of other potential murderers. Indeed, that sort of calculus is at the opposite end of the spectrum from behavior of mentally retarded offenders. . . . Thus, executing the mentally retarded will not measurably further the goal of deterrence.

The reduced capacity of mentally retarded offenders provides a second justification for a categorical rule making such offenders ineligible for the death penalty. The risk that the death penalty will be imposed in spite of factors which may call for a less severe penalty is enhanced, not only by the possibility of false confessions, but also by the lesser ability of mentally retarded defendants to make a persuasive showing of mitigation in the face of prosecutorial evidence of one or more aggravating factors. Mentally retarded defendants may be less able to give meaningful assistance to their counsel and are typically poor witnesses, and their demeanor may create an unwarranted impression of lack of remorse for their crimes. . . . Mentally retarded defendants in the aggregate face a special risk of wrongful execution.

Our independent evaluation of the issue reveals no reason to disagree with the judgment of the legislatures that have recently addressed the matter and concluded that death is not a suitable punishment for a mentally retarded criminal. We are not persuaded that the execution of mentally retarded criminals will measurably advance the deterrent or the retributive purpose of the death penalty. Construing and applying the Eighth Amendment in the light of our evolving standards of decency, we therefore conclude that such punishment is excessive and that the Constitution places a substantive restriction on the State's power to take the life of a mentally retarded offender.

CHIEF JUSTICE REHNQUIST, joined by JUSTICES SCALIA and THOMAS, filed a dissenting opinion. [Omitted]

JUSTICE SCALIA, joined by CHIEF JUSTICE REHNQUIST and JUSTICE THOMAS, filed a dissenting opinion.

Today's decision . . . find[s] no support in the text or history of the Eighth Amendment; it does not even have support in current social attitudes regarding the conditions that render an otherwise just death penalty inappropriate. Seldom has an opinion of this Court rested so obviously upon nothing but the personal views of its members. . . .

I respectfully dissent.

In 2005, a Virginia jury decided that Atkins's IQ had improved and that he was now intelligent enough to be executed. In 2008 while reconsidering whether or not Atkins was retarded, Ninth Circuit Court of Appeals judge Prentis Smiley received evidence of prosecutorial misconduct in the case. He commuted Atkins's sentence to life imprisonment.

Who Can Levy a Death Sentence?

Ring v. Arizona

June 24, 2002

INTRODUCTION

This case examined Arizona's capital-sentencing procedure. Arizona provided that juries determined guilt or innocence but that judges alone decided on punishment. The Supreme Court ruled that Arizona's sentencing procedures violate the Sixth Amendment right to trial by jury. Juries, not judges, should bear the responsibility for deciding whether or not to impose the death penalty. Justice Ginsburg wrote the opinion for the Court. The decision was joined by conservative justices as well as by some who generally opposed the death penalty. The only two dissenters were Chief Justice Rehnquist and Justice O'Connor, both from Arizona.

JUSTICE GINSBURG delivered the opinion of the Court.

This case concerns the Sixth Amendment right to a jury trial in capital prosecutions. In Arizona, following a jury adjudication of a defendant's guilt of first-degree murder, the trial judge, sitting alone, determines the presence or absence of the aggravating factors required by Arizona law for imposition of the death penalty.

In *Walton v. Arizona* (1990), this Court held that Arizona's sentencing scheme was compatible with the Sixth Amendment because the additional facts found by the judge qualified as sentencing considerations, not as element[s] of the offense of capital murder. Ten years later, however, we decided *Apprendi v. New Jersey* (2000), which held that the Sixth Amendment does not permit a defendant to be expose[d] to a penalty exceeding the maximum he would receive if punished according to the facts reflected in the jury verdict alone. This prescription governs, *Apprendi* determined, even if the State characterizes the additional findings made by the judge as sentencing factor[s].

Apprendi's reasoning is irreconcilable with *Walton*'s holding in this regard, and today we overrule *Walton* in relevant part. Capital defendants, no less than non-capital defendants, we conclude, are entitled to a jury determination of any fact on which the legislature conditions an increase in their maximum punishment.

At the trial of petitioner Timothy Ring for murder, armed robbery, and related charges . . . the jury [found] the facts here recounted. On November 28, 1994, a Wells Fargo armored van pulled up to the Dillard's department store at Arrowhead Mall in Glendale, Arizona. Courier Dave Moss left the van to pick up money inside the store. When he returned, the van, and its driver, John Magoch, were gone.

Later that day, Maricopa County Sheriff's Deputies found the van—its doors locked and its engine running—in the parking lot of a church in Sun City, Arizona. Inside the vehicle they found Magoch, dead from a single gunshot to the head. According to Wells Fargo records, more than $562,000 in cash and $271,000 in checks were missing from the van.

Prompted by an informant's tip, Glendale police sought to determine whether Ring and his friend James Greenham were involved in the robbery. The police investigation [resulted in criminal charges]. . . .

The trial judge instructed the jury on alternative charges of premeditated murder and felony murder. The jury deadlocked on premeditated murder, with 6 of 12 jurors voting to acquit, but convicted Ring of felony murder occurring in the course of armed robbery. . . .

As later summed up by the Arizona Supreme Court, the evidence admitted at trial failed to prove, beyond a reasonable doubt, that [Ring] was a major participant in the armed robbery or that he actually murdered Magoch. Although clear evidence connected Ring to the robbery's proceeds, nothing submitted at trial put him at the scene of the robbery. Furthermore, [f]or all we know from the trial evidence, the Arizona court stated, [Ring] did not participate in, plan, or even expect the killing. This lack of evidence no doubt explains why the jury found [Ring] guilty of felony, but not premeditated, murder.

Under Arizona law, Ring could not be sentenced to death, the statutory maximum penalty for first-degree murder, unless further findings were made. The State's first-degree murder statute . . . directs the judge who presided at trial to conduct a separate sentencing hearing to determine the existence or nonexistence of [certain enumerated] circumstances for the purpose of determining the sentence to be imposed. The statute further instructs: The hearing shall be conducted before the court alone. The court alone shall make all factual

"Under Arizona law, Ring could not be sentenced to death, the statutory maximum penalty for first-degree murder, unless further findings were made."

determinations required by this section or the constitution of the United States or this state.

At the conclusion of the sentencing hearing, the judge is to determine the presence or absence of the enumerated aggravating circumstances and any mitigating circumstances. The State's law authorizes the judge to sentence the defendant to death only if there is at least one aggravating circumstance and there are no mitigating circumstances sufficiently substantial to call for leniency. . . .

On October 29, 1997, the trial judge entered his Special Verdict sentencing Ring to death. Because Ring was convicted of felony murder, not premeditated murder, the judge recognized that Ring was eligible for the death penalty only if he was Magoch's actual killer or if he was a major participant in the armed robbery that led to the killing and exhibited a reckless disregard or indifference for human life. . . .

"Citing Greenham's testimony at the sentencing hearing, the judge concluded that Ring is the one who shot and killed Mr. Magoch."

Citing Greenham's testimony at the sentencing hearing, the judge concluded that Ring is the one who shot and killed Mr. Magoch. The judge also found that Ring was a major participant in the robbery and that armed robbery is unquestionably a crime which carries with it a grave risk of death.

The judge then turned to the determination of aggravating and mitigating circumstances. He found two aggravating factors. First, the judge determined that Ring committed the offense in expectation of receiving something of "pecuniary value" . . . "[t]aking the cash from the armored car was the motive and reason for Mr. Magoch's murder and not just the result." . . . Second, the judge found that the offense was committed in an especially heinous, cruel or depraved manner. In support of this finding, he cited Ring's comment, as reported by Greenham at the sentencing hearing, expressing pride in his marksmanship. The judge found one nonstatutory mitigating factor: Ring's minimal criminal record. In his judgment, that mitigating circumstance did not call for leniency; he therefore sentenced Ring to death.

On appeal, Ring argued that Arizona's capital sentencing scheme violates the Sixth and Fourteenth Amendments to the U.S. Constitution because it entrusts to a judge the finding of a fact raising the defendant's maximum penalty. The State, in response, noted that this Court had upheld Arizona's system in *Walton v. Arizona* and had stated in *Apprendi* that *Walton* remained good law.

. . . [T]he Arizona Supreme Court . . . rejected Ring's constitutional attack on the State's capital murder judicial sentencing system . . . and affirmed the death sentence.

We granted Ring's petition for a *writ of certiorari*. . . . We now reverse the judgment of the Arizona Supreme Court.

The central question: Can a judge impose a death sentence, overriding a jury's recommendation of life imprisonment?

Based solely on the jury's verdict finding Ring guilty of first-degree felony murder, the maximum punishment he could have received was life imprisonment. This was so because, in Arizona, a death sentence may not legally be imposed unless at least one aggravating factor is found to exist beyond a reasonable doubt. The question presented is whether that aggravating factor may be found by the judge, as Arizona law specifies, or whether the Sixth Amendments jury-trial guarantee, made applicable to the States by the Fourteenth Amendment, requires that the aggravating factor determination be entrusted to the jury. . . .

. . . [In] *Apprendi v. New Jersey* . . . [t]he defendant-petitioner . . . was convicted of second-degree possession of a firearm, an offense carrying a maximum penalty of 10 years under New Jersey law. On the prosecutor's motion, the sentencing judge found by a preponderance of the evidence that Apprendi's crime had been motivated by racial animus. That finding triggered application of New Jersey's hate crime enhancement, which doubled Apprendi's maximum authorized sentence. The judge sentenced Apprendi to 12 years in prison, 2 years over the maximum that would have applied but for the enhancement.

We held that Apprendi's sentence violated his right to a jury determination that [he] is guilty of every element of the crime with which he is charged, beyond a reasonable doubt. That right attached not only to Apprendi's weapons offense but also to the hate crime aggravating circumstance. New Jersey, the Court observed, threatened Apprendi with certain pains if he unlawfully possessed a weapon and with additional pains if he selected his victims with a purpose to intimidate them because of their race. Merely using the label sentence enhancement to describe the [second act] surely does not provide a principled basis for treating [the two acts] differently.

The dispositive question, we said, is one not of form, but of effect. If a State makes an increase in a defendant's authorized punishment contingent on the finding of a fact, that fact, no matter how the State labels it, must be found by a jury beyond a reasonable doubt. A defendant may not be expose[d] to a penalty exceeding the maximum he would receive if punished according to the facts reflected in the jury verdict alone. . . .

Arizona suggests that judicial authority over the finding of aggravating factors may be a better way to guarantee against the arbitrary imposition of the death penalty. The Sixth Amendment jury-trial right, however, does not turn on the relative rationality, fairness, or efficiency of potential fact finders. Entrusting to a judge the finding of facts necessary to support a death sentence might be an admirably fair and efficient scheme of criminal justice designed for a society that is prepared to leave criminal justice to the State. The founders of the American Republic were not prepared to leave it to the State, which is why the jury-trial guarantee was one of the least controversial provisions of the Bill of Rights. It has never been efficient; but it has always been free.

"If a State makes an increase in a defendant's authorized punishment contingent on the finding of a fact, that fact, no matter how the State labels it, must be found by a jury beyond a reasonable doubt."

In any event, the superiority of judicial fact finding in capital cases is far from evident. Unlike Arizona, the great majority of States responded to this Court's Eighth Amendment decisions requiring the presence of aggravating circumstances in capital cases by entrusting those determinations to the jury. . . .

Because Arizona's enumerated aggravating factors operate as the functional equivalent of an element of a greater offense, the Sixth Amendment requires that they be found by a jury.

The guarantees of jury trial in the Federal and State Constitutions reflect a profound judgment about the way in which law should be enforced and justice administered. If the defendant preferred the common sense judgment of a jury to the more tutored but perhaps less sympathetic reaction of the single judge, he was to have it.

... The judgment of the Arizona Supreme Court is therefore reversed, and the case is remanded for further proceedings not inconsistent with this opinion.

JUSTICE SCALIA, with whom JUSTICE THOMAS joins, concurring. [Omitted]

JUSTICE KENNEDY, concurring. [Omitted]

JUSTICE BREYER, concurring in the judgment. [Omitted]

JUSTICE O'CONNOR, with whom the CHIEF JUSTICE joins, dissenting. [Omitted]

The Sixth Amendment requires a jury, not a judge, to find the aggravating factors necessary for the death penalty.

Congress enacts major crime legislation at infrequent intervals. One major piece of modern federal law, the Sentencing Reform Act of 1984, moved away from a rehabilitation-oriented criminal law and did away with parole. More important, Congress created the U.S. Sentencing Commission to help reign in the widely disparate sentences imposed by different judges for the same crime and had the commission publish a compendium of sentencing guidelines. This effort made the sentencing proceeding an often tedious exercise in computing the precise intersection of the criminal history of the defendant and the specific characteristics of the offense in a 258-box grid. Most significant, under the Sentencing Reform Act the sentence that the defendant received might be determined on evidence not even presented to the jury and even evidence of crimes where the jury had not found guilt, as long as the sentencing judge found by a preponderance of the evidence, not proof beyond a reasonable doubt, that the defendant was responsible. Similar sentencing reforms with similar procedures were enacted by many states at the same time.

Federal judges chafed for more than a decade at the mandatory nature of the sentencing guidelines, while state and federal defense lawyers complained about the low threshold of evidence sufficient to impose lengthy sentences. In *Apprendi v. New Jersey* (2000) and eventually in *Blakely v. Washington* (2004), the Supreme Court ruled that the Sixth Amendment requires the jury to find all the facts necessary to impose sentence on a defendant beyond a reasonable doubt. *United States v. Booker* (2004) applied *Apprendi* and *Blakely* to the federal sentencing procedures and further held that mandatory sentencing guidelines were unconstitutional. *Ring v. Arizona* (2002) is a stepping stone along the way from *Apprendi* to *Booker*. Though important in its own right concerning the imposition of the death penalty, *Ring v. Arizona* is the rare capital punishment case that is perhaps best described as a skirmish in a jurisprudential war having little to do with the death penalty itself.

Chapter 7

Issues and Prospects for the 21st Century: Are Death Rows Facing Death Throes?

Execution of Minors

Roper v. Simmons

March 1, 2005

INTRODUCTION

Since 2000, developments in capital punishment can best be described as trench warfare in the courts and a gradual turn away from support for the death penalty by the public, as crime rates that peaked in the 1990s continue to drop. There was more than a 50 percent decrease in the number of executions nationwide from 1999 (98 executions) to 2012 (43 executions).[1] New capital sentences also diminished but at a slower rate than executions, so death rows continued to grow.

The Supreme Court has shifted its emphasis to reviewing how the lower federal courts influence death penalty decisions by their handling of habeas corpus petitions. As you will see in this chapter and the following one, the Court upheld Kentucky's lethal injection protocols against challenges in *Baze and Bowling v. Rees* (2008). But in several other cases—*Roper v. Simmons* (2005), *Kennedy v. Louisiana* (2008), and *Graham v. Florida* (2010), *Miller v. Alabama* (2012), and its companion case, *Jackson v. Hobbs* (2012)—the Court was receptive toward constitutional claims raised by condemned criminals.

In *Roper v. Simmons,* the Supreme Court again considered the death penalty for juvenile offenders. Justice Kennedy, joined by Justices Stevens, Souter, Ginsburg, and Breyer, delivered the opinion of the Court. Justices O'Connor, Scalia, and Thomas and Chief Justice Rehnquist dissented. The lineup of justices demonstrates the persisting importance of Justice Kennedy as the swing vote in 5–4 decisions. The case also illustrates the importance given to consensus and international law by Justices Kennedy and Breyer and the contrasting rejection of those two influences by Justices Scalia and Thomas.

JUSTICE KENNEDY delivered the opinion of the Court.

This case requires us to address, for the second time in a decade and a half, whether it is permissible under the Eighth and Fourteenth Amendments . . . to execute a juvenile offender who was older than 15 but younger than 18 when he committed a capital crime.

In *Stanford* v. *Kentucky* (1989), a divided Court rejected the proposition that the Constitution bars capital punishment for juvenile offenders in this age group. We reconsider the question.

At the age of 17, when he was still a junior in high school, Christopher Simmons . . . committed murder. About nine months later, after he had turned 18, he was tried and sentenced to death. . . . There is little doubt that Simmons was the instigator of the crime. Before its commission Simmons said he wanted to murder someone. Simmons assured his friends they could "get away with it" because they were minors.

. . . Simmons and Benjamin entered the home of the victim, Shirley Crook, after reaching through an open window and unlocking the back door. Simmons turned on a hallway light. Awakened, Mrs. Crook called out, "Who's there?" In response Simmons entered Mrs. Crook's bedroom, where he recognized her from a previous car accident involving them both. Simmons later admitted this confirmed his resolve to murder her.

Using duct tape to cover her eyes and mouth and bind her hands, the two perpetrators put Mrs. Crook in her minivan and drove to a state park. They reinforced the bindings, covered her head with a towel, and walked her to a railroad trestle spanning the Meramec River. There they tied her hands and feet together with electrical wire, wrapped her whole face in duct tape and threw her from the bridge, drowning her in the waters below.

. . . During closing arguments, both the prosecutor and defense counsel addressed Simmons' age, which the trial judge had instructed the jurors they could consider as a mitigating factor. Defense counsel reminded the jurors that juveniles of Simmons' age cannot drink, serve on juries, or even see certain movies, because "the legislatures have wisely

The Missouri Supreme Court had set aside Simmons's death sentence in favor of life imprisonment without eligibility for parole. The court acknowledged that *Stanford v. Kentucky* (1989) had rejected the claim that the Constitution bars capital punishment for offenders younger than 18, but Missouri's high court held that there is now a national consensus against the execution of juveniles. The U.S. Supreme Court granted certiorari, signaling that at least four justices—and probably a majority—agreed.

Consider the prosecutor's argument that youth is an aggravating factor, contrary to the holding of Missouri's highest court, and to the statement by the Supreme Court in *Johnson v. Texas* (1993) that "There is no dispute that a defendant's youth is a relevant mitigating circumstance." Prosecutors are in most states elected at the county or city level and have the power to charge or not charge a matter as a capital case, to offer a plea to a lesser offense, and to make deals with some defendants in order to convict others. The Supreme Court's review of some of these decisions can only take place after the fact. This does not mean that there are no efforts outside the judiciary to introduce consistency and proportionality in the death penalty process. In federal law, capital punishment is authorized by the Drug Kingpin Act of 1988, the Federal Death Penalty Act of 1994, and the Antiterrorism and Effective Death Penalty Act of 1996. Since 1995, the Department of Justice has centralized the decision of whether to seek the death penalty in federal court: for the stated goals of ensuring fairness and national consistency, the attorney general must approve or disapprove capital federal prosecutions. All 93 U.S. attorneys must submit for review all cases charging a capital offense, whether the U.S. attorney seeks the death penalty or not, to the Capital Review Committee—a group of senior attorneys within the department—that then makes a recommendation to the attorney general. The views of the family of the victim of the crime, if any, along with the defendant's background and criminal record, aggravating factors, and defense counsel's position as to mitigating factors, are part of the information that U.S. attorneys are required to submit.

In making its decision, the Court reviewed *Thompson v. Oklahoma* (1988), *Stanford v. Kentucky* (1989), *Penry v. Lynaugh* (1989), and *Atkins v. Virginia* (2002).

decided that individuals of a certain age aren't responsible enough."

Defense counsel argued that Simmons' age should make "a huge difference to [the jurors] in deciding just exactly what sort of punishment to make." In rebuttal, the prosecutor gave the following response: "Age, he says. Think about age. Seventeen years old. Isn't that scary? Doesn't that scare you? Mitigating? Quite the contrary I submit. Quite the contrary."

The Missouri Supreme Court . . . set aside Simmons' death sentence and resentenced him to "life imprisonment without eligibility for probation, parole, or release except by act of the Governor."

We granted *certiorari* and now affirm.

. . . The evidence of national consensus against the death penalty for juveniles is similar, and in some respects parallel, to the evidence *Atkins* held sufficient to demonstrate a national consensus against the death penalty for the mentally retarded. . . . Since *Stanford*, six States have executed prisoners for crimes committed as juveniles. In the past 10 years, only three have done so: Oklahoma, Texas, and Virginia. . . . In December 2003 the Governor of Kentucky decided to spare the life of Kevin Stanford, and commuted his sentence to one of life imprisonment without parole, with the declaration that "'[w]e ought not be executing people who, legally, were children.'" By this act the Governor ensured Kentucky would not add itself to the list of States that have executed juveniles within the last 10 years even by the execution of the very defendant whose death sentence the Court had upheld in *Stanford v. Kentucky.*

There is, to be sure, at least one difference between the evidence of consensus in *Atkins* and in this case. Impressive in *Atkins* was the rate of abolition of the death penalty for the mentally retarded. Sixteen States that permitted the execution of the mentally retarded at the time of *Penry* had prohibited the practice by the time we heard *Atkins*. By contrast, the rate of change in reducing the incidence of the juvenile death penalty, or in taking specific steps to abolish it, has been slower. Five States that allowed the juvenile death penalty at the time of *Stanford* have abandoned it in the intervening 15 years—four through legislative enactments and one through judicial decision.

Though less dramatic than the change from *Penry* to *Atkins* . . . , we still consider the change from *Stanford* to this case to be significant. . . . Since *Stanford,* no State that previously prohibited capital punishment for juveniles has reinstated it. . . .

When we heard *Stanford,* . . . 12 death penalty States had already prohibited the execution of any juvenile under 18, and 15 had prohibited the execution of any juvenile under 17. If anything, this shows that the impropriety of executing juveniles between 16 and 18 years of age gained wide recognition earlier than the impropriety of executing the mentally retarded. In the words of the Missouri Supreme Court: "It would be the ultimate in irony if the very fact that the inappropriateness of the death penalty for juveniles was broadly recognized sooner than it was recognized for the mentally retarded were to become a reason to continue the execution of juveniles now that the execution of the mentally retarded has been barred." . . .

As in *Atkins,* the objective *indicia* of consensus in this case— the rejection of the juvenile death penalty in the majority of States; the infrequency of its use even where it remains on the books; and the consistency in the trend toward abolition of the practice—provide sufficient evidence that today our society views juveniles, in the words *Atkins* used respecting the mentally retarded, as "categorically less culpable than the average criminal."

A majority of States have rejected the imposition of the death penalty on juvenile offenders under 18, and we now hold this is required by the Eighth Amendment.

. . . Once the diminished culpability of juveniles is recognized, it is evident that the penological justifications for the death penalty apply to them with lesser force than to adults. We have held there are two distinct social purposes served by the death penalty: "'retribution and deterrence of capital crimes by prospective offenders.'" . . . Whether viewed as an attempt to express the community's

"A majority of States have rejected the imposition of the death penalty on juvenile offenders under 18, and we now hold this is required by the Eighth Amendment."

moral outrage or as an attempt to right the balance for the wrong to the victim, the case for retribution is not as strong with a minor as with an adult. Retribution is not proportional if the law's most severe penalty is imposed on one whose culpability or blameworthiness is diminished, to a substantial degree, by reason of youth and immaturity.

As for deterrence, it is unclear whether the death penalty has a significant or even measurable deterrent effect on juveniles. . . . In general we leave to legislatures the assessment of the efficacy of various criminal penalty schemes. . . . [T]he same characteristics that render juveniles less culpable than adults suggest as well that juveniles will be less susceptible to deterrence. In particular, as the plurality observed in *Thompson,* "[t]he likelihood that the teenage offender has made the kind of cost-benefit analysis that attaches any weight to the possibility of execution is so remote as to be virtually nonexistent." To the extent the juvenile death penalty might have residual deterrent effect, it is worth noting that the punishment of life imprisonment without the possibility of parole is itself a severe sanction, in particular for a young person.

> "... [T]he United States is the only country in the world that continues to give official sanction to the juvenile death penalty."

. . . Our determination that the death penalty is disproportionate punishment for offenders under 18 finds confirmation in the stark reality that the United States is the only country in the world that continues to give official sanction to the juvenile death penalty. This reality does not become controlling, for the task of interpreting the Eighth Amendment remains our responsibility. Yet at least from the time of the Court's decision in *Trop,* the Court has referred to the laws of other countries and to international authorities as instructive for its interpretation of the Eighth Amendment's prohibition of "cruel and unusual punishments." . . .

As respondent and a number of *amici* emphasize, Article 37 of the United Nations Convention on the Rights of the Child, which every country in the world has ratified save for the United States and Somalia, contains an express prohibition on capital punishment for crimes committed by juveniles under 18. . . . No ratifying country has entered a reservation to the provision prohibiting the execution of juvenile offenders. . . .

Respondent and his *amici* have submitted, and petitioner does not contest, that only seven countries other than the United States have executed juvenile offenders since 1990: Iran, Pakistan, Saudi Arabia, Yemen, Nigeria, the Democratic Republic of Congo, and China. Since then each of these countries has either abolished capital punishment for juveniles or made public disavowal of the practice. In sum, it is fair to say that the United States now stands alone in a world that has turned its face against the juvenile death penalty.

. . . [I]t is instructive to note that the United Kingdom [also] abolished the juvenile death penalty. . . . The United Kingdom's experience bears particular relevance here in light of the historic ties between our countries and in light of the Eighth Amendment's own origins. . . .

It is proper that we acknowledge the overwhelming weight of international opinion against the juvenile death penalty, resting in large part on the understanding that the instability and emotional imbalance of young people may often be a factor in the crime. The opinion of the world community, while not controlling our outcome, does provide respected and significant confirmation for our own conclusions.

"It is proper that we acknowledge the overwhelming weight of international opinion against the juvenile death penalty, . . ."

Over time, from one generation to the next, the Constitution has come to earn the high respect and even, as Madison dared to hope, the veneration of the American people. . . . It does not lessen our fidelity to the Constitution or our pride in its origins to acknowledge that the express affirmation of certain fundamental rights by other nations and peoples simply underscores the centrality of those same rights within our own heritage of freedom.

JUSTICE STEVENS, with whom JUSTICE GINSBURG joins, concurring. [Omitted]

JUSTICE SCALIA, with whom THE CHIEF JUSTICE and JUSTICE THOMAS join, dissenting.

In urging approval of a constitution that gave life-tenured judges the power to nullify laws enacted by the people's representatives, Alexander Hamilton assured the citizens of New York that there was little risk in this, since "[t]he judiciary . . . ha[s] neither FORCE nor WILL but merely judgment." *The Federalist* No. 78. But Hamilton had in mind a traditional judiciary, "bound down by strict rules and precedents which serve to define and point out their duty in every particular case that comes before them." Bound down, indeed. What a mockery today's opinion makes of Hamilton's expectation, announcing the Court's conclusion that the meaning of our Constitution has changed over the past 15 years—not, mind you, that this Court's decision 15 years ago was wrong, but that the Constitution has changed. The Court reaches this implausible result by purporting to advert, not to the original meaning of the Eighth Amendment, but to "the evolving standards of decency" of our national society. It then finds, on the flimsiest of grounds, that a national consensus which could not be perceived in our people's laws barely 15 years ago now solidly exists. Worse still, the Court says in so many words that what our people's laws say about the issue does not, in the last analysis, matter: "[I]n the end our own judgment will be brought to bear on the question of the acceptability of the death penalty under the Eighth Amendment."

The Court thus proclaims itself sole arbiter of our Nation's moral standards—and in the course of discharging that awesome responsibility purports to take guidance from the views of foreign courts and legislatures.

Because I do not believe that the meaning of our Eighth Amendment, any more than the meaning of other provisions of our Constitution, should be determined by the subjective views of five Members of this Court and like-minded foreigners, I dissent. . . .

JUSTICE O'CONNOR, dissenting.

The Court's decision today establishes a categorical rule forbidding the execution of any offender for any crime committed before his 18th birthday, no matter how deliberate, wanton, or cruel the offense. Neither the objective evidence of contemporary societal values, nor the Court's moral proportionality analysis, nor the two in tandem suffice to justify this ruling.

. . . Nevertheless, I disagree with Justice Scalia's contention that foreign and international law have no place in our

---

It is important to distinguish between international law and the laws of individual foreign countries. Since its earliest days, the Supreme Court has recognized that customary international law, even though unwritten, is part of federal law. Furthermore, the Supreme Court has from the beginning looked upon international law as subject to change by consensus: at the beginning of the 19th century the slave trade was legal, then it was a violation of federal law, and then it was recognized as a violation of international law. Challenges to the status of the death penalty in international law are beginning to be advanced regularly in capital prosecutions. So far no judge has accepted the argument that international rejection of capital punishment is consistent or widespread enough to establish a new norm of behavior, making capital punishment like the slave trade. The Supreme Court has signaled its increasing awareness of the issue: striking down the death penalty for mentally retarded defendants in *Atkins v. Virginia* (2002), Justice Stevens's opinion contained a footnote observing that international practice was "additional" evidence that capital punishment for the retarded was unconstitutional. Justice Kennedy refers to international agreements as having "particular relevance" to the legality of executing juvenile murderers here in *Roper*. Other justices, particularly Justice Scalia who in 2005 engaged in a rare off-the-Court debate with Justice Breyer at American University on the subject, reject the relevance of modern international law to interpretation of the U.S. Constitution or the Bill of Rights because they believe that those documents had a definite meaning when enacted and that meaning should not be changed by judicial interpretation. During Sonia Sotomayor's confirmation hearing, she was asked by Senator Tom Coburn (R-Okla.) whether she believed that the Supreme Court could use "foreign" law to interpret the Constitution. Sotomayor adroitly responded in the negative.

Eighth Amendment jurisprudence. Over the course of nearly half a century, the Court has consistently referred to foreign and international law as relevant to its assessment of evolving standards of decency. . . .

[T]his Nation's evolving understanding of human dignity certainly is neither wholly isolated from, nor inherently at odds with, the values prevailing in other countries. On the contrary, we should not be surprised to find congruence between domestic and international values, especially where the international community has reached clear agreement—expressed in international law or in the domestic laws of individual countries— that a particular form of punishment is inconsistent with fundamental human rights. At least, the existence of an international consensus of this nature can serve to confirm the reasonableness of a consonant and genuine American consensus. The instant case presents no such domestic consensus, however, and the recent emergence of an otherwise global consensus does not alter that basic fact.

In December 2012, the United Nations General Assembly approved a resolution by a 111–41 vote (with 34 abstentions) that called on members "to progressively restrict the death penalty's use and not impose capital punishment for offenses committed by persons under age 18 or pregnant women." This followed a 2007 General Assembly call for a moratorium.

In determining whether the Eighth Amendment permits capital punishment of a particular offense or class of offenders, we must look to whether such punishment is consistent with contemporary standards of decency. We are obligated to weigh both the objective evidence of societal values and our own judgment as to whether death is an excessive sanction in the context at hand. In the instant case, the objective evidence is inconclusive; standing alone, it does not demonstrate that our society has repudiated capital punishment of 17-year-old offenders in all cases. Rather, the actions of the Nation's legislatures suggest that, although a clear and durable national consensus against this practice may in time emerge, that day has yet to arrive. By acting so soon after our decision in *Stanford*, the Court both pre-empts the democratic debate through which genuine consensus might develop and simultaneously runs a considerable risk of inviting lower court reassessments of our Eighth Amendment precedents. . . .

Justice O'Connor's dissent deftly balances her deference to legislative choices, her belief in the relevance of international law, and her respect for the Court's precedents.

Reasonable minds can differ as to the minimum age at which commission of a serious crime should expose the defendant to the death penalty, if at all. Many jurisdictions have abolished capital punishment altogether, while many others have determined that even the most heinous crime, if committed before the age of 18, should not be punishable by death. Indeed, were my office that of a legislator, rather than a judge, then I, too, would be inclined to support legislation setting a minimum age of 18 in this context. But a significant number of States, including Missouri, have decided to make the death penalty potentially available for 17-year-old capital murderers such as respondent.

Without a clearer showing that a genuine national consensus forbids the execution of such offenders, this Court should not substitute its own "inevitably subjective judgment" on how best to resolve this difficult moral question for the judgments of the Nation's democratically elected legislatures. I respectfully dissent.

Note

1. "Facts about the Death Penalty," Death Penalty Information Center, http://www.deathpenaltyinfo.org/documents/FactSheet.pdf.

Death by Lethal Injection

Baze and Bowling v. Rees

April 14, 2008

INTRODUCTION

Developments since the turn of the century suggest that state by state, abolition movements will again play an important role in America's use of capital punishment. Six states have abolished the death penalty since 2007: New Jersey (2007), New York (2007), New Mexico (2009), Illinois (2011), Connecticut (2012), and Maryland (2013). Governors have found themselves in the spotlight on the issue as well. In signing Connecticut's death penalty repeal bill, Governor Dannel Malloy said that when he served as a prosecutor, he "learned firsthand that our system of justice is very imperfect" and that it is "subject to the fallibility of those who participate in it."[1] In 2003, Governor Robert L. Ehrlich Jr. of Maryland rescinded a moratorium on executions that had been imposed the previous year by his predecessor, Governor Parris Glendening. In 2006, however, a Maryland appellate court suspended executions until the manual that sets protocols for lethal injections was reviewed by a legislative committee.

In 2003, Governor George Ryan commuted the death sentences of 167 inmates on the Illinois death row and declared the Illinois death penalty system to be "arbitrary, capricious, and . . . immoral." At the same time, speaking in opposition to Governor Ehrlich's rescission of the Maryland moratorium, Maryland attorney general J. Joseph Curran Jr. said that mistakes are inevitable and that the death penalty should be eliminated. In 2003, Kentucky governor Paul Patton commuted the death sentence of Kevin L. Stanford. This is the same Kevin Stanford who was 17 years old when he committed a capital crime, the same Kevin Stanford's whose death sentence was affirmed by the Supreme Court in *Stanford v. Kentucky* (1989). In 2004, the governors of South Dakota and Wyoming signed legislation raising the minimum age for imposition of the death penalty to 18 at the time of the crime.

Other developments suggest that capital punishment may be falling out of favor. Public opinion polls reveal that capital punishment continues to enjoy majority support. Gallup Poll results showed that 74 percent of survey respondents favored the death penalty in 2003. But by 2011, public support for capital punishment had dropped to 61 percent—the lowest level of support since 1972 when the Supreme Court struck down challenged death penalty laws in *Furman v. Georgia.*[2]

In 2007, the American Bar Association published a report recommending a moratorium on the death penalty in Indiana. In 2007, the General Assembly of the United Nations voted in favor of a moratorium on the death penalty. Concerns about rising costs associated with the death penalty compared to life sentences were voiced in many states, including California, Maryland, New York, Washington, New Jersey, Tennessee, Kansas, Indiana, North Carolina, Florida, and Texas. Restrictions, suspensions, and moratoriums on capital punishment were effected in North Carolina, California, Nebraska, Kentucky, Oregon, and Arkansas.

In 2008, the Supreme Court considered a challenge to Kentucky's lethal injection protocols and procedures in *Baze and Bowling v. Rees* (2008). In *Baze,* two inmates challenged Kentucky's three-drug lethal injection protocol claiming that it was inhumane. They conceded that the procedure was "humane" when performed correctly but maintained that incorrect administration of the drugs would be cruel and unusual punishment. In a 7–2 decision, the Court disagreed.

CHIEF JUSTICE ROBERTS announced the judgment of the Court and delivered an opinion, in which JUSTICE KENNEDY and JUSTICE ALITO join.

Like 35 other States and the Federal Government, Kentucky has chosen to impose capital punishment for certain crimes. . . .

[E]ach of these States and the Federal Government . . . has altered its method of execution over time to more humane means of carrying out the sentence. That progress has led to the use of lethal injection by every jurisdiction that imposes the death penalty.

Petitioners in this case—each convicted of double homicide—acknowledge that the lethal injection procedure, if applied as intended, will result in a humane death. They nevertheless contend that the lethal injection protocol is unconstitutional under the Eighth Amendment's ban on "cruel and unusual punishments," because of the risk that the protocol's terms might not be properly followed, resulting in significant pain. They propose an alternative protocol, one that they concede has not been adopted by any State and has never been tried.

The trial court held extensive hearings and entered detailed Findings of Fact and Conclusions of Law. It recognized that "[t]here are no methods of legal execution that are satisfactory to those who oppose the death penalty on moral, religious, or societal grounds," but concluded that Kentucky's procedure "complies with the constitutional requirements against cruel and unusual punishment." The State Supreme Court affirmed. We too agree that petitioners have not carried their burden of showing that the risk of pain from maladministration of a concededly humane lethal injection protocol, and the failure to adopt untried and untested alternatives, constitute cruel and unusual punishment. . . .

Lethal injection is currently the most common method used for executions. Most states use a three-drug combination: an anesthetic (either pentobarbital or sodium thiopental), a paralytic agent (pancuronium bromide or Pavulon), and a drug that stops the heart and causes death (potassium chloride). Twelve states have used pentobarbital instead of sodium thiopental (Alabama, Arizona, Delaware, Florida, Georgia, Idaho, Mississippi, Ohio, Oklahoma, South Carolina, Texas, and Virginia), and four additional states (Kentucky, Louisiana, Montana, and South Dakota) have announced plans to do so. Nine states (Arizona, Georgia, Idaho, Kentucky, Missouri, Ohio, South Dakota, Texas, and Washington) provide for a single-drug method of execution, administering a lethal dosage of an anesthetic instead of using a lethal cocktail. Missouri plans to use propofol (Diprivan) in its single-drug protocol. Texas was the first state to use lethal injection (December 7, 1982), Ohio was the first to use a one-drug method (December 8, 2009), Oklahoma was the first to substitute pentobarbital for sodium thiopental in a three-drug method (December 16, 2010), and Ohio was the first to use pentobarbital in its one-drug protocol (March 10, 2011).[3]

Lundbeck, Inc., the Danish producer of pentobarbital, restricted its distribution to prevent the use of this drug in executions. Additionally, the United Kingdom restricted exportation of propofol after Missouri officials announced their plans to use the anesthetic for one-drug executions. Exports of sodium thiopental were previously restricted when the drug was used in executions. United Kingdom business secretary Vince Cable explained that "This country opposes the death penalty. We are clear that the state should never be complicit in judiciary executions through the use of British drugs in lethal injections."[4]

Of [the] 36 States [that use lethal injection], at least 30 (including Kentucky) use the same combination of three drugs in their lethal injection protocols. The first drug, sodium thiopental (also known as Pentathol), is a fast-acting barbiturate sedative that induces a deep, coma-like unconsciousness when given in the amounts used for lethal injection. The second drug, pancuronium bromide (also known as Pavulon), is a paralytic agent that inhibits all muscular-skeletal movements and, by paralyzing the diaphragm, stops respiration. Potassium chloride, the third drug, interferes with the electrical signals that stimulate the contractions of the heart, inducing cardiac arrest. The proper administration of the first drug ensures that the prisoner does not experience any pain associated with the paralysis and cardiac arrest caused by the second and third drugs. . . .

After exhausting their state and federal collateral remedies, Baze and Bowling sued three state officials in the Franklin Circuit Court for the Commonwealth of Kentucky, seeking to have Kentucky's lethal injection protocol declared unconstitutional. . . . On appeal, the Kentucky Supreme Court . . . affirmed [the Kentucky protocol].

We granted *certiorari* to determine whether Kentucky's lethal injection protocol satisfies the Eighth Amendment. We hold that it does. . . .

This Court has never invalidated a State's chosen procedure for carrying out a sentence of death as the infliction of cruel and unusual punishment. In *Wilkerson v. Utah,* we upheld a sentence to death by firing squad . . . rejecting the argument that such a sentence constituted cruel and unusual punishment. We noted there the difficulty of "defin[ing] [cruel and unusual punishment] with exactness. . . ." Rather than undertake such an effort, the *Wilkerson* Court simply noted that "it is safe to affirm that punishments of torture . . . and all others in the same line of unnecessary cruelty, are forbidden" by the Eighth Amendment. By way of example, the Court cited cases from England in which "terror, pain, or disgrace were sometimes superadded" to the sentence, such as where the condemned was "embowelled alive, beheaded, and quartered," or instances of "public dissection in murder, and burning alive." In contrast, we observed that the firing squad was routinely used as a method of execution for military officers.

The Supreme Court announces broad principles of law. It is not primarily a court for the correction of errors. It is not uncommon for the Supreme Court to grant certiorari limited to only one of several issues presented in a case, and it is not necessarily the issue most important to the defendant. For instance, the defendant may wish the Court to hear an argument that he was not guilty or is guilty but should not be executed, but as in *Baze,* the Court can accept the case only for review of the question of whether the execution may be by lethal injection.

Therefore, knowing what issues to present to the Supreme Court to maximize the chances of review is an important, if esoteric, art. The Court seeks to provide uniformity in the interpretation of law, so an issue that has been decided several different ways in several different federal courts of appeals is typically a good candidate for review. The biggest single "customer" at the Supreme Court is the federal government. The nation's chief legal officer is the attorney general, but the government's arguments in the Supreme Court are usually presented by the solicitor general. The Court traditionally gives great weight to the views of the solicitor general in deciding whether review of an issue is urgent.

As an example, consider Justice Sotomayor's first published opinion in a capital case, *Wood v. Allen* (2010). Holly Wood broke into his ex-girlfriend's house and shot her as she lay in bed. After his death sentence was upheld, Wood claimed that his attorneys neglected to present to the jury evidence of his mental impairments. The state court found that Wood's attorneys knew about the evidence but made a strategic decision in refusing to present to the jury the doctor who examined Wood, because the doctor's report would have let the jury know about Wood's 19 previous arrests and his attempt to murder another ex-girlfriend. The Court granted certiorari simply to answer a question about the proper standard of proof: Did Wood have to disprove the state court's finding of fact by the ordinary preponderance of evidence or by the more demanding clear and convincing evidence standard? Once the Court held that even under the lower standard the state court's decision that Wood's counsel made a strategic decision in refusing to present the doctor's report was not unreasonable, it affirmed the denial of relief to Wood. The Court refused even to consider Wood's alternative claim, that counsel had failed to make a reasonable investigation before making its decision. Alabama executed Wood on September 9, 2010.

Although the Supreme Court has never invalidated a specific method of execution, lower federal courts and state supreme courts have ruled that executions in the electric chair and in the gas chamber are unconstitutionally cruel. These rulings have prompted changes in state procedures, making further review by the Supreme Court moot.

What each of the forbidden punishments had in common was the deliberate infliction of pain for the sake of pain—"superadd[ing]" pain to the death sentence through torture and the like.

. . . [I]n *In re Kemmler* . . . , we observed that "[p]unishments are cruel when they involve torture or a lingering death; but the punishment of death is not cruel within the meaning of that word as used in the Constitution. It implies there something inhuman and barbarous, something more than the mere extinguishment of life." We noted that the New York statute adopting electrocution as a method of execution "was passed in the effort to devise a more humane method of reaching the result."

Petitioners . . . concede that "if performed properly," an execution carried out under Kentucky's procedures would be "humane and constitutional." . . .

Instead, petitioners claim that there is a significant risk that the procedures will not be properly followed—in particular, that the sodium thiopental will not be properly administered to achieve its intended effect—resulting in severe pain when the other chemicals are administered. Our cases recognize that subjecting individuals to a risk of future harm—not simply actually inflicting pain—can qualify as cruel and unusual punishment.

Both *Helling v. McKinney* and *Farmer v. Brennan* upheld suits against prison officials for ignoring health and safety risks to inmates.

To establish that such exposure violates the Eighth Amendment, however, the conditions presenting the risk must be "sure or very likely to cause serious illness and needless suffering," and give rise to "sufficiently imminent dangers." *Helling v. McKinney*. . . . [T]o prevail on such a claim there must be a "substantial risk of serious harm," an "objectively intolerable risk of harm" that prevents prison officials from pleading that they were "subjectively blameless for purposes of the Eighth Amendment." *Farmer v. Brennan*.

Simply because an execution method may result in pain, either by accident or as an inescapable consequence of death, does not establish the sort of "objectively intolerable risk of harm" that qualifies as cruel and unusual. In *Louisiana ex rel. Francis v. Resweber*, a plurality of the Court upheld a second attempt at executing a prisoner by electrocution after a mechanical malfunction had interfered with the first attempt. The principal opinion noted that "[a]ccidents happen for which no man is to blame" and conclud[ing] that such "an accident, with no suggestion of malevolence" did not give rise to an Eighth Amendment violation.

As Justice Frankfurter noted in a separate opinion . . . , however, "a hypothetical situation" involving "a series of abortive attempts at electrocution" would present a different case. In terms of our present Eighth Amendment analysis, such a situation—unlike an "innocent misadventure"—would demonstrate an "objectively intolerable risk of harm" that officials may not ignore.

In other words, an isolated mishap alone does not give rise to an Eighth Amendment violation, precisely because such an event, while regrettable, does not suggest cruelty, or that the procedure at issue gives rise to a "substantial risk of serious harm." . . .

The majority rejected Baze and Reese's proposed "unnecessary risk" standard and the dissent's proposed "untoward" variation in favor of a requirement that any alternative procedure must be feasible, readily implemented, and "significantly reduce a substantial risk of severe pain."

In applying these standards to the facts of this case, we note at the outset that it is difficult to regard a practice as "objectively intolerable" when it is in fact widely tolerated. Thirty-six States that sanction capital punishment have adopted lethal injection as the preferred method of execution. The Federal Government uses lethal injection as well. This broad consensus goes not just to the method of execution, but also to the specific three-drug combination used by Kentucky. . . .

. . . Our society has . . . steadily moved to more humane methods of carrying out capital punishment. . . . The broad framework of the Eighth Amendment has accommodated this progress toward more humane methods of execution, and our approval of a particular method in the past has not precluded legislatures from taking the steps they deem appropriate, in light of new developments, to ensure humane capital punishment. There is no reason to suppose that today's decision will be any different.

The judgment below concluding that Kentucky's procedure is consistent with the Eighth Amendment is, accordingly, affirmed.

JUSTICE ALITO, concurring.

Justice Alito pointed out that guidelines issued by the American Medical Association state that "[a]n individual's opinion on capital punishment is the personal moral decision of the individual" but that "[a] physician, as a member of a profession dedicated to preserving life when there is hope of doing so, should not be a participant in a legally authorized execution." The American Nurses Association and the National Association of Emergency Medical Technicians take the same position: participation in an execution is a breach of medical ethics.

Challenges to lethal injection had by this time been litigated in Indiana, North Carolina, Tennessee, Texas, Virginia, Florida, Connecticut, Arizona, and Oklahoma. Justice Alito may have been thinking particularly about the litigation gridlock in state and federal courts in California. In 2006, condemned inmate Michael Angelo Morales filed a complaint alleging that California's lethal injection protocol violated the Eighth Amendment. His and other executions were stayed pending evidentiary hearing. Before *Baze* was decided, a federal judge had found that California's existing procedure would cause a demonstrated risk of severe pain but permitted executions to go forward if the state permitted an anesthesiologist to monitor the execution. California revised its three-drug procedure. While state court litigation challenging the new regulations under state law proceeded, Morales and other inmates scheduled for execution moved for federal court stays of execution pending challenges to the new procedure. In 2010, the federal district court denied a stay to inmate Albert Brown, giving him the option to choose whether he would be executed by one drug or three. This decision was reversed by the Ninth Circuit Court of Appeals, which observed that it appeared that California had begun scheduling executions simply because its inventory of sodium thiopental would reach its expiration date in October 2010. As of the end of 2012, the California's lower courts had held that the state's lethal injection procedures were invalid, and the federal courts ordered that its stays of executions remain in place pending further evidentiary hearing, which would not be scheduled until it was clear that California had a valid protocol.

In his separate concurring opinion, Justice Stevens for the first time stated his opposition to capital punishment. The "diminishing force of the principal rationales for retaining the death penalty" led Stevens to the conclusion that the death penalty represents "the pointless and needless extinction of life with only marginal contributions to any discernible social or public purposes." Such a penalty is excessive, cruel, and unusual. In spite of his personal reservations about capital punishment, however, Stevens concurred in the judgment out of respect for established precedents.

. . . The issue presented in this case—the constitutionality of a method of execution—should be kept separate from the controversial issue of the death penalty itself.

If the Court wishes to reexamine the latter issue, it should do so directly, as Justice Stevens now suggests. The Court should not produce a *de facto* ban on capital punishment by adopting method-of-execution rules that lead to litigation gridlock.

JUSTICE STEVENS, concurring in the judgment.

. . . [T]he recent rise in statutes providing for life imprisonment without the possibility of parole demonstrates that incapacitation is neither a necessary nor a sufficient justification for the death penalty. Moreover, a recent poll indicates that support for the death penalty drops significantly when life without the possibility of parole is presented as an alternative option. And the available sociological evidence suggests that juries are less likely to impose the death penalty when life without parole is available as a sentence.

The legitimacy of deterrence as an acceptable justification for the death penalty is also questionable, at best. Despite 30 years of empirical research in the area, there remains no reliable statistical evidence that capital punishment in fact deters potential offenders. In the absence of such evidence, deterrence cannot serve as a sufficient penological justification for this uniquely severe and irrevocable punishment.

We are left, then, with retribution as the primary rationale for imposing the death penalty. And indeed, it is the retribution rationale that animates much of the remaining enthusiasm for the death penalty. As Lord Justice Denning argued in 1950, "'some crimes are so outrageous that society insists on adequate punishment, because the wrong-doer deserves it, irrespective of whether it is a deterrent or not.'" Our Eighth Amendment jurisprudence has narrowed the class of offenders eligible for the death penalty to include only those who have committed outrageous crimes defined by specific aggravating factors. It is the cruel treatment of victims that provides the most persuasive arguments for prosecutors seeking the death penalty. A natural response to such heinous crimes is a thirst for vengeance.

"[A] penalty may be cruel and unusual because it is excessive and serves no valid legislative purpose." . . .

Justice White was exercising his own judgment in 1972 when he provided the decisive vote in *Furman,* the case that led to a nationwide reexamination of the death penalty. . . . [H]e correctly stated that the "needless extinction of life with only marginal contributions to any discernible social or public purposes . . . would be patently excessive" and violative of the Eighth Amendment. . . .

In sum, just as Justice White ultimately based his conclusion in *Furman* on his extensive exposure to countless cases for which death is the authorized penalty, I have relied on my own experience in reaching the conclusion that the imposition of the death penalty represents "the pointless and needless extinction of life with only marginal contributions to any discernible social or public purposes. A penalty with such negligible returns to the State [is] patently excessive and cruel and unusual punishment violative of the Eighth Amendment."

The conclusion that I have reached with regard to the constitutionality of the death penalty itself makes my decision in this case particularly difficult. It does not, however, justify a refusal to respect precedents that remain a part of our law. This Court has held that the death penalty is constitutional, and has established a framework for evaluating the constitutionality of particular methods of execution. Under those precedents, whether as interpreted by The Chief Justice or Justice Ginsburg, I am persuaded that the evidence adduced by petitioners fails to prove that Kentucky's lethal injection protocol violates the Eighth Amendment. Accordingly, I join the Court's judgment.

JUSTICE SCALIA, with whom JUSTICE THOMAS joins, concurring in the judgment.

I write separately to provide what I think is needed response to Justice Stevens' separate opinion.

Justice Stevens concludes as follows: "[T]he imposition of the death penalty represents the pointless and needless extinction of life with only marginal contributions to any discernible social or public purposes. A penalty with such negligible returns to the State [is] patently excessive and cruel and unusual punishment violative of the Eighth Amendment."

"The conclusion that I have reached with regard to the constitutionality of the death penalty itself makes my decision in this case particularly difficult."

This conclusion is insupportable as an interpretation of the Constitution, which generally leaves it to democratically elected legislatures rather than courts to decide what makes significant contribution to social or public purposes. Besides that more general proposition, the very text of the document recognizes that the death penalty is a permissible legislative choice. The Fifth Amendment expressly requires a presentment or indictment of a grand jury to hold a person to answer for "a capital, or otherwise infamous crime," and prohibits deprivation of "life" without due process of law. . . . There is simply no legal authority for the proposition that the imposition of death as a criminal penalty is unconstitutional. . . .

But actually none of this really matters. As Justice Stevens explains, "'objective evidence, though of great importance, [does] not wholly determine the controversy, for the Constitution contemplates that in the end our own judgment will be brought to bear on the question of the acceptability of the death penalty under the Eighth Amendment.'" "I have relied on my own experience in reaching the conclusion that the imposition of the death penalty" is unconstitutional. . . .

> *"Purer expression cannot be found of the principle of rule by judicial fiat. In the face of Justice Stevens' experience, the experience of all others is, it appears, of little consequence."*

Purer expression cannot be found of the principle of rule by judicial fiat. In the face of Justice Stevens' experience, the experience of all others is, it appears, of little consequence. The experience of the state legislatures and the Congress—who retain the death penalty as a form of punishment—is dismissed as "the product of habit and inattention rather than an acceptable deliberative process." The experience of social scientists whose studies indicate that the death penalty deters crime is relegated to a footnote. The experience of fellow citizens who support the death penalty is described, with only the most thinly veiled condemnation, as stemming from a "thirst for vengeance." It is Justice Stevens' experience that reigns over all.

JUSTICE THOMAS, with whom JUSTICE SCALIA joins, concurring in the judgment.

Although I agree that petitioners have failed to establish that Kentucky's lethal injection protocol violates the Eighth Amendment, I write separately because I cannot subscribe to the plurality opinion's formulation of the governing standard. As I understand it, that opinion would hold that a method of execution violates the Eighth Amendment if it poses a substantial risk of severe pain that could be significantly reduced by adopting readily available alternative procedures. This standard—along with petitioners' proposed "unnecessary risk" standard and the dissent's "untoward risk" standard—finds no support in the original understanding of the Cruel and Unusual Punishments Clause or in our previous method-of-execution cases; casts constitutional doubt on long-accepted methods of execution; and injects the Court into matters it has no institutional capacity to resolve. Because, in my view, a method of execution violates the Eighth Amendment only if it is deliberately designed to inflict pain, I concur only in the judgment. . . .

Judged under the proper standard, this is an easy case. It is undisputed that Kentucky adopted its lethal injection protocol in an effort to make capital punishment more humane, not to add elements of terror, pain, or disgrace to the death penalty. And it is undisputed that, if administered properly, Kentucky's lethal injection protocol will result in a swift and painless death. . . . Because Kentucky's lethal injection protocol is designed to eliminate pain rather than to inflict it, petitioners' challenge must fail. I accordingly concur in the Court's judgment affirming the decision below.

JUSTICE BREYER concurring in the judgment.

. . . The upshot is that I cannot find, either in the record or in the readily available literature that I have seen, sufficient grounds to believe that Kentucky's method of lethal injection creates a significant risk of unnecessary suffering. The death penalty itself, of course, brings with it serious risks, for example, risks of executing the wrong person, risks that unwarranted *animus* (in respect, e.g., to the race of victims) may play a role, risks that those convicted will find themselves on death row for many years, perhaps decades, to come. These risks in part explain why that penalty is so controversial. But the lawfulness of the death penalty is not before us. And petitioners' proof and evidence, while giving rise to legitimate concern, do not show that Kentucky's method of applying the death penalty amounts to "cruel and unusual punishmen[t]."

For these reasons, I concur in the judgment.

JUSTICE GINSBURG, with whom JUSTICE SOUTER joins, dissenting.

. . . The Court has considered the constitutionality of a specific method of execution on only three prior occasions. Those

> "Because, in my view, a method of execution violates the Eighth Amendment only if it is deliberately designed to inflict pain, I concur only in the judgment."

cases, and other decisions cited by the parties and *amici,* provide little guidance on the standard that should govern petitioners' challenge to Kentucky's lethal injection protocol.

In *Wilkerson v. Utah* [firing squad], . . . *In re Kemmler* [electrocution] . . . [and] *Lousiiana ex rel. Francis v. Reseweber* [reelectrocution], the Court rejected Eighth and Fourteenth Amendment challenges.

No clear standard for determining the constitutionality of a method of execution emerges from these decisions. Moreover, the age of the opinions limits their utility as an aid to resolution of the present controversy. The Eighth Amendment, we have held, "'must draw its meaning from the evolving standards of decency that mark the progress of a maturing society.'" *Wilkerson* was decided 129 years ago, *Kemmler* 118 years ago, and *Resweber* 61 years ago.

> "*Whatever little light our prior method-of-execution cases might shed is thus dimmed by the passage of time.*"

Whatever little light our prior method-of-execution cases might shed is thus dimmed by the passage of time. . . .

The dissenting justices regard the age of the Court's precedents as a reason to disregard them, which is exactly the opposite of the philosophy of the justices voting to uphold Kentucky's protocol. The justices tend to split the same way on whether the Court should try to guide public opinion, as Justice Goldberg once suggested, or defer to public opinion as it is reflected in legislation.

Kentucky's Legislature adopted lethal injection as a method of execution in 1998. Lawmakers left the development of the lethal injection protocol to officials in the Department of Corrections. Those officials, the trial court found, were "given the task without the benefit of scientific aid or policy oversight." "Kentucky's protocol," that court observed, "was copied from other states and accepted without challenge." Kentucky "did not conduct any independent scientific or medical studies or consult any medical professionals concerning the drugs and dosage amounts to be injected into the condemned." Instead, the trial court noted, Kentucky followed the path taken in other States that "simply fell in line" behind the three-drug protocol first developed by Oklahoma in 1977. . . .

Other than using qualified and trained personnel to establish IV access, however, Kentucky does little to ensure that the inmate receives an effective dose of sodium thiopental. After siting the catheters, the IV team leaves the execution chamber. From that point forward, only the warden and deputy warden remain with the inmate. Neither the warden nor the deputy warden has any medical training. . . .

"The easiest and most obvious way to ensure that an inmate is unconscious during an execution," petitioners argued to the Kentucky Supreme Court, "is to check for consciousness prior to injecting pancuronium [bromide]." . . . The court did not address petitioners' argument.

I would therefore remand with instructions to consider whether the failure to include readily available safeguards to confirm that the inmate is unconscious after injection of sodium thiopental, in combination with the other elements of Kentucky's protocol, creates an untoward, readily avoidable risk of inflicting severe and unnecessary pain.

Notes

1. "Connecticut Repeals Death Penalty," ABC News, April 25, 2012, http://abcnews.go.com/US/connecticut-repeals-death-penalty -governor-dannel-malloy-signs/story?id=16212552.

2. For more information about the above statistics, see "Facts about the Death Penalty," Death Penalty Information Center Web site, June 27, 2013, http://www.deathpenaltyinfo.org/documents/ FactSheet.pdf, and Frank Newport, "In U.S. Support for Death Penalty Falls to 39-Year Low," Gallup Politics, October 13, 2011, http://www.gallup.com/poll/150089/support-death-penalty-falls -year-low.aspx.

3. "State by State Lethal Injection," Death Penalty Information Center, http://www.deathpenaltyinfo.org/state-lethal-injection.

4. "United Kingdom Acts to Ban Export of Lethal Injection Drug," Death Penalty Information Center, http://www.deathpenaltyinfo .org/united-kingdom-acts-ban-export-lethal-injection-drug.

Litigation over the drugs used continues to be the most likely source of lower court decisions halting executions. In April 2013, Arkansas announced that it was switching to the use of phenobarbital in executions, then had to abandon that plan when the state's department of corrections was unable to obtain a stock of that drug. Phenobarbital, never yet employed in executions, is normally used as an antiseizure medication. Arkansas last executed anyone in 2005 and had no executions scheduled in the first half of 2013.

In July 2013, the Court of Appeals for the D.C. Circuit decided in *Cook v. Food & Drug Administration* that the Food and Drug Administration (FDA) must regulate the importation of sodium thiopental into the United States. The last domestic manufacturer of thiopental discontinued making the drug in 2009. Since then, states using thiopental for executions have purchased it from European companies not registered with the FDA. In 2011 the FDA announced that it would not review shipments of thiopental being ordered by states for use in executions. Inmates on death row in Arizona, California, and Tennessee sued the FDA to require it to refuse admission to the drugs. The D.C. Circuit held that the FDA could not refuse to examine thiopental manufactured in unregistered establishments but that the states need not turn over to the FDA the stocks of thiopental they had already acquired.

Also in July 2013, a state court judge in Georgia halted the scheduled execution of Warren Hill in order to review Georgia's switch of execution method from a three-drug protocol to the use of one drug, pentobarbital, and its provision that the identity of the drug supplier would be kept secret. Hill, already serving life for murdering his girlfriend, received the death penalty for murdering his cellmate in 1990.

Death Penalty for Rape of a Child

Kennedy v. Louisiana

June 25, 2008

INTRODUCTION

Gregg v. Georgia implied and *Coker v. Georgia* held that the death penalty could not be imposed for a crime not resulting in death. Because the American judicial system evolved from the common law, case by case, a declaration that a law is unconstitutional, although it has precedential force, does not repeal that law or even necessarily strike down similar laws. Louisiana was one of the few states after *Gregg* that permitted the death penalty for the rape of a child. Thirty years after *Coker,* Patrick Kennedy challenged that law.

JUSTICE KENNEDY delivered the opinion of the Court.

. . . Patrick Kennedy . . . was charged by . . . the State of Louisiana, with the aggravated rape of his then-8-year-old stepdaughter. After a jury-trial petitioner was convicted and sentenced to death under a state statute authorizing capital punishment for the rape of a child under 12 years of age. This case presents the question whether the Constitution bars [Louisiana] from imposing the death penalty for the rape of a child where the crime did not result, and was not intended to result, in death of the victim. We hold the Eighth Amendment prohibits the death penalty for this offense. The Louisiana statute is unconstitutional. . . .

Petitioner's crime was one that cannot be recounted in these pages in a way sufficient to capture in full the hurt and horror inflicted on his victim or to convey the revulsion society, and the jury that represents it, sought to express by sentencing petitioner to death.

. . . [At] trial . . . L. H. . . . testified that she "'woke up one morning and Patrick was on top of [her].'" She remembered petitioner bringing her "[a] cup of orange juice and pills chopped up in it" after the rape and overhearing him on the telephone saying she had become a "young lady." L. H. acknowledged that she had accused two neighborhood boys but testified petitioner told her to say this and that it was untrue.

The jury having found petitioner guilty of aggravated rape, the penalty phase ensued. The State presented the testimony of S. L., who is the cousin and goddaughter of petitioner's ex-wife. S. L. testified that petitioner sexually abused her three times when she was eight years old and that the last time involved sexual intercourse. She did not tell anyone until two years later and did not pursue legal action. . . .

The [Supreme Court of Louisiana] acknowledged that petitioner would be the first person executed for committing child rape since [the Louisiana statute] was amended in 1995 and that Louisiana is in the minority of jurisdictions that authorize the death penalty for the crime of child rape. But . . . [the court] found significant not the "numerical counting of which [S]tates . . . stand for or against a particular capital prosecution," but "the direction of change." Since 1993, the court explained, four more States—Oklahoma, South Carolina, Montana, and Georgia—had capitalized the crime of child rape and at least eight States had authorized capital punishment for other nonhomicide crimes. By its count, 14 of the then-38 States permitting capital punishment, plus the Federal Government, allowed the death penalty for nonhomicide crimes and 5 allowed the death penalty for the crime of child rape. . . .

We granted *certiorari.*

. . . The [U.S. Supreme] Court explained in *Atkins* and *Roper* that the Eighth Amendment's protection against excessive or cruel and unusual punishments flows from the basic "precept of justice that punishment for [a] crime should be graduated and proportioned to [the] offense." *Weems v. United States* (1910). Whether this requirement has been fulfilled is determined not by the standards that prevailed when the Eighth Amendment was adopted in 1791 but by the norms that "currently prevail." *Atkins.* The Amendment "draw[s] its meaning from the evolving standards of decency that mark the progress of a maturing society." *Trop v. Dulles* (1958). . . .

. . . [P]unishment is justified under one or more of three principal rationales: rehabilitation, deterrence, and retribution. It is the last of these, retribution, that most often can contradict the law's own ends. This is of particular concern when the Court interprets the meaning of the Eighth Amendment in capital cases. When the law punishes by death, it risks its

"[P]unishment is justified under one or more of three principal rationales: rehabilitation, deterrence, and retribution. It is the last of these, retribution, that most often can contradict the law's own ends."

own sudden descent into brutality, transgressing the constitutional commitment to decency and restraint.

For these reasons we have explained that capital punishment must "be limited to those offenders who commit 'a narrow category of the most serious crimes' and whose extreme culpability makes them 'the most deserving of execution.'" *Roper.* Though the death penalty is not invariably unconstitutional, the Court insists upon confining the instances in which the punishment can be imposed.

Applying this principle, we held in *Roper* and *Atkins* that the execution of juveniles and mentally retarded persons are punishments violative of the Eighth Amendment because the offender had a diminished personal responsibility for the crime. The Court further has held that the death penalty can be disproportionate to the crime itself where the crime did not result, or was not intended to result, in death of the victim. In *Coker,* for instance, the Court held it would be unconstitutional to execute an offender who had raped an adult woman. . . . And in *Enmund v. Florida* (1982), the Court overturned the capital sentence of a defendant who aided and abetted a robbery during which a murder was committed but did not himself kill, attempt to kill, or intend that a killing would take place. On the other hand, in *Tison v. Arizona* (1987), the Court allowed the defendants' death sentences to stand where they did not themselves kill the victims but their involvement in the events leading up to the murders was active, recklessly indifferent, and substantial.

In these cases the Court has been guided by "objective indicia of society's standards, as expressed in legislative enactments and state practice with respect to executions." . . . The inquiry does not end there, however. Consensus is not dispositive. Whether the death penalty is disproportionate to the crime committed depends as well upon the standards elaborated by controlling precedents and by the Court's own understanding and interpretation of the Eighth Amendment's text, history, meaning, and purpose.

The majority discussed the history of the death penalty for the crime of rape.

Based both on consensus and our own independent judgment, our holding is that a death sentence for one who raped but did not kill a child, and who did not intend to assist another in killing the child, is unconstitutional under the Eighth and Fourteenth Amendments. . . .

In 1925, 18 States, the District of Columbia, and the Federal Government had statutes that authorized the death penalty for the rape of a child or an adult. Between 1930 and 1964, 455 people were executed for those crimes. To our knowledge the last individual executed for the rape of a child was Ronald Wolfe in 1964.

In 1972, *Furman* invalidated most of the state statutes authorizing the death penalty for the crime of rape; and in *Furman*'s aftermath only six States reenacted their capital rape provisions. Three States—Georgia, North Carolina, and Louisiana—did so with respect to all rape offenses. Three States—Florida, Mississippi, and Tennessee—did so with respect only to child rape. All six statutes were later invalidated under state or federal law. . . .

Louisiana reintroduced the death penalty for rape of a child in 1995. . . . Five States have since followed Louisiana's lead: Georgia, Montana, Oklahoma, South Carolina, and Texas. Four of these States' statutes are more narrow than Louisiana's in that only offenders with a previous rape conviction are death eligible. Georgia's statute makes child rape a capital offense only when aggravating circumstances are present, including but not limited to a prior conviction.

By contrast, 44 States have not made child rape a capital offense. As for federal law, Congress in the Federal Death Penalty Act of 1994 expanded the number of federal crimes for which the death penalty is a permissible sentence, including certain nonhomicide offenses; but it did not do the same for child rape or abuse. Under [federal law], an offender is death eligible only when the sexual abuse or exploitation results in the victim's death. . . .

The evidence of a national consensus with respect to the death penalty for child rapists, as with respect to juveniles, mentally retarded offenders, and vicarious felony murderers, shows divided opinion but, on balance, an opinion against it. Thirty-seven jurisdictions—36 States plus the Federal Government—have the death penalty. As mentioned above, only 6 of those jurisdictions authorize the death penalty for rape of a child. Though our review of national consensus is not confined to tallying the number of States with applicable death penalty legislation, it is of significance that, in 45 jurisdictions, petitioner could not be executed for child rape of any kind. . . .

". . . Congress in the Federal Death Penalty Act of 1994 expanded the number of federal crimes for which the death penalty is a permissible sentence, including certain nonhomicide offenses; but it did not do the same for child rape or abuse."

Respondent insists that the six States where child rape is a capital offense, along with the States that have proposed but not yet enacted applicable death penalty legislation, reflect a consistent direction of change in support of the death penalty for child rape. Consistent change might counterbalance an otherwise weak demonstration of consensus. . . . But whatever the significance of consistent change where it is cited to show emerging support for expanding the scope of the death penalty, no showing of consistent change has been made in this case. . . .

There are measures of consensus other than legislation. Statistics about the number of executions may inform the consideration whether capital punishment for the crime of child rape is regarded as unacceptable in our society. These statistics confirm our determination from our review of state statutes that there is a social consensus against the death penalty for the crime of child rape.

Nine States—Florida, Georgia, Louisiana, Mississippi, Montana, Oklahoma, South Carolina, Tennessee, and Texas—have permitted capital punishment for adult or child rape for some length of time between the Court's 1972 decision in *Furman* and today. Yet no individual has been executed for the rape of an adult or child since 1964, and no execution for any other nonhomicide offense has been conducted since 1963. . . .

Louisiana is the only State since 1964 that has sentenced an individual to death for the crime of child rape; and petitioner and Richard Davis, who was convicted and sentenced to death for the aggravated rape of a 5-year-old child by a Louisiana jury in December 2007, are the only two individuals now on death row in the United States for a nonhomicide offense.

After rejecting the death penalty in the present case, the majority next advanced its theory that the Court's judgment should be an independent check on the constitutionality of state statutes.

After reviewing the authorities informed by contemporary norms, including the history of the death penalty for this and other nonhomicide crimes, current state statutes and new enactments, and the number of executions since 1964, we conclude there is a national consensus against capital punishment for the crime of child rape.

. . . "[T]he Constitution contemplates that in the end our own judgment will be brought to bear on the question of the acceptability of the death penalty under the Eighth

Amendment." . . . We turn, then, to the resolution of the question before us, which is informed by our precedents and our own understanding of the Constitution and the rights it secures.

. . . [W]e should be most reluctant to rely upon the language of the plurality in *Coker*, which posited that, for the victim of rape, "life may not be nearly so happy as it was" but it is not beyond repair. Rape has a permanent psychological, emotional, and sometimes physical impact on the child. . . . We cannot dismiss the years of long anguish that must be endured by the victim of child rape.

When *Coker* was decided, there were no women on the Supreme Court. In 2008 Justice O'Connor had left the Court, leaving Justice Ginsburg, who had been a lawyer for the National Organization of Women before becoming a law professor. *Coker*'s precedent was helpful to the majority, but its language was that of a bygone era.

It does not follow, though, that capital punishment is a proportionate penalty for the crime. The constitutional prohibition against excessive or cruel and unusual punishments mandates that the State's power to punish "be exercised within the limits of civilized standards." Evolving standards of decency . . . counsel us to be most hesitant before . . . allow[ing] the extension of the death penalty, a hesitation that has special force where no life was taken in the commission of the crime. It is an established principle that decency, in its essence, presumes respect for the individual and thus moderation or restraint in the application of capital punishment. . . .

Our concern here is limited to crimes against individual persons. We do not address, for example, crimes defining and punishing treason, espionage, terrorism, and drug kingpin activity, which are offenses against the State. As it relates to crimes against individuals, though, the death penalty should not be expanded to instances where the victim's life was not taken. . . .

As in *Coker*, here it cannot be said with any certainty that the death penalty for child rape serves no deterrent or retributive function. . . . This argument does not overcome other objections, however. The incongruity between the crime of child rape and the harshness of the death penalty poses risks of over-punishment and counsels against a constitutional ruling that the death penalty can be expanded to include this offense.

The goal of retribution, which reflects society's and the victim's interests in seeing that the offender is repaid for the hurt he caused, does not justify the harshness of the death penalty here. . . .

There is an additional reason for our conclusion that imposing the death penalty for child-rape would not further retributive purposes. . . . In considering the death penalty for nonhomicide offenses this inquiry necessarily also must include the question whether the death penalty balances the wrong to the victim.

It is not at all evident that the child rape victim's hurt is lessened when the law permits the death of the perpetrator. Capital cases require a long-term commitment by those who testify for the prosecution. . . . In cases like this the key testimony is not just from the family but from the victim herself. During formative years of her adolescence, made all the more daunting for having to come to terms with the brutality of her experience, L. H. was required to discuss the case at length with law enforcement personnel. In a public trial she was required to recount once more all the details of the crime to a jury as the State pursued the death of her stepfather. And in the end the State made L. H. a central figure in its decision to seek the death penalty, telling the jury in closing statements: "[L. H.] is asking you, asking you to set up a time and place when he dies."

Society's desire to inflict the death penalty for child rape by enlisting the child victim to assist it over the course of years in asking for capital punishment forces a moral choice on the child, who is not of mature age to make that choice. The way the death penalty here involves the child victim in its enforcement can compromise a decent legal system. . . .

There are, moreover, serious systemic concerns in prosecuting the crime of child rape that are relevant to the constitutionality of making it a capital offense.

This has been a perennial objection in all child witness cases. The members of the majority here, however, have not in noncapital cases been active in promoting enhanced scrutiny for such testimony.

The problem of unreliable, induced, and even imagined child testimony means there is a "special risk of wrongful execution" in some child-rape cases. This undermines, at least to some degree, the meaningful contribution of the death penalty to legitimate goals of punishment. Studies conclude that children are highly susceptible to suggestive questioning techniques like repetition, guided imagery, and selective reinforcement. . . .

With respect to deterrence, if the death penalty adds to the risk of nonreporting, that, too, diminishes the penalty's objectives. Underreporting is a common problem with respect to child sexual abuse. . . . Although we know little about what differentiates those who report from those who do not report, one of the most commonly cited reasons for nondisclosure is fear of negative consequences for the perpetrator, a concern that has special force where the abuser is a family member. . . . The experience of the *amici* who work with child victims indicates that, when the punishment is death, both the victim and the victim's family members may be more likely to shield the perpetrator from discovery, thus increasing underreporting. As a result, punishment by death may not result in more deterrence or more effective enforcement.

In addition, by in effect making the punishment for child rape and murder equivalent, a State that punishes child rape by death may remove a strong incentive for the rapist not to kill the victim. Assuming the offender behaves in a rational way, as one must to justify the penalty on grounds of deterrence, the penalty in some respects gives less protection, not more, to the victim, who is often the sole witness to the crime. . . .

Each of these propositions, standing alone, might not establish the unconstitutionality of the death penalty for the crime of child rape. Taken in sum, however, they demonstrate the serious negative consequences of making child rape a capital offense. These considerations lead us to conclude, in our independent judgment, that the death penalty is not a proportional punishment for the rape of a child. . . .

JUSTICE ALITO, with whom THE CHIEF JUSTICE, JUSTICE SCALIA, and JUSTICE THOMAS join, dissenting.

. . . In assessing current norms, the Court relies primarily on the fact that only 6 of the 50 States now have statutes that permit the death penalty for this offense. But this statistic is a highly unreliable indicator of the views of state lawmakers and their constituents. . . . [T]his Court's decision in *Coker v. Georgia* has stunted legislative consideration of the question whether the death penalty for the targeted offense of raping a young child is consistent with prevailing standards of decency. . . . *Coker* . . . gave state legislators and others good reason to fear that any law permitting the imposition of the death penalty for this crime would meet precisely the fate that has now befallen the Louisiana statute that is

". . . [B]y in effect making the punishment for child rape and murder equivalent, a State that punishes child rape by death may remove a strong incentive for the rapist not to kill the victim."

currently before us, and this threat strongly discouraged state legislators—regardless of their own values and those of their constituents—from supporting the enactment of such legislation. . . .

If anything can be inferred from state legislative developments, the message is very different from the one that the Court perceives. In just the past few years, despite the shadow cast by . . . *Coker* . . . , five States have enacted targeted capital child-rape laws. . . . If, as the Court seems to think, our society is "[e]volving" toward ever higher "standards of decency," these enactments might represent the beginning of a new evolutionary line.

. . . [T]he failure to enact capital child-rape laws cannot be viewed as evidence of a moral consensus against such punishment. . . .

Finally, the Court argues that statistics about the number of executions in rape cases support its perception of a "national consensus," but here too the statistics do not support the Court's position. The Court notes that the last execution for the rape of a child occurred in 1964, but the Court fails to mention that litigation regarding the constitutionality of the death penalty brought executions to a halt across the board in the late 1960s. In 1965 and 1966, there were a total of eight executions for all offenses, and from 1968 until 1977, the year when *Coker* was decided, there were no executions for any crimes. The Court also fails to mention that in Louisiana, since the state law was amended in 1995 to make child rape a capital offense, prosecutors have asked juries to return death verdicts in four cases. . . . In two of those cases, Louisiana juries imposed the death penalty. This 50% record is hardly evidence that juries share the Court's view that the death penalty for the rape of a young child is unacceptable under even the most aggravated circumstances. . . .

The Court is willing to block the potential emergence of a national consensus in favor of permitting the death penalty for child rape because, in the end, what matters is the Court's "own judgment" regarding "the acceptability of the death penalty." Although the Court has much to say on this issue, most of the Court's discussion is not pertinent to the Eighth Amendment question at hand. And once all of the Court's irrelevant arguments are put aside, it is apparent that the Court has provided no coherent explanation for today's decision. . . .

". . . [T]he Court fails to mention that litigation regarding the constitutionality of the death penalty brought executions to a halt across the board in the late 1960s."

A major theme of the Court's opinion is that permitting the death penalty in child-rape cases is not in the best interests of the victims of these crimes and society at large. In this vein, the Court suggests that it is more painful for child-rape victims to testify when the prosecution is seeking the death penalty. The Court also argues that "a State that punishes child rape by death may remove a strong incentive for the rapist not to kill the victim," and may discourage the reporting of child rape.

These policy arguments, whatever their merits, are simply not pertinent to the question whether the death penalty is "cruel and unusual" punishment. The Eighth Amendment protects the right of an accused. It does not authorize this Court to strike down federal or state criminal laws on the ground that they are not in the best interests of crime victims or the broader society. The Court's policy arguments concern matters that legislators should—and presumably do—take into account in deciding whether to enact a capital child-rape statute, but these arguments are irrelevant to the question that is before us in this case. . . .

With respect to the question of the harm caused by the rape of child in relation to the harm caused by murder, it is certainly true that the loss of human life represents a unique harm, but that does not explain why other grievous harms are insufficient to permit a death sentence. . . .

The harm that is caused to the victims and to society at large by the worst child rapists is grave. It is the judgment of the Louisiana lawmakers and those in an increasing number of other States that these harms justify the death penalty. The Court provides no cogent explanation why this legislative judgment should be overridden. Conclusory references to "decency," "moderation," "restraint," "full progress," and "moral judgment" are not enough. . . .

> *"The Eighth Amendment protects the right of an accused. It does not authorize this Court to strike down federal or state criminal laws on the ground that they are not in the best interests of crime victims or the broader society."*

Chapter 8

Locked Up for Life?: Juvenile Offenders and Ever-Evolving Standards of Decency

Juvenile Life without Parole for Nonhomicide Crimes

Graham v. Florida

May 17, 2010

INTRODUCTION

Terrance Jamar Graham was 17 years old when he was convicted of armed home robbery and sentenced to life in prison without parole. Is a sentence of life without parole for a juvenile convicted of an offense other than homicide cruel and unusual punishment? Advocates for retaining the death penalty have argued that abolitionists are insincere about their motives and that if the death penalty were not the ultimate sanction against crime, abolitionists would turn next to attacking life without parole. Some abolitionists indeed draw the line at the death penalty. From *Weems* in 1910 forward, however, the Court has applied the Eighth Amendment to cases other than the death penalty.

Justice Kennedy was joined by Justices Stevens, Ginsburg, Breyer, and Sotomayor. Chief Justice Roberts concurred separately.

JUSTICE KENNEDY delivered the opinion of the Court.

The issue before the Court is whether the Constitution permits a juvenile offender to be sentenced to life in prison without parole for a nonhomicide crime. . . .

[Graham was serving a 3-year term of probation for a robbery attempt in which he was prosecuted as an adult.] Graham . . . was released on June 25, 2004.

Less than 6 months later, on the night of December 2, 2004, Graham again was arrested . . . [for participating] in a home invasion robbery. His two accomplices were Meigo Bailey and Kirkland Lawrence, both 20-year-old men. According to the State . . . Graham, Bailey, and Lawrence knocked on the door of the home where Carlos Rodriguez lived. [They] . . . forcibly entered the home and held a pistol to Rodriguez's chest. For the next 30 minutes, the three held Rodriguez and another man, a friend of Rodriguez, at gunpoint while they ransacked the home searching for money. Before leaving, Graham and his accomplices barricaded Rodriguez and his friend inside a closet.

The State further alleged that Graham, Bailey, and Lawrence, later the same evening, attempted a second robbery, during which Bailey was shot. Graham, who had borrowed his father's car, drove Bailey and Lawrence to the hospital and left them there. As Graham drove away, a police sergeant signaled him to stop. Graham continued at a high speed but crashed into a telephone pole. He tried to flee on foot but was apprehended. Three handguns were found in his car.

When detectives interviewed Graham, he denied involvement in the crimes. He said he encountered Bailey and Lawrence only after Bailey had been shot. One of the detectives told Graham that the victims of the home invasion had identified him. He asked Graham, "Aside from the two robberies tonight how many more were you involved in?" Graham responded, "Two to three before tonight." The night that Graham allegedly committed the robbery, he was 34 days short of his 18th birthday. . . .

The trial court found Graham guilty of the earlier armed burglary and attempted armed robbery charges. It sentenced him to the maximum sentence authorized by law on each charge: life imprisonment for the armed burglary and 15 years for the attempted armed robbery. Because Florida has abolished its parole system, a life sentence gives a defendant no possibility of release unless he is granted executive clemency. . . .

. . . Embodied in the Constitution's ban on cruel and unusual punishments is the "precept of justice that punishment for crime should be graduated and proportioned to [the] offense." *Weems* v. *United States.*

"The night that Graham allegedly committed the robbery, he was 34 days short of his 18th birthday."

The Court discussed *Solem v. Helm, Harmelin v. Michigan,* and its other disproportionate sentence cases. The Court moved on to discuss *Roper v. Simmons* barring the execution of minors.

The Court's cases addressing the proportionality of sentences fall within two general classifications. The first involves challenges to the length of term-of-years sentences given all the circumstances in a particular case. The second comprises cases in which the Court implements the proportionality standard by certain categorical restrictions on the death penalty. . . .

In the cases adopting categorical rules the Court has taken the following approach. The Court first considers "objective indicia of society's standards, as expressed in legislative enactments and state practice" to determine whether there is a national consensus against the sentencing practice at issue. *Roper.* Next, guided by "the standards elaborated by controlling precedents and by the Court's own understanding and interpretation of the Eighth Amendment's text, history, meaning, and purpose," the Court must determine in the exercise of its own independent judgment whether the punishment in question violates the Constitution. *Roper.*

The present case involves an issue the Court has not considered previously: a categorical challenge to a term-of-years sentence. . . . Here, in addressing the question presented, the appropriate analysis is the one used in cases that involved the categorical approach, specifically *Atkins, Roper,* and *Kennedy.*

The analysis begins with objective indicia of national consensus. . . . Six jurisdictions do not allow life without parole sentences for any juvenile offenders. Seven jurisdictions permit life without parole for juvenile offenders, but only for homicide crimes. Thirty-seven States as well as the District of Columbia permit sentences of life without parole for a juvenile nonhomicide offender in some circumstances. Federal law also allows for the possibility of life without parole for offenders as young as 13. Relying on this metric, the State and its *amici* argue that there is no national consensus against the sentencing practice at issue.

This argument is incomplete and unavailing. . . . Here, an examination of actual sentencing practices in jurisdictions where the sentence in question is permitted by statute discloses a consensus against its use. Although these statutory schemes contain no explicit prohibition on sentences of life without parole for juvenile nonhomicide offenders, those sentences are most infrequent. . . .

> . . . [O]nly 12 jurisdictions nationwide in fact impose life-without-parole sentences on juvenile nonhomicide offenders—and most of those impose the sentence quite rarely—while 26 States as well as the District of Columbia do not impose them despite apparent statutory authorization. . . .

Juvenile courts became widespread in the United States at the beginning of the 20th century, at about the same time that the use of indeterminate sentences and parole rather than fixed sentences became common. The reasons for both practices derived in large part from the same mind-set of the era: that crime was a public health issue and that rehabilitation and cure should be foremost concerns in imposing sentence. By the time *Graham v. Florida* was decided, that era had long since ended in most jurisdictions.

. . . Many States have chosen to move away from juvenile court systems and to allow juveniles to be transferred to, or charged directly in, adult court under certain circumstances. Once in adult court, a juvenile offender may receive the same sentence as would be given to an adult offender, including a life without parole sentence. But the fact that transfer and direct charging laws make life without parole possible for some juvenile nonhomicide offenders does not justify a judgment that many States intended to subject such offenders to life without parole sentences.

. . . A sentence lacking any legitimate penological justification is by its nature disproportionate to the offense. With respect to life without parole for juvenile nonhomicide offenders, none of the goals of penal sanctions that have been recognized as legitimate—retribution, deterrence, incapacitation, and rehabilitation—provides an adequate justification.

Retribution is a legitimate reason to punish, but it cannot support the sentence at issue here. Society is entitled to impose severe sanctions on a juvenile nonhomicide offender to express its condemnation of the crime and to seek restoration of the moral imbalance caused by the offense. But "[t]he heart of the retribution rationale is that a criminal sentence must be directly related to the personal culpability of the criminal offender." *Tison.* . . .

Deterrence does not suffice to justify the sentence either. *Roper* noted that "the same characteristics that render juveniles less culpable than adults suggest . . . that juveniles will be less susceptible to deterrence." . . . Here, in light of juvenile nonhomicide offenders' diminished moral responsibility, any limited deterrent effect provided by life without parole is not enough to justify the sentence.

Incapacitation, a third legitimate reason for imprisonment, does not justify the life without parole sentence in question here. Recidivism is a serious risk to public safety, and so incapacitation is an important goal. . . . But while incapacitation may be a legitimate penological goal sufficient to justify life without parole in other contexts, it is inadequate to justify that punishment for juveniles who did not commit homicide. To justify life without parole on the assumption that the juvenile offender forever will be a danger to society requires the sentencer to make a judgment that the juvenile is incorrigible. The characteristics of juveniles make that judgment questionable. "It is difficult even for expert psychologists to differentiate between the juvenile offender whose crime reflects unfortunate yet transient immaturity, and the rare juvenile offender whose crime reflects irreparable corruption." *Roper.*

Here one cannot dispute that this defendant posed an immediate risk, for he had committed, we can assume, serious crimes early in his term of supervised release and despite his own assurances of reform . . . but it does not follow that he would be a risk to society for the rest of his life. Even if the State's judgment that Graham was incorrigible were later corroborated by prison misbehavior or failure to mature, the sentence was still disproportionate because that judgment was made at the outset. A life without parole sentence improperly denies the juvenile offender a chance to demonstrate growth and maturity. . . .

Finally . . . [a] sentence of life imprisonment without parole . . . cannot be justified by the goal of rehabilitation. The penalty forswears altogether the rehabilitative ideal. By denying the defendant the right to reenter the community, the State makes an irrevocable judgment about that person's value and place in society. This judgment is not appropriate in light of a juvenile nonhomicide offender's capacity for change and limited moral culpability. . . .

> *"By denying the defendant the right to reenter the community, the State makes an irrevocable judgment about that person's value and place in society."*

A State is not required to guarantee eventual freedom to a juvenile offender convicted of a nonhomicide crime. What the State must do, however, is give defendants like Graham some meaningful opportunity to obtain release based on demonstrated maturity and rehabilitation. It is for the State, in the first instance, to explore the means and mechanisms for compliance. It bears emphasis, however, that while the Eighth Amendment forbids a State from imposing a life without parole sentence on a juvenile nonhomicide offender, it does not require the State to release that offender during his natural life. Those who commit truly horrifying crimes as juveniles may turn out to be irredeemable, and thus deserving of incarceration for the duration of their lives. The Eighth

Amendment does not foreclose the possibility that persons convicted of nonhomicide crimes committed before adulthood will remain behind bars for life. It does forbid States from making the judgment at the outset that those offenders never will be fit to reenter society. . . .

There is support for our conclusion in the fact that, in continuing to impose life without parole sentences on juveniles who did not commit homicide, the United States adheres to a sentencing practice rejected the world over. . . .

Today we continue that longstanding practice in noting the global consensus against the sentencing practice in question. . . .

. . . [A]s petitioner contends and respondent does not contest, the United States is the only Nation that imposes life without parole sentences on juvenile nonhomicide offenders. We also note, as petitioner and his *amici* emphasize, that Article 37(a) of the United Nations Convention on the Rights of the Child, Nov. 20, 1989, 1577 U. N. T. S. 3 (entered into force Sept. 2, 1990), ratified by every nation except the United States and Somalia, prohibits the imposition of "life imprisonment without possibility of release . . . for offences committed by persons below eighteen years of age."

As we concluded in *Roper* with respect to the juvenile death penalty, "the United States now stands alone in a world that has turned its face against" life without parole for juvenile nonhomicide offenders.

. . . The question before us is not whether international law prohibits the United States from imposing the sentence at issue in this case. The question is whether that punishment is cruel and unusual. In that inquiry,

"the overwhelming weight of international opinion against" life without parole for nonhomicide offenses committed by juveniles "provide[s] respected and significant confirmation for our own conclusions." *Roper*. . . .

CHIEF JUSTICE ROBERTS, concurring in the judgment.

. . . I conclude that there is a strong inference that Graham's sentence of life imprisonment without parole was grossly disproportionate in violation of the Eighth Amendment. . . .

The criminal justice system in the United States and the Supreme Court's death penalty jurisprudence have been the subject of particular criticism in Europe. The European Union, which requires abolition of capital punishment as a condition for joining, funds the preparation of and files amicus curiae briefs—briefs expressing the views of persons interested in the outcome of a case but without a legal stake in the controversy—in the U.S. Supreme Court and around the world. The European Union actively sought the commutation of the sentence for Troy Davis, sentenced by Georgia in 1991 for the murder of a police officer. After the Supreme Court took the rare step in 2009 of remanding Davis's habeas corpus petition to the lower federal courts to conduct a hearing, the Supreme Court rejected further appeals. Georgia executed Davis on September 21, 2011. That same day, Texas executed Lawrence Brewer for kidnapping and murdering James Byrd Jr. in 1998 by dragging Byrd to death behind Brewer's truck. Brewer's execution drew relatively little protest in Europe or in the United States.

The Geneva Conventions of 1949 govern the treatment of prisoners of war and regulate the laws of war. Article 77 of Protocol I, added to the Geneva Conventions in 1977, prohibits the death penalty even for war crimes for "persons who had not attained the age of eighteen years at the time the offence was committed."

The United States ratified the International Covenant on Civil and Political Rights in 1994 but with the reservation that the covenant's prohibition of "cruel, inhuman or degrading treatment or punishment"—language that duplicated the text of the Universal Declaration of Human Rights adopted in 1948—did not prohibit capital punishment, including for murderers younger than 18 years of age.

So much for Graham. But what about Milagro Cunningham, a 17-year-old who beat and raped an 8-year-old girl before leaving her to die under 197 pounds of rock in a recycling bin in a remote landfill? Or Nathan Walker and Jakaris Taylor, the Florida juveniles who together with their friends gang-raped a woman and forced her to perform oral sex on her 12-year-old son? The fact that Graham cannot be sentenced to life without parole for his conduct says nothing whatever about these offenders, or others like them who commit non-homicide crimes far more reprehensible than the conduct at issue here. The Court uses Graham's case as a vehicle to proclaim a new constitutional rule—applicable well beyond the particular facts of Graham's case—that a sentence of life without parole imposed on *any* juvenile for *any* nonhomicide offense is unconstitutional. This categorical conclusion is as unnecessary as it is unwise.

> *"A holding this broad is unnecessary because the particular conduct and circumstances at issue in the case before us are not serious enough to justify Graham's sentence."*

A holding this broad is unnecessary because the particular conduct and circumstances at issue in the case before us are not serious enough to justify Graham's sentence. In reaching this conclusion, there is no need for the Court to decide whether that same sentence would be constitutional if imposed for other more heinous nonhomicide crimes.

A more restrained approach is especially appropriate in light of the Court's apparent recognition that it is perfectly legitimate for a juvenile to receive a sentence of life without parole for committing murder. This means that there is nothing *inherently* unconstitutional about imposing sentences of life without parole on juvenile offenders; rather, the constitutionality of such sentences depends on the particular crimes for which they are imposed. But if the constitutionality of the sentence turns on the particular crime being punished, then the Court should limit its holding to the particular offenses that Graham committed here, and should decline to consider other hypothetical crimes not presented by this case. . . .

Our system depends upon sentencing judges applying their reasoned judgment to each case that comes before them. . . . [T]he whole enterprise of proportionality review is premised on the "justified" assumption that "courts are competent to judge the gravity of an offense, at least on a relative scale." . . .

JUSTICE STEVENS, with whom JUSTICE GINSBURG and JUSTICE SOTOMAYOR join, concurring. [Omitted]

JUSTICE THOMAS, with whom JUSTICE SCALIA joins, and with whom JUSTICE ALITO joins as to Parts I and III, dissenting.

The Court holds today that it is "grossly disproportionate" and hence unconstitutional for any judge or jury to impose a sentence of life without parole on an offender less than 18 years old, unless he has committed a homicide. . . . [T]he Court insists that the standards of American society have evolved such that the Constitution now requires its prohibition.

The news of this evolution will, I think, come as a surprise to the American people. Congress, the District of Columbia, and 37 States allow judges and juries to consider this sentencing practice in juvenile nonhomicide cases, and those judges and juries have decided to use it in the very worst cases they have encountered.

The Court does not conclude that life without parole itself is a cruel and unusual punishment. It instead rejects the judgments of those legislatures, judges, and juries regarding what the Court describes as the "moral" question of whether this sentence can ever be "proportionat[e]" when applied to the category of offenders at issue here.

I am unwilling to assume that we, as members of this Court, are any more capable of making such moral judgments than our fellow citizens. Nothing in our training as judges qualifies us for that task, and nothing in Article III gives us that authority. . . .

The ultimate question in this case is not whether a life-without-parole sentence "fits" the crime at issue here or the crimes of juvenile nonhomicide offenders more generally, but to whom the Constitution assigns that decision. The Florida Legislature has concluded that such sentences should be available for persons under 18 who commit certain crimes, and the trial judge in this case decided to impose that legislatively authorized sentence here. Because a life-without-parole prison sentence is not a "cruel and unusual" method of punishment under any standard, the Eighth Amendment gives this Court no authority to reject those judgments.

It would be unjustifiable for the Court to declare otherwise even if it could claim that a bare majority of state laws supported its independent moral view. The fact that the Court

"I am unwilling to assume that we, as members of this Court, are any more capable of making such moral judgments than our fellow citizens."

categorically prohibits life-without-parole sentences for juvenile nonhomicide offenders in the face of an overwhelming legislative majority *in favor* of leaving that sentencing option available under certain cases simply illustrates how far beyond any cognizable constitutional principle the Court has reached to ensure that its own sense of morality and retributive justice pre-empts that of the people and their representatives. . . .

JUSTICE ALITO, dissenting. [Omitted]

Mandatory Life without Parole for Homicide by Juveniles

Miller v. Alabama and *Jackson v. Hobbs*

June 25, 2012

INTRODUCTION

Only two years after *Graham v. Florida,* the Court considered whether a sentence of life without parole for a juvenile convicted of homicide is cruel and unusual punishment.

In July 2003 when he was 14 years old, Evan Miller participated in the killing of Cole Cannon. Miller and a companion beat Cannon with a baseball bat and burned his trailer while Cannon was inside. Miller was convicted in Alabama of murder in the course of arson and sentenced to a mandatory term of life imprisonment without the possibility of parole. In the companion case, Kuntrell Jackson along with two companions, all of whom were 14 years old at the time, robbed a local movie rental store in Arkansas. During the robbery, one of the other boys shot and killed the store clerk with a sawed-off shotgun. Jackson was convicted of capital murder and aggravated robbery and sentenced to a mandatory term of life imprisonment without the possibility of parole.

Writing for a 5–4 majority, the most recent appointee, Justice Elena Kagan, wrote that the Constitution forbids mandatory sentences of life without the possibility of parole for juvenile offenders, even for murder. Justice Breyer, joined by Justice Sotomayor, issued a separate concurring opinion. Chief Justice Roberts Jr., joined by Justices Scalia, Thomas, and Alito, filed a dissenting opinion, as did Justice Alito.

JUSTICE KAGAN delivered the opinion of the Court.

The two 14-year-old offenders in these cases were convicted of murder and sentenced to life imprisonment without the possibility of parole. In neither case did the sentencing authority have any discretion to impose a different punishment. State law mandated that each juvenile die in prison even if a judge or jury would have thought that his youth and its attendant characteristics, along with the nature of his crime, made a lesser sentence (for example, life with the possibility of parole) more appropriate. Such a scheme prevents those meting out punishment from considering a juvenile's "lessened culpability" and greater "capacity for change," *Graham v. Florida,* and runs afoul of our cases' requirement of individualized sentencing for defendants facing the most serious penalties. We therefore hold that mandatory life without parole for those under the age of 18 at the time of their crimes violates the Eighth Amendment's prohibition on "cruel and unusual punishments." . . .

The Supreme Court's reliance on science and social science has a checkered history, as previous cases rejecting statistical studies reflect. The Court ordinarily defers to legislatures and administrative agencies as being the better organs of government to make decisions about technical and scientific matters. *In re Kemmler* (1890) was a good example of this approach. Even after a quarter century of evidence that electrocution was neither instantaneous nor painless, the Court observed in *Malloy v. South Carolina* (1915) that the legislature could reasonably conclude that electrocution was less painful and more humane than hanging.

On the other hand, the Supreme Court began receiving briefs packed with facts and figures in the generation before Louis Brandeis became a justice in 1916, and so-called Brandeis briefs appealing to the justices' sense that legal rules should change when the circumstances that gave rise to them disappear also have a long history of influencing the Court. How should the Court view those statistics? In dissent, Justice Alito quoted Bureau of Justice Statistics that 17-year-olds committed an average of 424 murders each year from 2002 to 2010. Those same statistics indicate that the overall homicide rate for 14–17-year-olds tripled between 1985 and 1993 and then fell as abruptly by 2000 to a level below that of 1985. It is likely that neither the rise nor the fall in homicides was in response to the penalty for homicide, and it is impossible for both to have been. From *Roper* to *Graham* to *Miller*, the majority of the Supreme Court has been confident that deterrence is not a meaningful rationale for penalties imposed on juveniles. It is likely that the Supreme Court would not have moved so quickly from *Graham* to *Miller* or at all if the youth crime wave had not already faded away.

The Eighth Amendment's prohibition of cruel and unusual punishment "guarantees individuals the right not to be subjected to excessive sanctions." . . . As we noted the last time we considered life-without-parole sentences imposed on juveniles, "[t]he concept of proportionality is central to the Eighth Amendment." *Graham*. And we view that concept less through a historical prism than according to "'the evolving standards of decency that mark the progress of a maturing society.'" *Estelle v. Gamble* (1976) (quoting *Trop v. Dulles*).

The cases before us implicate two strands of precedent reflecting our concern with proportionate punishment. The first has adopted categorical bans on sentencing practices based on mismatches between the culpability of a class of offenders and the severity of a penalty. So, for example, we have held that imposing the death penalty for nonhomicide crimes against individuals, or imposing it on mentally retarded defendants, violates the Eighth Amendment. Several of the cases in this group have specially focused on juvenile offenders, because of their lesser culpability. Thus, *Roper* held that the Eighth Amendment bars capital punishment for children, and *Graham* concluded that the Amendment also prohibits a sentence of life without the possibility of parole for a child who committed a nonhomicide offense. *Graham* further likened life without parole for juveniles to the death penalty itself, thereby evoking a second line of our precedents. In those cases, we have prohibited mandatory imposition of capital punishment, requiring that sentencing authorities consider the characteristics of a defendant and the details of his offense before sentencing him to death. See *Woodson v. North Carolina* (1976); *Lockett v. Ohio* (1978). Here, the confluence of these two lines of precedent leads to the conclusion that mandatory life-without-parole sentences for juveniles violate the Eighth Amendment.

. . . [C]hildren are constitutionally different from adults for purposes of sentencing. . . .

Our decisions rested not only on common sense—on what "any parent knows"—but on science and social science as well. . . .

Graham concluded from this analysis that life-without-parole sentences, like capital punishment, may violate the Eighth Amendment when imposed on children. To be sure,

Graham's flat ban on life without parole applied only to nonhomicide crimes, and the Court took care to distinguish those offenses from murder, based on both moral culpability and consequential harm. But none of what it said about children—about their distinctive (and transitory) mental traits and environmental vulnerabilities—is crime-specific. Those features are evident in the same way, and to the same degree, when (as in both cases here) a botched robbery turns into a killing. So *Graham*'s reasoning implicates any life-without-parole sentence imposed on a juvenile, even as its categorical bar relates only to nonhomicide offenses. . . .

. . . [T]he mandatory penalty schemes at issue here prevent the sentencer from taking account of these central considerations. By removing youth from the balance—by subjecting a juvenile to the same life-without-parole sentence applicable to an adult—these laws prohibit a sentencing authority from assessing whether the law's harshest term of imprisonment proportionately punishes a juvenile offender.

That contravenes *Graham*'s (and also *Roper*'s) foundational principle: that imposition of a State's most severe penalties on juvenile offenders cannot proceed as though they were not children. . . .

So *Graham* and *Roper* and our individualized sentencing cases alike teach that in imposing a State's harshest penalties, a sentencer misses too much if he treats every child as an adult. To recap: Mandatory life without parole for a juvenile precludes consideration of his chronological age and its hallmark features—among them, immaturity, impetuosity, and failure to appreciate risks and consequences. It prevents taking into account the family and home environment that surrounds him—and from which he cannot usually extricate himself—no matter how brutal or dysfunctional. It neglects the circumstances of the homicide offense, including the extent of his participation in the conduct and the way familial and peer pressures may have affected him. Indeed, it ignores that he might have been charged and convicted of a lesser offense if not for incompetencies associated with youth—for example, his inability to deal with police officers or prosecutors (including on a plea agreement) or his incapacity to assist his own attorneys.

Originally, children and adults were tried under the same rules and were subject to the same punishments. The early 20th century was the era of the rehabilitative ideal for all criminals, but juvenile courts were founded on the special idea that children were essentially good and needed only to be reformed. Many states and the federal government would not allow children below a certain age to be tried as adults. The rehabilitative system, because it often dispensed with basic rights to notice of the charges, to counsel, to cross-examination of accusers, and to protection against self-incrimination, could nevertheless be an instrument of injustice too. The Court recognized this in the application of *In re Gault* (1967), in which a juvenile court judge committed a 15-year-old to reform school for six years for making a lewd phone call (an adult could have received two months in jail) and held that the juvenile system had to provide most of the elements of due process. Over the next three decades, the increase in the number of state and federal laws permitting or requiring juveniles to be tried as adults meant that a juvenile certified as an adult was in the adult world of punishments too. After the early 1980s, that world grew increasingly harsh. In effect, *Miller* tries to preserve the original idea of the juvenile court system—that retribution is inappropriate for children—in the post-*Gault*, postrehabilitative era.

The majority does not mean that rehabilitation is a constitutionally required goal of a sentence for a juvenile but does come close to suggesting that rehabilitation must be somewhere in the overall sentencing scheme.

The majority has progressively drawn the line at higher and higher ages, and the inevitable question is whether there is anything talismanic about one or another particular birthday as the dividing line between eligibility for death, life without parole, or a lesser sentence. Consider the case of Jose Ernesto Medellin, sentenced to death for the rape and murder of two teenage girls in Houston in 1993. Medellin was only a few months past his 18th birthday. He was also a Mexican national who had not been informed that he had the right to assistance from the Mexican consulate, a step required in the United States under the Vienna Convention on Consular Relations.

The United States, one of the original advocates of the International Court of Justice (ICJ) after World War II, has in recent years been sued by Paraguay, by Germany, and by Mexico in the ICJ over the imposition of the death penalty on foreign citizens. In each case, the claim was that foreign nationals were prosecuted in the United States without their consulate being informed, in violation of the Vienna Convention. In each case the ICJ decided that the United States had violated its treaty responsibilities: in each case the Supreme Court held that the treaty violation was no reason to halt the execution. Texas courts had held they had no legal obligation to hear Medellin's Vienna Convention claim because it had not been raised properly. The ICJ disagreed, holding in the *Avena* (2004) case that the United States was bound by the treaty to consider Medellin's claim and the claim of approximately 50 other Mexican citizens on American death rows. As a result of the *Avena* decision, the governor of Oklahoma, Brad Henry, commuted the death sentence of Osbaldo Torres to life imprisonment in May 2004. Texas did not follow suit. In March 2008, the Supreme Court decided *Medellin v. Texas* (2008), holding that Texas had no obligation to obey the decision of the ICJ and that in the absence of legislation by Congress, Texas was not even obliged to heed President George W. Bush's written memorandum stating that the United States would comply with the ICJ's decision. Texas executed Medellin on August 5, 2008. If Medellin had been only a few months younger, he would have been made eligible for parole in 2012 by the same Court that permitted his execution in 2008.

And finally, this mandatory punishment disregards the possibility of rehabilitation even when the circumstances most suggest it.

Both cases before us illustrate the problem. Take Jackson's first. As noted earlier, Jackson did not fire the bullet that killed Laurie Troup; nor did the State argue that he intended her death. Jackson's conviction was instead based on an aiding-and-abetting theory. . . . To be sure, Jackson learned on the way to the video store that his friend Shields was carrying a gun, but his age could well have affected his calculation of the risk that posed, as well as his willingness to walk away at that point. All these circumstances go to Jackson's culpability for the offense. And so too does Jackson's family background and immersion in violence: Both his mother and his grandmother had previously shot other individuals. At the least, a sentencer should look at such facts before depriving a 14-year-old of any prospect of release from prison.

That is true also in Miller's case. No one can doubt that he and Smith committed a vicious murder. But they did it when high on drugs and alcohol consumed with the adult victim. And if ever a pathological background might have contributed to a 14-year-old's commission of a crime, it is here. Miller's stepfather physically abused him; his alcoholic and drug-addicted mother neglected him; he had been in and out of foster care as a result; and he had tried to kill himself four times, the first when he should have been in kindergarten. Nonetheless, Miller's past criminal history was limited— two instances of truancy and one of "second-degree criminal mischief." That Miller deserved severe punishment for killing Cole Cannon is beyond question. But once again, a sentencer needed to examine all these circumstances before concluding that life without any possibility of parole was the appropriate penalty.

We therefore hold that the Eighth Amendment forbids a sentencing scheme that mandates life in prison without possibility of parole for juvenile offenders.

JUSTICE BREYER, with whom JUSTICE SOTOMAYOR joins, concurring.

I join the Court's opinion in full. I add that,

if the State continues to seek a sentence of life without the possibility of parole for Kuntrell Jackson, there will have to be a determination whether Jackson "kill[ed] or intend[ed] to kill" the robbery victim. *Graham v. Florida.* In my view, without such a finding, the Eighth Amendment as interpreted in *Graham* forbids sentencing Jackson to such a sentence, regardless of whether its application is mandatory or discretionary under state law. . . .

Justice Breyer refers to the reasoning that Jackson, who did not shoot, was guilty of murder under the traditional rule that death caused in the course of a felony is caused by all participants who intended to commit the felony, regardless of whether they killed or intended to kill. This idea of transferred intent is based on the ability to consider the full consequences of a course of action, precisely what Justice Breyer said "we know juveniles lack capacity to do effectively."

CHIEF JUSTICE ROBERTS, with whom JUSTICE SCALIA, JUSTICE THOMAS, and JUSTICE ALITO join, dissenting.

Determining the appropriate sentence for a teenager convicted of murder presents grave and challenging questions of morality and social policy. Our role, however, is to apply the law, not to answer such questions. The pertinent law here is the Eighth Amendment to the Constitution, which prohibits "cruel and unusual punishments." Today, the Court invokes that Amendment to ban a punishment that the Court does not itself characterize as unusual, and that could not plausibly be described as such. I therefore dissent.

The parties agree that nearly 2,500 prisoners are presently serving life sentences without the possibility of parole for murders they committed before the age of 18. The Court accepts that over 2,000 of those prisoners received that sentence because it was mandated by a legislature. And it recognizes that the Federal Government and most States impose such mandatory sentences. Put simply, if a 17-year-old is convicted of deliberately murdering an innocent victim, it is not "unusual" for the murderer to receive a mandatory sentence of life without parole. That reality should preclude finding that mandatory life imprisonment for juvenile killers violates the Eighth Amendment. . . .

In this case, there is little doubt about the direction of society's evolution. . . . [M]ost States have changed their laws relatively recently to expose teenage murderers to mandatory life without parole. . . .

The Court also advances another reason for discounting the laws enacted by Congress and most state legislatures. Some of the jurisdictions that impose mandatory life without parole on juvenile murderers do so as a result of two statutes: one providing that juveniles charged with serious crimes may be tried as adults, and another generally mandating that those convicted of murder be imprisoned for life. According to the Court, our cases suggest that where the sentence results from the interaction of two such statutes, the legislature can be considered to have imposed the resulting sentences "inadvertent[ly]." . . .

It is a fair question whether this Court should ever assume a legislature is so ignorant of its own laws that it does not understand that two of them interact with each other, especially on an issue of such importance as the one before us. . . . [H]ere the widespread and recent imposition of the sentence makes it implausible to characterize this sentencing practice as a collateral consequence of legislative ignorance.

Nor do we display our usual respect for elected officials by asserting that legislators have accidentally required 2,000 teenagers to spend the rest of their lives in jail. This is particularly true given that our well-publicized decision in *Graham* alerted legislatures to the possibility that teenagers were subject to life with parole only because of legislative inadvertence. I am aware of no effort in the wake of *Graham* to correct any supposed legislative oversight. Indeed, in amending its laws in response to *Graham* one legislature made especially clear that it does intend juveniles who commit first-degree murder to receive mandatory life without parole. . . .

I respectfully dissent.

JUSTICE ALITO, with whom JUSTICE SCALIA joins, dissenting.

The Court now holds that Congress and the legislatures of the 50 States are prohibited by the Constitution from identifying any category of murderers under the age of 18 who must be sentenced to life imprisonment without parole.

Even a 17½-year-old who sets off a bomb in a crowded mall or guns down a dozen students and teachers is a "child" and must be given a chance to persuade a judge to permit his release into society. Nothing in the Constitution supports this arrogation of legislative authority.

JUSTICE THOMAS, with whom JUSTICE SCALIA joins, dissenting. [Omitted]

Justice Alito's choice of a hypothetical 17-year-old bomber may have been more than a rhetorical device in the post-9/11 era. Both the majority and the dissent remark on the disparities between sentencing practices in the United States and Europe, particularly with respect to use of sentences for juveniles and use of the death penalty. Those disparities have already led to collateral legal problems.

The European Court of Human Rights decided in the case of *Soering v. United Kingdom* (1989) that the United Kingdom could not legally extradite Soering, a German, to Virginia as long as he was subject to a risk that the death penalty could be imposed for two murders he committed in 1985. Virginia promised to forego seeking the death penalty to have Soering extradited. Soering was convicted and sentenced to two consecutive life sentences in 1990. Since *Soering*, Canada, Italy, Portugal, and Mexico have refused extradition of accused murderers based on the possibility of capital punishment. This has become a significant issue due to the global scope of the war on terror. After the bombings of the U.S. embassies in Kenya and Tanzania on August 7, 1998, German authorities would not extradite Al-Qaeda member Mamdouh Mahmud Salim (Osama bin Laden's finance manager, suspected of organizing the bombings) to the United States without guarantees that he would not be subject to the death penalty; Salim is serving a life sentence. South Africa's Constitutional Court ruled in May 2001 that it had been improper to surrender Khalfan Khamis Mohamed (the bomb manufacturer) to the United States without a guarantee against a capital sentence. The extradition of Khalid al-Fawwaz (Al-Qaeda's head of media) from Great Britain took more than a decade, the delay due in part to disputes over the possibility that he could be sentenced to death.

These national policies continue to hamper many formal extraditions for terrorism and other crimes. It is important to note that informal extraditions, or kidnappings, although frequently the source of diplomatic protests, do not under U.S. law deprive a court of jurisdiction over the defendant brought before it. In 1993 Mir Aimal Kasi, a Pakistani, opened fire on CIA employees in Fairfax, Virginia, killing two. FBI agents located him in 1997 and abducted him from Pakistan to stand trial in Virginia state court. Kasi was convicted and sentenced to death. After state and federal courts rejected his argument that his abduction violated a treaty with Pakistan and the Supreme Court denied a stay of execution, Kasi was executed on November 14, 2002. Two years later in an unrelated case, the Supreme Court held that cross-border kidnapping to obtain a defendant for trial was not a violation of international law.

Conclusions

Chapter 9

Concluding Observations

Moving into the 21st century, the Supreme Court continues to be, as it has been for 50 years, the most significant gatekeeper for the death penalty in America. The Court is not likely to surrender its role as the foremost interpreter of the Eighth Amendment's prohibition of cruel and unusual punishment or to abandon "evolving standards of decency" as its philosophical touchstone for that interpretation. For the foreseeable future, to understand capital punishment in the United States means to take a course in judicial politics and constitutional law. But stepping back from skirmishes of the last few decades between Justices Brennan, Marshall, Powell, and Blackmun, who at different stages in their careers maintained that capital punishment is categorically prohibited by the Constitution, and Chief Justice Rehnquist and Justices Scalia and Thomas, who have maintained that judicial overreaching on essentially political questions of crime and punishment is constitutionally forbidden, we can see larger trends and decode more complex interactions.

To reflect properly on capital punishment, we need to be conscious of three levels of analysis: facts, philosophy, and worldviews. "The Supreme Court decided 5–4 that the death penalty for persons who commit murder before the age of 18 is unconstitutional" is a factual statement. Such facts are straightforward and indispensable, but they should not be the exclusive focus of our understanding. Whatever our views on capital punishment, we should honestly acknowledge the sincerity and merit of arguments on all sides of the issue, not just predict rulings based on a lineup of which president appointed which justice at a particular time in history.

Consider some of the most important questions addressed by the Court in recent years. What crimes deserve the death penalty—murder, child rape, treason? What offenders are eligible for the death penalty? Those who are over 16, 17, or 18? Those who are not insane or not seriously mentally ill? Those who are not mentally retarded? And how, precisely, is mental retardation defined? Who should decide on capital sentences—legislators, judges, or juries, prosecutors, appellate courts, boards of pardons, or governors? How certain should we be before someone is executed? Should executions be carried out in public? Should executions be witnessed by the press, the victim's family, and/or the condemned's family? How many levels of appellate review do we need? How long should all this take? Is capital punishment worth the costs? When the Eighth Amendment was ratified in 1791, such questions might have been met by puzzled stares or elicited brief replies. Today, we regard each of these questions as reasonable and necessary. The preceding Supreme Court cases represent some of the most important documents on the death penalty and convey the complexity of the issue in the United States in contemporary times.

Next we come to a philosophical approach, a search for consistent principles based on reasons known and explainable, a search for perspectives deeper than mere factual descriptions. We seek neutral principles that are broadly conceded to be legitimate. Capital punishment, like criminal punishment generally, serves several different and sometimes conflicting ends, ends that rise and fall in importance, ends that sometimes cease to matter at all.

From the earliest days of recorded history, as the quote that began this book records, the death penalty was explained in quasi-religious terms as atonement or expiation. That the shedding of blood required the shedding of more blood was an obvious bit of magical correspondence to both Aeschylus and Moses. Public discourse no longer uses the vocabulary of Greek tragedy or the book of Exodus. This does not mean that secular traces of the concept of punishment as expiation have vanished: we often hear of "paying one's debt to society" as well as explanations and denunciations of the death penalty as giving or not giving "closure" to the collateral victims of horrific crimes.

In the early modern era, capital punishment carried quasi-religious overtones. There was the formal and traditional recitation of the capital sentence, ending with the words "may God have mercy on your soul." The executioner, masked and garbed in black, carried out his work in public view. The condemned's last words were offered as a ritual warning to the young. Society was being purged of its impiety. Eventually, capital punishment came to be more a reflection of the king's concern for deterring challenges to his order than atonement for sin. Governments commonly claim to have a monopoly on the legitimate use of force. From 1200 to 1800, the death penalty was part of the staking out of that claim. Although modern executions no longer employ the gibbet to exhibit the bodies of the executed or display the heads cut off by the guillotine to impress the public with the sovereign's power, supporters of the death penalty continue to defend it as the only acceptable alternative to vigilantism or anarchy—"if the Law doesn't provide justice Judge Lynch will!" Opponents of the death penalty from Thomas Paine in *The Rights of Man* (1791) onward counter that one of the evils of the death penalty is its coarsening effect on public morals. Critics maintain that by killing people, we are only teaching people to kill. Sometimes a slogan such as "Here in Texas, if you kill someone we will kill you back" can be used by either side of an argument because neither side is sure what it means.

"Incapacitation," "interdiction," "specific deterrence"—such terms are used interchangeably to refer to attempts to stop the criminal himself, an unchanging goal of all societies in all times. The death penalty has throughout history drawn the line for the offender, often between the neck and the shoulders, like nothing else can. Of course the *finality* of that interdiction has impelled speculation and a considerable amount of literature (e.g., Sir Thomas More's *Utopia,* Edward Bellamy's *Looking Backward,* and Anthony Burgess's *Clockwork Orange,* to name a few) into considering whether there are equally effective alternatives. The debate over interdiction is whether any punishment short of death is equally effective as a deterrent that the negative aspects of the death penalty make it obsolete. An important recent development in this area is the alteration in the Catholic Church's position. For the first time in several centuries, the church published a new catechism in 1994. Discussing capital punishment within the context of punishment generally, the first draft expressed the traditional view that the death penalty was morally licit for governments but advised that "if bloodless means are sufficient to defend human lives against an aggressor . . . public authority should limit itself to such means." This statement could be interpreted in two ways: capital punishment should (but need not) be limited to the crime of murder, and it should (but need not be) limited to cases of defending future human lives (for instance, where the murderer had confederates on the outside who would take hostages or murder to free him). Three years later, the official edition of the catechism was issued. For the most part, its changes consisted of corrections to minor translation errors. As for the section on crime and punishment, however, the 1997 edition expressly advised that the death penalty is permissible "if this is the only possible way" to "defend human lives." Furthermore, to dispel any attempt to quibble about sufficiency and possibility, the revision went on to say that in the modern world, "cases in which the execution of the offender is an absolute necessity are very rare, if not practically nonexistent." European countries with Catholic cultural traditions had already abolished the death penalty, but the effect of the catechism in the United States may yet be significant. Several states with significant percentages of Catholic legislators began repealing their death penalty statutes in the 21st century, beginning with New Jersey in 2007.

Closely related to specific deterrence or interdiction is rehabilitation. The idea that punishment has a "medicinal effect" is one with a long tradition in Western thought. Some religious thinkers continue as an academic exercise to discuss whether capital punishment encourages or prevents repentance by a condemned prisoner, but most public figures regardless of politics would find it politically embarrassing to talk about a murderer's soul. Even though that philosophical consideration no longer influences legislation (provisions in the Geneva Conventions requiring delay in the execution of death sentences even for war criminals are responses to the prospect that an innocent person might be too hastily executed), it should be noted that the idea of nobly facing even a justifiable death penalty is one that continues to resonate in popular culture. Every reader or moviegoer of the *Furman* generation is familiar with Sydney Carton, the hero of Charles Dickens's *Tale of Two Cities,* who proves his transformation from self-indulgent lawyer to romantic hero by going gallantly to the guillotine during the French Revolution. In France during the post–World War II era, one of the last uses of the guillotine was to execute Jaques Fesch for the 1954 murder of a Paris policeman as Fesch fled from a robbery. Jailhouse conversions often occur conveniently prior to sentencing, but Fesch's conversion prior to his 1957 execution was regarded as serious enough that three decades later the archbishop of Paris proposed that he be considered for sainthood. At the other end of the cultural scale, the 1990s movies *Dead Man Walking* (a fictionalized account based on an actual execution) and *The Green Mile* (based on a fictional story by Stephen King) and the 2008 young adult novel by Jodi Picoult, *Change of Heart,* advance the same themes: there is redemption and more even on death row and maybe *especially* on death row.

Nevertheless, by definition, death clearly does not rehabilitate an offender even in the sense of Dr. Samuel Johnson's quip that the prospect of being hanged serves to concentrate one's mind. We now reject the idea that rehabilitation is advanced by the prospect of death, and we must also admit that the idea of effective rehabilitative punishment as a basis for any criminal penalty has fallen out of favor too. The United States was formed during the era when rehabilitative punishment became not just an ideal but a stated goal of the criminal justice system. The changing names of our prisons tell the story. Through the 1800s, workhouses (places of work), penitentiaries (places of penance), and reformatories (places of reform) were built across America, even as use of the death penalty was being pared down almost solely to cases of murder and forcible rape. By 1900, separate juvenile courts were no novelty, and the use of parole to transition criminals back into the community was beginning to be widespread. Some criminologists expressly compared crime to disease and suggested that the causes of epidemics, like poverty and crowded slums, were the same in both cases. They also argued that the same treatments, like education and professional social service, could "cure" both ills. Influential educator John Dewey stated the prevailing wisdom at the beginning of the 20th century that "where the moral opinion of the community is highly developed and where scientific penology has made considerable progress [the death penalty] is likely to be more harmful than helpful." By the middle of the century, the Supreme Court confidently proclaimed in *New York v. Williams* (1949) that the purpose of punishment was no longer solely retribution but rehabilitation. Ironically enough, the Court *affirmed* a death sentence in that case.

Fifty years later, it was much harder to convince the Supreme Court or the public that much rehabilitation was taking place in or out of prisons. Just as fears of anarchists and immigrants had led to a brief resurgence in the use of the death penalty in the 1920s, the turbulent society of the 1960s with its urban riots and the assassinations of President John F. Kennedy, Martin Luther King Jr., and Robert Kennedy alarmed even idealists and utopians. Unrest spread to prisons, with fatal riots at Soledad Prison in California in 1970 and at San Quentin in California and Attica in New York in 1971. Also in the 1970s, the wider dissemination of statistics about recidivism among paroled offenders was accompanied by a boom of movies such as *Dirty Harry* (1971) and *Death Wish* (1974) that were commercial successes because they featured unsanctioned protagonists giving irredeemable criminals their fatal comeuppance. The decade ended with the launch in 1980 of the first 24-hours-per-day news source, Cable News Network.

Since the birth of the very concept of the news cycle, crimes of paroled or recidivist criminals have been spotlighted. By 1988, publicity over the crimes of furloughed murderer Willie Horton contributed to derailing the presidential campaign of Massachusetts governor Michael Dukakis. The potential for a candidate to be "Willie Hortoned" by a political opponent altered the status of rehabilitation as a goal for punishment in America. This shift was illustrated only four years later when Arkansas governor Bill Clinton took time off from his presidential campaign to preside over the January 1992 execution of Ricky Ray Rector. Although Willie Horton and Ricky Ray Rector were not solely responsible for the election results, Dukakis was defeated, and Clinton was elected.

As a coda to these developments, in 1984 Congress enacted a sweeping overhaul of the federal sentencing law, expressly directing judges that punishment should serve "retributive, educational, deterrent and incapacitative goals." Note that the word "rehabilitation" was not even used by Congress except in the language of a Senate report criticizing the "outmoded rehabilitation model." In *Tapia v. United States* (2011), a unanimous Supreme Court held that federal judges no longer have the power to consider a defendant's need for rehabilitation in imposing imprisonment or in setting the length of a sentence of imprisonment or even to order offenders to participate in prison rehabilitation programs. It is safe to say that the decline of the rehabilitative ideal means that alternatives to capital punishment are not going to be justified by their potential to reform murderers.

When this nation was founded, Europe and its colonies were going through a philosophical era known as the Enlightenment. One of the hallmarks of this philosophical movement was its reliance on a few simple assumptions, most particularly that Man was a rational creature and that although the physical world was a large and complicated mechanism, perfection of society could be brought about by application of relatively small number of commonsense rules. Our written Constitution, only 4,223 words long, is a spectacularly fortunate reflection of this philosophy. As applied to crime and punishment, the Enlightenment philosophy of deterrence relied on simple ideas of cause and effect: would-be offenders would see the severity of punishment, multiply it by the likelihood of getting caught, and compare the product against the expected gain from any crime. Deterring crime was a purely mathematical exercise in checks and balances. During and after this era, liberal thinkers from Cesare Beccaria to John Stuart Mill argued for abolition or reduced use of the death penalty on the ground that life imprisonment was a much harsher penalty than the short sharp shock of execution and so would be more of a deterrent than widespread use of capital punishment. As for the certainty of punishment, in the era of the founding of this country legal minds such as William Blackstone and William Bradford (attorney general for Pennsylvania and later for the United States) argued that because juries were reluctant to return guilty verdicts when death was a possible penalty, reducing the number of death-eligible offenses would deter more crime by encouraging more convictions. More than a century later, wardens, legislators, and judges in Colorado, Kansas, and Massachusetts, including future Supreme Court justice Oliver Wendell Holmes Jr., were making the same argument.

The 18th and 19th centuries' simple reasoning about deterrence relied on untestable intuitions about human nature, such as the inherent goodness and rationality of Man, and guesses about the real-world prevalence of crime. Accurate records of crime or even punishment were impossible to compile when there was no central repository of data or even a government or academic body with the personnel to collect the data. The mathematical discipline of statistics did not begin to mature until the late 19th century, and reliable records are scarcely older than the establishment in the 1930s of the Federal Bureau of Prisons and the Federal Bureau of Investigation. The three simple comparisons most commonly used in the pre-*Furman* era were comparisons of homicide rates between states with and without the death penalty, comparisons of homicide rates within a state after repeal or enactment of capital punishment laws, and comparison of homicide rates before and after an execution. None could be considered a reasonable basis for drawing a valid conclusion today. Even as late as *Furman,* death penalty opponents such as Hugo Bedau acknowledged that criminologists who were skeptical of the deterrent effect of capital punishment reached their conclusions by assuming congenial theories of behavior and not by examining evidence. After *Gregg,* the number of executions has been such a small proportion of total criminal punishments, even for murder, that most econometricians find it impossible to separate the effect of the death penalty from background noise.

Deterrence theory has come under two related philosophical attacks. The morality of using punishment to "send a message" or "scare straight" patently relies on punishing a criminal not because he deserves it but because it might benefit someone else. This involuntary moral servitude becomes most problematic when the punishment is death. In the extreme, this view could be used to justify ritualistic executions of innocent people to scare the citizenry into good behavior—sacrificing the few for the greater good! The second problem is that the Enlightenment-era conception of persons as rational actors and the subsequent fashion of considering persons as engaged in simple utility maximization have been thoroughly tested, found wanting, and discarded. Midway between *Furman* and *Gregg,* an article titled, "Judgment under Uncertainty: Heuristics and Biases" by Professors Amos Tversky and Daniel Kahneman appeared in the journal *Science.* The authors asserted that in the real world, people were not the rational and calculating machines that classical theorists assumed them to be. Instead, people were susceptible to cognitive illusions, biases, and counterfactual hunches about rewards and punishments. In the academic world, this article was as influential a piece as Beccaria's essay was in its day. The article caused a revolution in scholarship and won Kahneman a Nobel Prize. Its greater impact, however, has been as the forerunner of a new consensus in the academic community that deterrence is not the chief reason for criminal punishment and often does not work at all. One powerful alternative explanation for successes and failures in crime prevention is the simple insight that ordinarily people obey criminal laws for the same reason they stop at red lights even at 2:30 a.m.: it's the right thing to do, whether or not they might get caught. It is an insight as old as Plato that a good person does not need laws to act responsibly, while a bad person will find a way around the law. Laws that are seen as legitimate, however, act as a greater deterrent than ones that are not perceived as legitimate. As a result, regardless of the statistical evidence, widespread popular perception that the death penalty is biased against whites, blacks, Hispanics, the poor, the mentally ill, or young offenders call into question its legitimacy and undermine arguments that the death penalty has a greater deterrent effect than imprisonment.

One last anecdotal point about the success or failure of deterrence is of interest. By now, the phenomenon of criminals committing "suicide by cop" is widely recognized. Some criminals deliberately stage violent crimes without any attempt to escape. The notion that some criminals want to die is old news on death row. Of the few inmates executed in the years just before *Furman,* one was a murderer serving a life sentence in Oklahoma who strangled his cellmate in order to request the death penalty. Another was a murderer who killed four members of his family in Colorado and then fired his attorney to speed up the execution. Since *Gregg,* many states have had executions of inmates who fired their lawyers and discontinued their appeals, typically with the public statement that they find the prospect of death more inviting than further existence. In effect, they volunteer for death. Death is hardly a deterrent to them after being faced with the prospect for years. It is unlikely to have been much of a deterrent at the time they committed the murder that exposed them to the penalty, either.

Even more damaging to the credibility of deterrence is what may be called the Columbine phenomenon. While most of us would not murder even if we could get away with it, and while a "rational murderer" would calculate that in the absence of aggravating circumstances his chances of being executed for murder are about zero, for the small sliver of humanity governed neither by charity nor logic, the death penalty might be an *incentive* to kill, to kill a police officer or to kill in large numbers or grisly ways so as to achieve the celebrity status of death row. Death penalty organizations, pro or anti, have Web sites with every execution listed and every crime that led to the inmate being eligible for the death penalty detailed. Some even have pictures of the condemned. Comparing the 30 years of celebrity for death row cop-killer Mumia Abu-Jamal—invited to speak to a college commencement assembly and engaged to broadcast his opinions on public radio—to the relative anonymity of the life-sentenced Abu-Jamal after the Philadelphia district attorney gave up efforts to defend Abu-Jamal's sentence for murdering Officer Daniel Faulkner in 1981, a mentally unstable attention-seeker might reasonably seek out states that nominally retain the death penalty but hardly ever execute anyone to achieve a notoriety they could never achieve any other way.

This leaves retribution as the basis for punishment. It is the only rationale that applies to all criminal sentences: we punish sophisticated embezzlers such as Bernie Madoff with significant jail terms not because we believe that he would be able to steal billions again if not imprisoned or because we believe other would-be white-collar criminals are waiting to see what penalty is imposed before deciding not to steal but simply because we believe that he deserves it. Retribution becomes particularly controversial when it leads to the possible conclusion that some crimes are so heinous that the only appropriate penalty is death. Opponents of the death penalty admit the force of the *urge* to retribution but argue that if anyone has the right to seek vengeance, it is not the state and not in cold blood. Supporters of the death penalty, on the contrary, assert that since some crimes deserve death, the state *must,* not may, be the instrument of retribution. As all the other rationales for or against capital punishment come into or go out of fashion, retribution endures. In the 1930s, the Lindbergh baby kidnapping and murder commanded public attention and drove several states to amend their laws to punish similar crimes. In the last decade, the Petit murders in Connecticut in 2007—a home invasion during which a mother and two daughters were murdered after the mother and one of the daughters had been raped by two career criminals who met while released on parole—certainly persuaded Governor Jodi Rell to veto a 2009 bill repealing the death penalty in Connecticut. A subsequent bill was signed in 2012 by Dannel Malloy, the state's next governor, but it is doubtful that he could have survived the political backlash if the repeal had not applied only to future crimes and left the two murderers of the Petit family on death row.

The federal government has had the death penalty since 1790, even before the Bill of Rights was ratified in 1791. *Furman* applied to the federal death penalty, of course, but because the federal government as a matter of policy had almost ceased to seek the death sentence, there was no immediate response to *Furman* in Congress: the Drug Kingpin Act nominally restored the death penalty in 1988 for a few narcotics-related offenses, but the general Federal Death Penalty Act was not signed into law until 1994. Today, only about half of 1 percent of death sentences imposed in the United States are imposed in federal court. Nonetheless, just as federal judges wield the single most potent veto on state executions, federal legislators and prosecutors are and will be key forces in the 21st-century history of capital prosecutions. As history shows, Congress lagged behind the states in responding to *Furman*. Even if the current trend toward abolition represented by New Jersey, New Mexico, Illinois, Connecticut, and Maryland continues, Congress's slower reaction to social trends means that the federal death penalty is unlikely to be repealed quickly. Furthermore, due to the Supremacy Clause in Article VI of the Constitution, the federal death penalty is available even in states that have repealed their death penalty laws. High-profile *federal* prosecutions in Idaho (which has the death penalty) of Joseph Duncan for the 2005 kidnapping and murder of a 9-year-old boy and sexual assault of an 8-year-old girl and in Vermont (which repealed its death penalty in 1965) of Michael Jacques for the 2008 rape and murder of his 12-year-old niece pose questions about federalism and the proper role of the national government in prosecuting local crime, but the horrific nature of the crimes tends to overshadow debate over legal niceties. The ultimate importance of these federal prosecutions may be that they signal a shift in capital prosecutions solely on the grounds of ability to follow through. Duncan's and Jacques's prosecutions have not been completed as of 2013 due to the inevitable appeals and collateral attacks.

That a death sentence takes a long time to carry out is a commonplace of American law, but the length of time that it takes to even get a capital prosecution over with is becoming a factor. And time is money in legal matters. Beginning in the 1980s, newspapers began to report that the typical capital case could cost the taxpayer millions. By the 2000s, appeals to the fiscal conservatism of legislatures proved much more successful than legal or ethical arguments in successful repeal campaigns in New Jersey and New Mexico. One federal study estimates that in 2010, the defense costs in federal trials for cases in which the death penalty was permitted but not sought were about $55,000, while costs for trials in which the death penalty was sought were about $431,000. There is reason to believe that the costs to the prosecution side of the courtroom are similar. Since indigent defendants commit the overwhelming majority of death-eligible crimes and the cost of criminal prosecutions has traditionally been borne at the county or city level, imposing a level of financial distress by raising the costs of defense is an acknowledged part of the arsenal of an attorney opposing the death penalty. The financial strain of death penalty litigation, rather than the legal merit of a case, is what often moves a defendant off death row. Since the decision-making process in seeking the federal death penalty is centralized in Washington, D.C., and the budget available to a U.S. attorney in an approved prosecution is much greater than to the typical district attorney in a state court, it is not surprising that in capital cases in Philadelphia the federal rate of obtaining a death penalty verdict (26 percent) is about 20 times higher than in state court (1.3 percent). Federal prosecutions may increasingly be seen as the remedy of last resort (or the first resort in states such as Vermont) where there is a significant public revulsion toward the facts of a particular crime.

Changes in worldview have a subtle but powerful influence on the future of the death penalty. Worldviews are the soil from which philosophies grow. To distinguish worldview from philosophy and to show how worldview interacts with philosophy, consider that both Locke and Hobbes constructed their ideal government from the same social contract philosophy. Hobbes's approach, based on fear, the fear that life is nasty, brutish, solitary, and short, led him to justify absolute monarchy. Locke's approach, based on a belief that government was ordained to secure life, liberty, and property, led him to justify deposing a king in favor of constitutionally limited government. To illustrate how the same worldview can underlie apparent opposites, consider that in the 1970s there was great popular anxiety over global cooling, over-population, and nuclear warfare. Popular stories in 2010 used the same adjectives to fan anxiety, but this time the end of the world as we know it would come from global warming, demographic winter, and asteroid collisions. As was the case in the 1970s, scientists and politicians of today sincerely believe that they are acting on the latest and best science, but their seeming lurches are based on the same worldview: catastrophic events dominate in history, and the only things certain are chaos and disaster. By contrast, the country parson of the 19th century who believed that the world was 6,000 years old and that dinosaur bones were left by Noah's flood took an inherently calmer and indeed a Whiggish view of the future: the world would not change, society would get better, and both would certainly do so gradually. It is no surprise that the 19th century was one of steady, gradually increasing lenience in capital punishment laws, while the last 50 years have seen the United States lurch from abolition to restoration and back with comparative rapidity. Although abolition has been the dominant trend for the last decade, it would be unwise to bet that a future *Furman* would not be followed by a future *Gregg*.

As far as the death penalty is concerned, we can trace the impact of worldview almost to the beginnings of history. To early societies, death for serious crimes was the only option, whether fast by execution or slow by the more unpleasant jobs done by slave labor. Religious and political acceptance of the death penalty reflected the worldview that the law was given, not made, and that the way things are is the way they have always been and always would be. Abraham might debate boldly with God over whether the citizens of Sodom and Gomorrah deserved to die, but to question the death penalty itself was unthinkable. This static conception of society, even in the face of dramatic changes caused by the collapse of empires, the migration of peoples, and the invention of new technologies, persisted from the earliest times to the Middle Ages.

The Renaissance, the Reformation, and the revival of the study of Roman law were bound together by a new worldview that life existed not simply as a testing ground for the *next* life. How to order society for the greatest good in *this* world was a proper subject for study. Of course, philosophers, kings, and churchmen reached different conclusions, and the 16th- and 17th-century religious wars that followed did no credit to anyone, but post-Reformation lack of agreement on a single religious philosophy opened the field for a secular explanation of laws, including the laws of crime and punishment. International commerce led to a commercial worldview. In the first treatise to explain law in other than religious terms, Dutch jurist Hugo Grotius explained early in the 17th century that pagan and biblical justice alike could be explained as a transaction, that "every penalty is considered as a debt arising out of a crime, which the offender is bound to pay to the aggrieved party." Although death for religious disputes was inconsistent with the precepts of Christ, capital punishment for murder "and similar crimes" could surely be part of human laws. For the next 200 years, advocates of milder or more severe punishments would debate how many "similar crimes" there were, but their debate was firmly grounded in the worldview of society as a business venture, not a religious pilgrimage.

This is not to say that religious philosophies were less than important. The United States was settled and the Constitution was written by Calvinist dissidents and their children who firmly believed that nature was corrupted by sin. Men were by nature corruptible and would tend to abuse power. And, in the persons of the British king and his ministers, they were abusing power. Constitutional safeguards against such abuse of power resulted.

Meanwhile, a more romantic worldview was blossoming in Europe: according to Jean-Jacques Rousseau, that Man was born free but everywhere was in chains was the fault of easily correctable flaws in society. Nature itself is good. The appeal of this view is obvious and became a dominant worldview in 19th-century Europe and 20th-century America. Although conservatives and liberals argued over deterrence, both assumed that by adjusting incentives and disincentives, the crime problem could be solved. Indeed, the sense that crime was curable like a disease arose at about the same time that Louis Pasteur was discovering that germs caused disease. The sense that murder, robbery, and rape came from an external source like Rousseau's imperfect society meant that rehabilitation and a medical approach to punishment would allow social progress. Progress itself was assumed to be possible and directional: toward less evil and more good.

The 20th century witnessed unprecedented slaughter by warfare on an industrial scale and genocides committed by governments against their own citizens. For the first time in history, the truism that even an unjust government was safer than anarchy was demonstrated to be false on three continents. The very idea of law came to be suspect. The early Progressive-era philosophy of Oliver Wendell Holmes Jr. denying that law was anything other than a prediction about what the judge would do and deriding the concepts of natural law and natural rights as the superstition of a brooding omnipresence in the sky found fertile ground. Scientific discoveries such as relativity and quantum physics as filtered through the popular media contributed to a sense that the right and wrong of crime and punishment were subjective and very much dependent on the observer. The United States was founded on the idea of popular sovereignty. The consent of the people was the source of all governmental authority. The people would devise relatively mild criminal laws that should be obeyed because the people imposed these laws on themselves. Yet in the 21st century, skeptics and cynics echo the complaints of the 18th-century American colonists that criminal laws are things that "they" do to "us."

And the divided world of us and them—individuals bound together by temporary coincidence of interests—looks very different from a unified world of "us." Roughly half of the readers of this sentence are male, and half are female. Throughout history, men have committed the overwhelming majority of all crimes. Until recently, women had almost nothing to do with punishment because they had little to do with governing. Even after women began voting in the Western democracies, their behavior often could be predicted by their husbands' behavior. One of the significant shifts that has taken place in recent times has been that women constitute a major force in political society and do so in significantly different ways than men do. Calls for more law and order have significantly less appeal to women than do other political messages. Although the 1994 election of George Pataki as governor of New York on a promise to restore the death penalty shows that in local politics the death penalty is still a potent divider of the electorate, candidates on the national level have had mixed results. Richard Nixon pledged to "get tough on crime" in 1968, and George H. W. Bush successfully used Willie Horton's crimes as a campaign issue in 1988. But such messages resonate more strongly with conservative white males than they do with other segments of the electorate. No national candidate in the last 25 years has made crime and punishment a major campaign issue because it is not important to the voters who matter. Decisions about capital punishment therefore continue to be made almost exclusively by judges and the small bar of death penalty lawyers. In fact, the very worldview of criminal punishment in a democracy as the product of political consensus has undergone change. Shortly after the war crimes trials following World War II, most European nations followed West Germany in abolishing capital punishment, despite the consistent support of large majorities of each country's population for the death penalty. Why? It has been a truism for the past 100 years that organizational elites are more liberal than the rank-and-file members, regardless of the organization. In parliamentary systems throughout much of Europe, the opinions of the electorate about issues such as the death penalty may have little impact on election results.

The United States parted course with Europe on the death penalty when it was reinstated in *Gregg*. The United States features significantly more state, local, and federal elections than in European countries. Public opinion is expressed frequently in polling places across the United States, leading to a veritable checkerboard of state options regarding the death penalty. Elite opinion in the United States, represented by Justice Goldberg's adage that it was the Supreme Court's duty to *lead* public opinion, continues to be pressured by other nations' criticism of the American retention of capital punishment. Some recent Supreme Court decisions discussed in this book reflect an increased receptiveness to international opinion. The European Union now forbids member countries to use capital punishment, even in wartime. International tribunals prosecuting war crimes in Yugoslavia and investigating atrocities in the internecine war in Rwanda do not have the power to impose a death sentence, nor does the International Criminal Court created by the Rome Statute in 2002. While the ruling class in Europe once imposed the death penalty on the lower classes, who mostly saw criminal punishment as a tool of oppression, the ruling elites in Europe now prohibit the lower classes from imposing the death penalty on *anyone,* regardless of the reason and regardless of the support of the lower classes for capital punishment. Elite opinion in the United States has recently taken a decisive shift toward abolition, while the population at large remains divided, largely on the basis of geography, not class. Only time will tell whether the United States will take the path of Europe or whether even after years of Supreme Court rulings the death penalty will remain the crazy quilt of varying state practices, subject to the vetoes of federal judges not chosen for their views on capital punishment. Such is the virtue and vice of federalism.

Chapter 10
Chronology

1600s

In England, religious and political conflicts lead to increased tension between the first Stuart monarchs (James I and Charles I) and Parliament. Adventurers from England and refugees from the English Civil War (1642–1649) and the Thirty Years' War (1618–1648) settle North America. The first use of the death penalty occurs in the American colonies when Virginia executes George Kendall for spying (1608) and then Daniel Frank for theft (1622).

1641

The Massachusetts code titled Body of Liberties forbids "cruel and inhuman" punishments but permits limited use of torture as well as the death penalty for crimes, including witchcraft.

1660–1690s

Mary Dyer (1660) and others are hanged in Boston for defying laws against Quakers being found in Massachusetts. Ann Glover (1688) is hanged in Boston for being a Catholic and a witch. Eighteen witches are hanged at Salem (1692); Giles Cory is pressed to death for refusing to plead either guilty or not guilty.

1682

Charles II grants the colony of Pennsylvania to William Penn, a Quaker. Penn's Great Law permits the death penalty only for murder and treason. (Under pressure from England, Pennsylvania abandons the Great Law in 1718 and readopts English common-law crimes.)

1688

A bloodless coup known as the Glorious Revolution replaces James II with William III of Orange and Mary II as joint monarchs of England. In 1689 Parliament passes the Bill of Rights, forbidding cruel and unusual punishments.

1723

In England, interest in modernization of the common law and concern over vagrancy, theft, and poaching by persons dislocated by the Industrial Revolution lead to enactment of the Black Act, which adds scores of new capital offenses. Jury nullification and the practice of pardoning and "transporting" convicted criminals to American colonies as indentured servants save many capital defendants from execution. Parliament makes returning to England after transportation a felony.

1764

Cesare Beccaria publishes *On Crimes and Punishments,* calling for the abolition of torture and capital punishment. European countries in response abolish judicial use of torture and restrict use of the death penalty.

1776–1787

American colonies declare their independence from England over dissatisfaction with taxation and political representation and fight the American Revolutionary War (1775–1781). English criminal law is a minor issue in the Declaration of Independence (1776). The Articles of Confederation (adopted in 1781 and effective in 1783) leave crime and punishment to state governments. Most states adopt written constitutions and declarations or bills of rights outlawing but not defining cruel and unusual punishments.

1787–1791

The inadequacy of the Articles of Confederation to retire debt incurred during the Revolutionary War and to regulate foreign trade and interstate commerce leads to the Constitutional Convention in Philadelphia. The last Confederation Congress enacts the Northwest Ordinance (1787) outlawing but not defining cruel or unusual punishments in the Northwest Territory. The Constitution is ratified based on a political promise by Federalists to propose the Bill of Rights in the First Congress (1789). The First Congress enacts the federal crime bill (1790) with a mandatory death penalty for treason, murder, and rape on federal property; counterfeiting; and piracy on the high seas. The Fifth Amendment forbids denial of life, liberty, or property without due process, and the Eighth Amendment forbids the federal government from imposing cruel and unusual punishments (1791). Due process and cruel and unusual punishments are not defined.

1787

Dr. Benjamin Rush delivers a speech on prison reform at the home of Benjamin Franklin. Published as *An Enquiry into the Effects of Public Punishments upon Criminals and upon Society,* it contains the first American argument for total abolition of the death penalty. In 1788, Rush follows with *An Enquiry into the Justice and Policy of Punishing Murder by Death.* Pennsylvania attorney general William Bradford argues in a 1793 pamphlet that juries hesitate to convict when the death penalty is a possible sentence.

1830s

Laws restricting and abolishing imprisonment for debt reduce jail populations. Connecticut (1830), Rhode Island (1833), Pennsylvania (1834), and New York,

New Jersey, and Massachusetts (1835) end public executions in favor of hangings in prison with either only official witnesses or a few members of the public chosen as representative witnesses. Public hangings remain popular spectacles on the frontier.

1833

Barron v. Baltimore (1833) holds that the Bill of Rights is a restraint only on the federal government.

1859

Abolitionist John Brown is hanged for treason, conspiracy, and murder on December 2, 1859, at Charles Town, Virginia. He rejects counsel's suggestion to attempt an insanity defense.

1873

The *Slaughterhouse Cases* (1873) hold that the Fourteenth Amendment's Due Process Clause does not generally restrict what state governments do.

1878

Wilkerson v. Utah (1878) holds that execution by firing squad does not violate the Eighth Amendment's prohibition of cruel and unusual punishment.

1889

For the first time, federal law allows a right to appeal all death sentences imposed in federal trial courts. The Supreme Court later holds in *McKane v. Durston* (1894) that the Constitution does not require a state to allow criminal appeals.

1890

In re Kemmler (1890) holds that New York's legislation adopting electrocution as a method of execution does not violate the Due Process Clause. Murderer William Kemmler is the first person executed in the electric chair, on August 6 at Auburn Prison. The chair is later installed at Sing Sing Prison.

Holden v. Minnesota (1890) holds that Minnesota's switch from public hangings to hangings within a county jail or other building designed to "exclude the view of persons outside" violates no constitutional right of Clifton Holden.

1891

Federal law creates courts of appeal, an intermediate appeals court below the Supreme Court with jurisdiction to hear appeals in federal criminal cases.

1895

The Supreme Court begins to rule that the Due Process Clause makes portions of the Bill of Rights applicable to state and local governments.

State governments begin an era of rehabilitative punishments, increasingly using indeterminate sentences with eligibility for parole when an administrative parole board believes that an inmate is ready to be released. Separate courts for juvenile offenders also become widespread.

1896

Ohio joins New York in using electrocution as its method of execution, as do Massachusetts (1898), New Jersey (1907), Virginia (1908), North Carolina (1909), Kentucky (1910), South Carolina (1912), and Arkansas, Indiana, Pennsylvania, and Nebraska (1913).

1897

Federal law is amended to reduce the number of offenses eligible for the death penalty to three: treason, murder, and rape. The mandatory death penalty is abolished in favor of jury discretion to choose capital punishment or life imprisonment. *Winston v. United States* (1899) holds that this gives federal juries complete discretion over choice between the death sentence and life imprisonment and overturns convictions because judges instructed juries to vote for death unless a good reason not to had been shown.

1907

Kansas abolishes capital punishment. Eight states (Minnesota, Washington, Oregon, North Dakota, South Dakota, Tennessee, Arizona, and Missouri) also abolish or sharply restrict the death penalty in the decade before World War I. All except Minnesota later reinstate some death penalty provisions.

1915

Malloy v. South Carolina (1915) holds that South Carolina's switch from execution by hanging to execution in the electric chair violates no constitutional right of Joe Malloy because South Carolina's preference for use of electrocution "is the consequent of a well grounded belief that electrocution is less painful and more humane than hanging."

1923

The Nevada Supreme Court decides *State v. Gee Jon* (1923), upholding Nevada's statute providing for executions in the gas chamber. The court writes that "[t]he Legislature has determined that the infliction of the death penalty by the administration of lethal gas is humane, and it would indeed be not only presumptuous, but boldness on our part, to substitute our judgment for theirs, even if we thought differently upon the matter." Gee Jon becomes the first person executed by gas.

1924

Chicago attorney Clarence Darrow pleads Richard Loeb and Nathan Leopold Jr. guilty to the kidnapping and murder of Leopold's 14-year-old cousin because state law requires a jury convicting of first-degree murder to impose the death sentence but permits a judge to set a lesser sentence. Darrow obtains life sentences for his teenaged clients after a marathon argument including the assertion that "it is unfair to hang a nineteen-year-old boy for the philosophy that was taught him at the university." Loeb is later murdered in jail. Leopold is paroled after 33 years.

1927

Fear of immigrants, crime, and violent political movements leads to increased use of the death penalty in the post–World War I era. On August 27, Massachusetts electrocutes Nicola Sacco and Bartolomeo Vanzetti, Italian immigrants with anarchist sympathies, for two murders in 1920.

1936

The rate of executions reaches an all-time peak in the United States in this decade at an average of 167 per year. New Jersey electrocutes Bruno Hauptmann for the 1932 kidnapping and murder of the infant son of aviation pioneer Charles Lindbergh. The media coverage of the trial is widely criticized by judges and lawyers as creating a "carnival atmosphere." Congress enacts the Lindbergh Law only months after the kidnapping, making death in the course of an interstate kidnapping a capital offense.

A crowd estimated at from 10,000 to 20,000 watches the hanging of Rainey Bethea in Owensboro, Kentucky.

1937

A crowd estimated at 1,500 watches the hanging of Roscoe Jackson for murder in Galena, Missouri, the last known public execution in the United States.

1947

Louisiana ex rel. Francis v. Resweber (1947) holds that Louisiana's repeated attempts to electrocute Willie Francis do not deprive him of due process of law by inflicting cruel and unusual punishment. The Court does not hold that the Due Process Clause makes the Eighth Amendment binding on the states.

1948

On December 10, 1948, the United Nations adopts by a vote of 48–0 (with 8 abstentions from Saudi Arabia, South Africa, and 6 Soviet-controlled nations) the Universal Declaration of Human Rights. The death penalty is not expressly mentioned, but Article 5 provides that "[n]o one shall be subject to torture or to cruel, inhuman, or degrading treatment or punishment."

1949

West Virginia becomes the last state to switch to electrocution as its method of execution.

1950

Oscar Callazo and Grisello Torresola attempt to assassinate President Harry Truman, killing a Secret Service agent. Torresola is killed, and Callazo is sentenced to death. In 1952 Truman commutes Callazo's sentence to life imprisonment.

1953

Julius and Ethel Rosenberg are electrocuted in Sing Sing Prison for espionage. The federal government does not at this time have a separate death row and uses whatever form of execution is legal in the state where the trial was held. The federal government opens the new federal death row at the United States Penitentiary in Terra Haute, Indiana, in 1999.

1957

Alaska, Hawaii, and Delaware abolish the death penalty.

Reid v. Covert (1957) holds that court-martial for murder cannot be used in times of peace to deprive civilian defendants of the right to jury trial. Justices Frankfurter and Harlan concur, stressing that the possibility of capital punishment requires special safeguards.

1958

Trop v. Dulles (1958) holds that loss of citizenship as a punishment for deserting a military post in time of war is cruel and unusual punishment in violation of the Eighth Amendment. Four justices distinguish capital punishment for murder as a separate issue but comment that there are weighty arguments against capital punishment too.

1959

Sociologist Thorsten Sellin publishes *The Death Penalty,* asserting that statistical comparison of states with and without the death penalty show that the death penalty does not deter homicide.

1960

After 11 years on death row, eight stays of execution, and seven trips to the Supreme Court, Caryl Chessman is executed in California's gas chamber for the kidnapping and sexual assault of women he stopped while impersonating a police officer. Petitions for clemency were signed by millions in the United States and Europe.

1961

Delaware readopts the death penalty.

1962

Robinson v. California (1962) holds that the Due Process Clause does make the Eighth Amendment applicable to the states.

1963

The federal government hangs Victor Feguer at Fort Madison, Iowa, on March 15 for interstate kidnapping and murder. It is the last federal execution for 38 years.

Justice Arthur Goldberg circulates a memorandum to the Supreme Court recommending review of six capital cases and abolition of the death penalty as a violation of the Eighth Amendment. The Court denies review in all six cases.

Lee Harvey Oswald assassinates President John F. Kennedy. Jack Ruby murders Oswald on live television as Oswald is being transported by police. A Texas jury finds Ruby guilty of murder and recommends the death penalty, but Ruby dies of cancer in prison in 1967 while awaiting a new trial.

The Court decides *Fay v. Noia* (1963) and *Townsend v. Sain* (1963), decisions expanding the scope of issues reviewable by federal courts in habeas corpus proceedings alleging that state court convictions and sentences deprived a petitioner of constitutional rights.

1964

Oregon abolishes the death penalty.

1965

Kansas hangs Richard Hickox and Perry Smith on April 14 for the murders of the Clutter family in 1959. Truman Capote publishes the best-selling book *In Cold Blood,* recounting the murders in the form of a novel.

Iowa and West Virginia abolish the death penalty.

Great Britain abolishes the death penalty.

1966

Only one person is executed in the United States this year. Oklahoma electrocutes James French on August 10 for the murder of his cellmate in 1961. French, who had been serving a life sentence for a 1958 murder, sought execution.

1967

California executes Aaron Mitchell in its gas chamber on April 12, and Colorado executes Luis Jose Monge in its gas chamber on June 2. An unofficial moratorium on executions begins as class actions challenging the death penalty are litigated nationwide.

Canada sharply restricts the death penalty.

1968

United States v. Jackson (1968) holds that the federal law death penalty for kidnapping is unconstitutional because it coerces a defendant to waive the right to a jury trial: after a guilty plea a judge can only impose a life sentence, while a jury can recommend death after a guilty verdict.

1969

Witherspoon v. Illinois (1969) holds that jurors who have objections to the death penalty but could nevertheless follow the judge's instructions cannot be excluded for cause from jury service.

Boykin v. Alabama (1969) holds that the death sentence cannot be imposed on a defendant who pleaded guilty to five armed robberies because the guilty plea was not shown to be made voluntarily and with understanding of the potential penalty. Boykin neither spoke at his guilty plea nor presented evidence about his character or background at his sentencing.

1970

Maxwell v. Bishop (1970) holds that a death penalty imposed in 1962 in Arkansas for rape was invalid because jurors opposed to the death penalty had been excluded in violation of *Witherspoon v. Illinois* (1969), which is applied retroactively.

1971

McGautha v. California (1971) holds that California law giving the jury complete discretion over the decision to return a death sentence or lesser punishment and Ohio law allowing determination of guilt and imposition of the death penalty without separate penalty phase do not violate due process of law.

1972

On February 18 the California Supreme Court decides *People v. Anderson,* holding that California's death penalty is cruel and unusual under California law. There are 104 inmates removed from death row, including Charles Manson and Sirhan Sirhan.

On June 29 the U.S. Supreme Court decides *Furman v. Georgia.* States respond by reenacting death penalty statutes, many of which are copied from the Model Penal Code published in 1962.

1975

The *American Economic Review* publishes Isaac Ehrlich's "The Deterrent Effects of Capital Punishment: A Matter of Life and Death," which asserts that statistical studies show that each death penalty execution causes "7 or 8 fewer murders."

1976

Solicitor General Robert Bork argues that death penalty statutes are constitutional. On July 2, the Supreme Court agrees in *Gregg v. Georgia* (1976), *Profitt v. Florida* (1976), and *Jurek v. Texas* (1976). *Woodson v. North Carolina* (1976) and *Roberts v. Louisiana* (1976) hold that mandatory death sentences are unconstitutional.

Gilmore v. Utah (1976) holds that Gary Gilmore's mother cannot challenge the death sentence imposed on her son after a showing that his waiver of appeals was knowing and intelligent.

Canada, which last executed anyone in 1962, abolishes the death penalty.

1977

Utah executes Gary Gilmore by firing squad on January 17, 1977. He is the first person executed in the United States in almost 10 years.

Oklahoma becomes the first state to adopt lethal injection as its method of execution.

1982

On December 7, Texas executes Charles Brooks in the first use of lethal injection in the United States.

1984

Strickland v. Washington (1984) sets a formal standard for effective assistance of counsel under the Sixth Amendment and requires a defendant to show a reasonable probability that an attorney's mistake made a difference in the outcome. Florida electrocutes David Washington on July 13.

1985

Ake v. Oklahoma (1985) holds that in capital cases where there is evidence that the defendant's sanity is in question, the state must provide a psychiatric expert to assist the defense.

1986

Skipper v. South Carolina (1986) holds that the defendant sentenced to death for murder must be permitted to introduce mitigating evidence that he adjusted well to prison while awaiting trial.

Roger "Animal" DeGarmo announces an auction for witness seats to his execution. Although DeGarmo claims that he received two $1,500 bids, Texas Department of Correction officials refuse to allow the sales.

Ford v. Wainwright (1986) holds that because an insane person cannot be executed, the Eighth Amendment requires adequate procedures to ascertain whether a condemned prisoner has become insane while awaiting execution.

California judicial retention elections result in Chief Justice Rose Bird and Justices Joseph Grodin and Cruz Reynoso being removed from office as a result of popular hostility to their opposition to the death penalty.

1988

The *Miami Herald* reports that Florida has spent an average of $3.2 million per execution carried out from 1973 to 1988.

Chief Justice William Rehnquist appoints retired justice Lewis Powell to head a commission to study reform of federal habeas corpus procedures.

1989

Penry v. Lynaugh (1989) holds that the Eighth Amendment does not forbid the execution of mentally retarded persons.

Stanford v. Kentucky (1989) holds that the Eighth Amendment permits the death penalty for murderers who commit their crimes at age 16 or older. In June 2003, Governor Paul Patton of Kentucky commutes Stanford's sentence to life imprisonment.

Teague v. Lane (1989) holds that with rare exceptions, federal courts cannot announce new rules of constitutional law in habeas corpus cases.

Murray v. Giarratano (1989) holds that inmates, even if they are condemned to death, are not guaranteed the assistance of counsel after their direct appeals end.

1990

Pennsylvania, which has not executed anyone since 1962, switches its method of execution from electrocution to lethal injection.

1992

After an all-night exchange of faxes between the Ninth Circuit Court of Appeals granting stays of execution and the U.S. Supreme Court overruling the stays of execution, California executes Robert Alton Harris in the gas chamber at San Quentin Prison for murdering two teenagers.

Peter Neufeld and Barry Scheck begin the Innocence Project at Cardozo Law School to study cases where DNA evidence might be able to exonerate convicted defendants.

The *Dallas Morning Herald* reports that Texas has spent an average of $2.3 million per death penalty prosecution.

1993

On January 5, Washington executes Westley Dodd by hanging.

On June 28, Kirk Bloodsworth becomes the first person exonerated by DNA evidence. After nine years in prison (two of them on death row) for the 1984 murder of a nine-year-old girl, Bloodsworth is set free by a Maryland judge and later pardoned by the governor of Maryland. Kimberly Ruffner pleads guilty to the murder and receives a life sentence on May 20, 2004.

Helen Prejean, CSJ, writes *Dead Man Walking: An Eyewitness Account of the Death Penalty in the United States*. Made into a hit movie in 1995 (Academy Award for Best Actress for Susan Sarandon as Prejean, Best Actor nomination for Sean Penn as Matthew Poncelet, the condemned murderer based on Elmo Sonnier, executed by Louisiana in 1984 for the murder in 1977 of two teenagers), the movie changes the actual method of execution used from electrocution to lethal injection.

Arave v. Creech (1993) holds that the aggravating factor that the defendant showed "utter disregard for human life" is not unconstitutionally vague. The Supreme Court had previously held in *Godfrey v. Georgia* (1980) and *Maynard v. Cartwright* (1988) that "especially heinous atrocious or cruel" and "outrageously or wantonly vile, horrible or inhuman" were too vague to support a death sentence.

1994

According to a Gallup Poll, support for the death penalty in the United States reaches a peak, at 80 percent.

President Bill Clinton signs the Federal Death Penalty Act of 1994 on September 15, 1994, making dozens of federal crimes subject to the death penalty "if death results" in the course of the crime.

On May 10, Illinois executes by lethal injection John Wayne Gacy, who was convicted in 1980 of 33 murders, mostly of young boys whose bodies were buried under the crawlspace of Gacy's residence.

A federal judge holds that Washington may not execute Mitchell Edward Rupe by hanging because Rupe had gained so much weight in prison that he likely would be decapitated during a hanging. Rupe dies in prison of natural causes in 2006.

Kansas reinstates the death penalty as a punishment for murder.

Justice Harry Blackmun, in *Callins v. Collins* (1994), declares his opposition to the death penalty in all cases.

Simmons v. South Carolina (1994) holds that a jury must be informed of life without parole as an alternative to the death penalty where state law provides for that as the alternative sentence and the defendant is not eligible for parole.

1995

On March 7, New York reinstates the death penalty as a punishment for murder after a campaign centering on crime and punishment elects George Pataki as governor.

In *Lackey v. Texas* (1995), Justice John Paul Stevens comments that excessive time on death row awaiting capital punishment may itself be a violation of the Eighth Amendment. In subsequent cases, Justice Stephen Breyer agrees with Stevens and Justice Clarence Thomas criticizes both, arguing that excessive delays are the result of the Supreme Court's "Byzantine death penalty jurisprudence."

Pennsylvania executes Keith Zettlemoyer by lethal injection for the 1980 murder of a witness against him. A few months later, Pennsylvania executes Leon Moser. Zettlemoyer and Moser are executed only because, over the opposition of their attorneys, they have discontinued all appeals. Pennsylvania's execution of Gary Heidnik, its third execution in 1999 (and last as of 2013), is likewise possible because he volunteers for death. Depending on the state, executions of inmates who prefer execution over continued appeals are from 8 percent to 100 percent of all executions.

1996

The number of new death sentences imposed by juries reaches a peak for the post-*Gregg* era, at 315.

Responding to public support for the death penalty and the first World Trade Center bombing in 1993, Congress enacts the Antiterrorism and Effective Death Penalty Amendments Act (AEDPA), effective April 24, 1996. The AEDPA creates several new federal capital offense, but its primary effect is on state habeas corpus petitions. The AEDPA limits state prisoners in most cases to one federal habeas corpus petition, provides for a one-year time limit to file in federal court after state appeals are exhausted, and requires federal courts to defer to state court rulings unless they are unreasonably wrong. *Felker v. Turpin* (1996) holds that the AEDPA does not suspend the writ of habeas corpus in violation of the Constitution. Georgia executes Ellis Felker by electrocution on November 15.

On January 25, Delaware executes Billy Bailey by hanging after he declines the option of lethal injection.

On January 26, Utah executes John A. Taylor by firing squad after he chooses that option.

The Ninth Circuit Court of Appeals holds in *Fierro v. Gomez* that California cannot execute David Fierro (or anyone else) in the gas chamber because it inflicts cruel and unusual punishment. California amends its law to make lethal injection the primary method of execution.

1997

In February, the American Bar Association calls for a moratorium on executions until death penalty fairness is ensured. Timothy McVeigh is convicted and sentenced to death in federal court for causing 168 deaths in the 1995 bombing of the Oklahoma City federal building.

1999

The number of executions per year reaches a peak in the post-*Gregg* era, at 98.

Journalism students at Northwestern University research and report on many cases in Illinois of innocent defendants being convicted and sentenced to death. Anthony Porter is freed from death row as a result.

Arizona executes Karl LaGrand by lethal injection. Arizona executes his brother, Walter LaGrand, in the gas chamber after the Supreme Court holds, in *Stewart v. Lagrand,* that he has waived any claim that it is cruel and unusual punishment by choosing that as his method of execution.

Russia abolishes the death penalty.

On April 20, Eric Harris and Dylan Klebold murder 13 persons at their high school in Columbine, Colorado, and then commit suicide. Their crimes punctuate a dramatic rise in homicide by males in the 14–17- and 18–24-year-old cohorts that begins in the late 1980s, peaks around 1995, and drops to much lower levels by 2000.

2000

Illinois governor George Ryan declares a moratorium on executions.

New Hampshire governor Jeanne Shaheen vetoes legislation that would have repealed the death penalty. The move is symbolic only: New Hampshire's last execution was in 1939.

Governor Frank O'Bannon orders a commission to study Indiana's death penalty system to ensure that innocent persons are not executed.

2001

On his last day in office, President Bill Clinton commutes the federal death sentence of drug kingpin Ronnie Chandler to life imprisonment. On June 11, Timothy McVeigh becomes the first person executed by the federal government since 1963. Juan Raul Garza becomes the second on June 19. (The third and most recent execution, of Louis Jones, was on March 18, 2003.)

2002

Ray Krone leaves an Arizona prison, the 100th person given the death penalty to be freed as innocent, after DNA testing establishes probable guilt of another person. He and Kirk Bloodsworth (see 1993) are invited to testify before the United States Senate.

Atkins v. Virginia (2002) holds that the Eighth Amendment forbids the execution of mentally retarded murderers.

Governor Parris Glendenning declares a moratorium on executions in Maryland.

Ohio executes Alton Coleman by lethal injection on April 26 for a murder committed during a crime spree in 1984 that resulted in Coleman receiving death sentences from Illinois, Indiana, and Ohio.

A federal trial judge in New York City declares the Federal Death Penalty Act of 1994 unconstitutional because of the risk that innocent defendants might be executed. The Second Circuit Court of Appeals reverses his ruling five months later.

2003

On his last day in office, Governor George Ryan commutes to life imprisonment the death sentences of all 167 inmates on death row in Illinois.

On his first day in office, Governor Robert Ehrlich rescinds the moratorium on executions in Maryland.

A Virginia jury finds that John Allen Muhammed should die for the first-degree murder of 10 persons killed in sniper attacks during three weeks in October 2002. A separate jury convicts his teenage accomplice, Lee Malvo, but declines to recommend the death penalty.

2004

Maryland executes Steven Oken for rape and murder in 1987.

New York's Court of Appeals holds in *People v. LaValle* that New York's death penalty statute is unconstitutional under the state constitution because it contains an improper jury instruction. The court orders death penalty cases to be brought only as noncapital first-degree murder cases until the legislature enacts a valid sentencing statute. No statutory amendment has been enacted; with no executions ever carried out under New York's decade-old statute, the last condemned murderer leaves death row in 2007.

2005

President George W. Bush, in his State of the Union address, announces an expansion of federal efforts to use DNA evidence to prevent wrongful convictions.

Roper v. Simmons (2005) holds that the Eighth Amendment forbids the death penalty for murderers who commit their crimes before age 18.

2006

Richard Moore, age 76, dies of old age after 26 years on Indiana's death row for the shotgun murders of his ex-wife, his father-in-law, and a police officer responding to the crime.

Virginia executes Roger Keith Coleman for a rape and murder committed in 1981. In *Coleman v. Thompson* (1991), the Supreme Court had held that Coleman had no constitutional right to the effective assistance of an attorney in a habeas corpus appeal that was dismissed for being filed three days late. Despite media claims asserting that executing Coleman risked killing an innocent man, postmortem DNA testing confirms that Coleman was in fact guilty.

New Jersey governor Richard Codey imposes a moratorium on executions.

Litigation in California state and federal courts results in a stay of execution for Michael Angelo Morales, sentenced for the rape and murder of a 17-year-old girl. As of 2013, no hearing has been scheduled in federal court on whether California's lethal injection protocol is constitutional, because state courts have held California's attempt to revise its procedure invalid under state law.

2007

South Dakota executes Elijah Page by lethal injection for the robbery, torture, and murder of a teenager, Chester Allen Poage. It is South Dakota's first execution in 60 years, made possible by Page's abandonment of all appeals.

The United Nations General Assembly votes 104–54 in favor of a nonbinding recommendation for a moratorium on the death penalty.

New Jersey repeals its death penalty statute, the first state to do so since 1976.

2008

The Nebraska Supreme Court decides, in *State v. Mata,* that use of the electric chair is cruel and unusual punishment under the state constitution but affirms Raymond Mata's death sentence.

Iowa adopts lethal injection as its method of execution.

Baze v. Rees (2008) holds that the Eighth Amendment permits Kentucky's use of a three-drug method of lethal injection because there is no proof that it causes substantial risk of pain.

Kennedy v. Louisiana (2008) holds that the Eighth Amendment forbids the death penalty for rape of a child not resulting in death.

On August 5, Texas executes Jose Ernesto Medellin, a Mexican national living in Houston, Texas, since childhood, for the 1993 gang rape and murder of two teenage girls. Medellin's case draws international attention after Mexico sues the United

States in the International Court of Justice, which rules that Medellin and other Mexican citizens were denied information about their right to contact the Mexican consulate.

Law professor Jon Gould and attorney Lisa Greenman publish a study for the Judicial Conference of the United States examining the costs of defending federal death penalty cases in 119 cases in which the federal death penalty was authorized between 1998 and 2004. Their *Report on the Cost Quality and Availability of Defense Representation in Federal Death Penalty Cases* concludes that the median cost of defense when the prosecution seeks the death penalty is approximately $353,000, seven times the median cost when the death penalty is not sought.

2009

New Mexico repeals its death penalty statute, the second state to do so since 1976.

The Washington Supreme Court stays executions in that state pending a hearing on whether its lethal injection method inflicts cruel and unusual punishment.

2010

Ohio executes eight death row inmates.

2011

Reacting to shortages of sodium thiopental, Ohio, Arizona, Oklahoma, Texas, Alabama, and Mississippi plan to switch to pentobarbital for lethal injections. Death penalty opponents note that the latter drug is used to euthanize animals.

The death penalty is repealed in Illinois. Governor Pat Quinn also commutes sentences of Illinois death row inmates.

2012

The death penalty is repealed in Connecticut.

2013

The death penalty is repealed in Maryland, effective October 1, 2013.

Chapter 11

Links and Resources

Selected Online Resources

We want to highlight several links and electronic sites that we have found to be extremely useful in conducting research about capital punishment. Several of the following Web sites serve as gateways, including extensive links to print and electronic resources. The following list is intended to be suggestive rather than comprehensive.

Amnesty International, http://www.amnestyusa.org/our-work/campaigns/abolish-the-death-penalty/death-penalty-campaign-resources. This site includes fact sheets, background materials, and other information compiled by Amnesty International.

Bureau of Justice Statistics, http://bjs.gov/. This site provides statistics about crime and victims, drugs and crime, criminal offenders, the justice system in the United States, law enforcement, prosecution, courts, and related matters.

Death Penalty Information center, http://www.deathpenaltyinfo.org/. This site includes updated fact sheets, regularly updated statistics, information about upcoming executions, an execution database, state-by-state comparisons, podcasts, and lists or relevant resources.

Death Penalty Links, Clark County, Indiana, Prosecutors Office, http://www.clarkprosecutor.org/html/links/dplinks.htm. This site includes a wealth of information on timelines, methods of execution, public opinion polls, and so on. The list of links to other resources is very comprehensive. See "1000+ Death Penalty Links."

Fascinating Facts about the Constitution, http://www.constitutionfacts.com. This site provides an assortment of facts about the U.S. Constitution. The site includes famous quotes, crossword puzzles, a glossary of terms, the Declaration of Independence, the Articles of Confederation, the Bill of Rights, state constitutions, foreign constitutions, dates, the Founding Fathers, and information about the U.S. Supreme Court.

The Federalist Papers, http://federalist.freeservers.com/papers.html. This is a Web site for the Federalist Papers. Madison's Federalist Number 51 and Hamilton's Federalist Numbers 78 and 84 are most directly relevant to the federal judiciary.

Human Rights: Death Penalty, http://www.derechos.org/dp/. This site provides international perspectives on the death penalty.

Kruglick's Death Penalty Links, http://www.bioforensics.com/kruglaw/dp_links .htm. Kruglick's Forensic Resource and Criminal Law Search Site provides a wide variety of relevant links. The site is sponsored by Forensic Bioinformatics, offering evaluations of DNA evidence and consulting services.

Legal Information Institute, http://www.law.cornell.edu/. This website provides access to historical and recent Supreme Court decisions.

National Constitution Center, http://www.constitutioncenter.org. This Web site includes educational resources, lesson plans, and other materials related to constitutional issues.

Oyez: U.S. Supreme Court Media, http://www.oyez.org. This Web site provides links to cases, upcoming arguments, and other information concerning the U.S. Supreme Court.

Report of the Advisory Committee on Wrongful Convictions, September 2011, John T. Rago, Esq. (Chair), http://jsg.legis.state.pa.us/resources/documents/ftp/documents/ 9–15–11%20rpt%20-%20Wrongful%20Convictions.pdf. This report for the Pennsylvania General Assembly's Joint State Government Commission chronicled wrongful convictions and reasons, including mistaken eyewitness identification, false confessions, incriminating admissions, interrogation practices, postconviction relief, adequacy of legal representation, and prosecutorial misconduct. The report discusses best practices and includes reform suggestions and redress for wrongful convictions.

Supreme Court of the United States, http://www.supremecourt.gov. This official Web site for the Supreme Court of the United States provides access to schedules of upcoming cases as well as briefs, transcripts, audio recordings of selected oral arguments, and judicial opinions.

Top Ten Pros and Cons: Should the Death Penalty be Allowed?, http://deathpenalty. procon.org/view.resource.php?resourceID=002000. ProCon.org is an independent, nonpartisan, nonprofit public charity. This Web site is a useful introduction to the capital punishment debate.

Web guide to U.S. Supreme Court Research, http://www.llrx.com/features/ supremectwebguide.htm. Gail Partin, associate law librarian at Dickinson School of Law, prepared this Web guide to Supreme Court research.

Selected Print Resources

For original source documents relevant to the Eighth Amendment, the Supreme Court, and the Court's role in constitutional law, see:

Adler, Mortimer, ed. 1976. *The Annals of America, 1493–1754,* Vol. 1. Chicago: Encyclopedia Britannica.

American Law Institute. 1980. *Model Penal Code and Commentaries, Part II.* 3 vols. Philadelphia: American Law Institute.

Beccaria, Cesare. 1963 [1764]. *On Crimes and Punishments.* Translated by Henry Paolucci. Englewood Cliffs, NJ: Prentice Hall.

Blackstone, William. 1979 [1765–1769]. *Commentaries on the Laws of England.* 4 vols. Chicago: University of Chicago Press.

Cogan, Neil H., ed. 1997. *The Complete Bill of Rights.* New York: Oxford University Press.

Elliot, Jonathan, ed. 1937 [1836]. *Debates in the Several State Conventions on the Adoption of the Federal Constitution.* 5 vols. Philadelphia: J. B. Lippincott.

Ford, Paul L., ed. 1968. *Pamphlets on the Constitution of the United States.* New York: Da Capo.

Goldberg, Arthur J. 1986. "Memorandum to the Conference Re: Capital Punishment." *South Texas Law Review* 27: 493.

Kaminski, John P., ed. 2008. *The Founders on the Founders: Word Portraits from the American Revolutionary Era.* Charlottesville: University of Virginia Press.

Kenyon, J. P., ed. 1966. *The Stuart Constitution, 1603–1688: Documents and Commentary.* London: Cambridge University Press.

Schwartz, Bernard, ed. 1980. *The Roots of the Bill of Rights.* 5 vols. New York: Chelsea House.

Story, Joseph. 1987. *Commentaries on the Constitution of the United States.* With an introduction by Ronald D. Rotunda and John E. Nowak. Durham, NC: Carolina Academic Press.

United States Department of Justice. 2000. *Survey of the Federal Death Penalty System, 1988–2000.* Washington, DC: Department of Justice.

For American constitutional law, the history of ideas, and the transformation of American legal thinking, see:

Abraham, Henry J. 1993. *The Judicial Process.* 6th ed. New York: Oxford University Press.

Bailyn, Bernard. 1992. *The Ideological Origins of the American Revolution.* Enlarged ed. Cambridge, MA: Belknap Press of Harvard University Press.

Berger, Raoul. 1977. *Government by Judiciary: The Transformation of the Fourteenth Amendment.* Cambridge, MA: Harvard University Press.

Berkin, Carol. 2003. *A Brilliant Solution: Inventing the American Constitution.* Orlando, FL: Harcourt.

Bork, Robert H. 1996. "Our Judicial Oligarchy." *First Things* 67 (November): 21.

Brant, Irving. 1965. *The Bill of Rights: Its Origin and Meaning.* Indianapolis: Bobbs-Merrill.

Cardozo, Benjamin N. 1921. *The Nature of the Judicial Process.* New Haven, CT: Yale University Press.

Clinton, Robert. 1999. "How the Court Became Supreme." *First Things* 89 (January): 13.

Closen, Michael L., and Robert J. Dzielak. 1996. "The History and Influence of the Law Review Institution." *Akron Law Review* 30 (Fall): 15.

Corwin, Edward S. 1958. *The Constitution and What It Means Today.* Princeton, NJ: Princeton University Press.

Cover, Robert M., and T. Alexander Aleinikoff. 1977. "Dialectical Federalism: Habeas Corpus and the Court." *Yale Law Journal* 86: 1035.

Douglas, William O. 1961. *A Living Bill of Rights.* New York: Doubleday.

Fairman, Charles. 1949. "Does the Fourteenth Amendment Incorporate the Bill of Rights?" *Stanford Law Review* 2 (December): 5.

Frankfurter, Felix. 1958. "The Supreme Court in the Mirror of Justices." *ABA Journal* 44: 723.

Friedman, Lawrence M. 1973. *A History of American Law.* New York: Touchstone Books and Simon and Schuster.

Gunther, Gerald. 1964. "The Subtle Vices of the 'Passive Virtues': A Comment on Principle and Expediency in Judicial Review." *Columbia Law Review* 64: 1.

Holmes, Oliver Wendell, Jr. 1881. *The Common Law.* Boston: Little, Brown.

Maine, Henry S. 1970 [1861]. *Ancient Law: Its Connection with the Early History of Society and Its Relation to Modern Ideas.* Gloucester, MA: Peter Smith.

Maitland, F. W. 1908. *The Constitutional History of England.* Edited by H. A. L. Fisher. Cambridge, UK: Cambridge University Press.

Melusky, Joseph. 2000. *The American Political System: An Owner's Manual.* Boston: McGraw-Hill.

O'Brien, David M. 2005. *Storm Center: The Supreme Court in American Politics.* 7th ed. New York: Norton.

Posner, Richard A. 2008. *How Judges Think.* Cambridge, MA: Harvard University Press.

Pound, Roscoe. 1957. *The Development of Constitutional Guarantees of Liberty.* New Haven, CT: Yale University Press.

Pound, Roscoe. 1999 [1921]. *The Spirit of the Common Law.* New Brunswick, NJ: Transaction Publishers.

Rehnquist, William H. 2001. *The Supreme Court.* New York: Knopf.

Silverstein, Mark. 1994. *Judicious Choices: The New Politics of Supreme Court Nominations.* New York: Norton.

Stannard, David E. 1977. *The Puritan Way of Death.* New York: Oxford University Press.

Sutherland, Arthur E. 1965. *Constitutionalism in America.* New York: Blaisdell.

Watson, Bradley C. S. 2009. *Living Constitution, Dying Faith: Progressivism and the New Science of Jurisprudence.* Wilmington, DE: ISI Books.

For treatment of the death penalty and the problem of crime and punishment in general, see:

Allen, Francis A. 1981. *The Decline of the Rehabilitative Ideal.* New Haven, CT: Yale University Press.

Banner, Stuart. 2002. *The Death Penalty: An American History.* Cambridge, MA: Harvard University Press.

Bedau, Hugo A., ed. 1982. *The Death Penalty in America.* 3rd ed. New York: Oxford University Press.

Berns, Walter. 1979. *For Capital Punishment: Crime and the Morality of the Death Penalty.* New York: Basic Books.

Carrington, Frank. 1978. *Neither Cruel nor Unusual.* New Rochelle, NY: Arlington House.

Cohen, Bernard L. 1970. *Law without Order: Capital Punishment and the Liberals.* New Rochelle, NY: Arlington House.

Cohen, Morris R. 1940. "Moral Aspects of the Criminal Law." *Yale Law Journal* 49 (April): 987.

Coyne, Randall, and Lyn Entzeroth. 2006. *Capital Punishment and the Judicial Process.* 3rd ed. Durham, NC: Carolina Academic Press.

DeGrandis, Michael P. 2003. "*Atkins v. Virginia*: Nothing Left of the Independent Legislative Power to Punish and Define Crime." *George Mason Law Review* 11 (Summer): 805.

Demleitner, Nora V. 2005. "Is There a Future for Leniency in the U.S. Criminal Justice System?" *Michigan Law Review* 103 (May): 1231.

Dershowitz, Alan M. 2004. *America on Trial: Inside the Legal Battles That Transformed Our Nation.* New York: Warner Books.

Dezhbaksh, Hashem, Paul H. Rubin, and Joanna Shepherd. 2003. "Does Capital Punishment Have a Deterrent Effect? New Evidence from Postmoratorium Panel Data." *American Law and Economics Review* 5 (August): 344.

Donohue, John J., and Justin Wolfers. 2005. "Uses and Abuses of Empirical Evidence in the Death Penalty Debate." *Stanford Law Review* 58 (December): 791.

Douglas, Davison M. 2000. "God and the Executioner: The Influence of Western Religion on the Death Penalty." *William and Mary Bill of Rights Journal* 9 (December): 137.

Dubber, Markus D. 1998. "The Right to Be Punished: Autonomy and Its Demise in Modern Penal Thought." *Law and History Review* 16 (Spring): 113.

Dulles, Avery. 2001. "Catholicism and Capital Punishment." *First Things* 112 (April): 30.

Garland, David. 2010. *Peculiar Institution: America's Death Penalty in an Age of Abolition.* Cambridge, MA: Belknap Press of Harvard University Press.

Greenberg, Jack. 1986. "Against the American System of Capital Punishment." *Harvard Law Review* 99 (May): 1670.

Greenlee, Harry, and Shelia P. Greenlee. 2008. "Women and the Death Penalty: Racial Disparities and Differences." *William and Mary Journal of Women and the Law* 14 (Winter): 319.

Grossman, Mark. 1998. *Encyclopedia of Capital Punishment.* Santa Barbara, CA: ABC-CLIO.

Hoeflich, M.H. 1986. "Law and Geometry: Legal Science from Leibniz to Langdell." *American Journal of Legal History* 30 (April): 95.

Hood, Roger, and Carolyn Hoyle. 2008. *The Death Penalty: A Worldwide Perspective.* 4th ed. Oxford: Oxford University Press.

Ignatieff, Michael. 1978. *A Just Measure of Pain: The Penitentiary in the Industrial Revolution, 1750–1850.* New York: Pantheon Books.

Jackson, Bruce, and Diane Christian. 1980. *Death Row.* Boston: Beacon.

Jackson, Jesse. 1996. *Legal Lynching: Racism, Injustice and the Death Penalty.* New York: Marlowe.

Joyce, James A. 1961. *Capital Punishment: A World View.* New York: Thomas Nelson.

Katz, Lawrence, Steven D. Levitt, and Ellen Shustorovich. 2003. "Prison Conditions, Capital Punishment, and Deterrence." *American Law and Economics Review* 5 (August): 318.

Kearns, Timothy S. 2005. "The Chair, the Needle and the Damage Done: What the Electric Chair and the Rebirth of the Method-of-Execution Challenge Could Mean for the Future of the Eighth Amendment." *Cornell Journal of Law and Public Policy* 15 (Fall): 197.

Kirchmeier, Jeffrey L. 2002. "Another Place beyond Here: The Death Penalty Moratorium Movement in the United States." *University of Colorado Law Review* 73 (Winter): 1.

Kozinski, Alex, and Sean Gallagher. 1995. "Death: The Ultimate Run-On Sentence." *Case Western Reserve Law Review* 46 (Fall): 1.

Kronenwetter, Michael. 1993. *Capital Punishment.* Santa Barbara, CA: ABC-CLIO.

Lanier, Charles S., William Bowers, and James R. Acker, eds. 2008. *The Future of America's Death Penalty: An Agenda for the Next Generation of Capital Punishment Research.* Durham, NC: Carolina Academic Press.

Laurence, John. 1960. *A History of Capital Punishment.* New York: Citadel Press.

Ledewitz, Bruce, and Scott Staples. 1993. "No Punishment without Cruelty." *George Mason University Civil Rights Law Journal* 4 (Winter): 41.

Lee, Robert W. 1990. "Deserving to Die," *New American* (13 August). Reprinted in George McKenna and Stanley Feingold, *Taking Sides: Clashing Views on Controversial Political Issues,* 142–149. McGraw-Hill, 2007.

Liebman, James S., Jeffrey Fagan, Valerie West, and Jonathan Lloyd. 2000. "Capital Attrition: Error Rates in Capital Cases, 1973–1995." *Texas Law Review* 78 (June): 1839.

Lifton, Robert J., and Greg Mitchell. 2000. *Who Owns Death? Capital Punishment, the American Conscience, and the End of Executions.* New York: HarperCollins.

Lindgren, James. 1996. "Why the Ancients May Not Have Needed a System of Criminal Law." *Boston University Law Review* 76 (February–April): 29.

Little, Rory K. 1999. "The Federal Death Penalty: History and Some Thoughts about the Department of Justice's Role." *Fordham Urban Law Journal* 26 (March): 347.

McCafferty, James A. 1972. *Capital Punishment.* Chicago: Aldine-Atherton.

McClellan, Grant S., ed. 1961. *Capital Punishment.* New York: H. W. Wilson.

Mencken, H. L. 1926. "The Penalty of Death." In *Elements of Argument,* edited by Annette T. Rottenberg, 394–396. 1985. New York: St. Martin's.

Mocan, H. Naci, and R. Kaj Gittings. 2003. "Getting Off Death Row: Commuted Sentences and the Deterrent Effect of Capital Punishment." *Journal of Law and Economics* 46 (October): 453.

Packer, Herbert L. 1964. "Making the Punishment Fit the Crime." *Harvard Law Review* 77 (April): 1071.

Pope John Paul II. 1995. "Evangelium Vitae (The Gospel of Life)." In *John Paul II: The Encyclicals in Everyday Language,* edited by Joseph G. Donders, 1997. Maryknoll, NY: Orbis Books.

Presser, Stephen B. 1982. *Studies in the History of the United States Courts of the Third Circuit.* Washington, DC: U.S. Government Printing Office.

Radelet, Michael, and Marian T. Borg. 2000. "The Changing Nature of the Death Penalty Debates." *Annual Review of Sociology* 26: 43.

Roleff, Tamara, ed. 1999. *Crime and Criminals: Opposing Viewpoints.* San Diego: Greenhaven.

Sellin, Thorsten. 1959. *The Death Penalty.* Philadelphia: Lippincott.

Sellin, Thorsten, ed. 1967. *Capital Punishment.* New York: Harper and Row.

Shapiro, Barbara J. 1969. "Law and Science in Seventeenth-Century England." *Stanford Law Review* 21 (April): 727.

Skelton, Meghan S. 1997. "Lethal Injection in the Wake of Fierro v. Gomez." *Thomas Jefferson Law Review* 19 (Spring): 1.

Smith, Bruce P. 2005. "The History of Wrongful Execution." *Hastings Law Journal* 56 (June): 1185.

Stack, Steven. 1987. "Publicized Executions and Homicide." *American Sociological Review* 52 (August): 532.

Standen, Jeffrey. 2005. "The New Importance of Maximum Penalties." *Drake Law Review* 53 (Spring): 575.

Stephenson, D. Grier. 1994. "Justice Blackmun's Eighth Amendment Pilgrimage." *BYU Journal of Public Law* 8: 271.

Stinneford, John F. 2008. "The Original Meaning of 'Unusual': The Eight Amendment as Bar to Cruel Innovation." *Northwestern University Law Review* 102 (Fall): 1739.

Stras, David R. 2007. "The Supreme Court's Gatekeepers: The Role of Law Clerks in the Certiorari Process." *Texas Law Review* 85 (March): 947.

Student Note. 1910. "What Is Cruel and Unusual Punishment." *Harvard Law Review* 24: 54.

Student Note. 1966. "The Cruel and Unusual Punishment Clause and the Substantive Criminal Law." *Harvard Law Review* 79: 635.

van den Haag, Ernest, and John P. Conrad. 1983. *The Death Penalty: A Debate.* New York: Plenum.

Wekesser, Carol, ed. 1991. *The Death Penalty: Opposing Viewpoints.* San Diego: Greenhaven.

Wiener, Scott. 1996. "Popular Justice: State Judicial Elections and Procedural Due Process." *Harvard Civil Rights–Civil Liberties Law Review* 31 (Winter): 187.

Zimmerman, Paul R. 2006. "Estimates of the Deterrent Effect of Alternative Execution Methods in the United States, 1978–2000." *American Journal of Economics and Sociology* 65 (October): 909.

For personal accounts, see:

Bennett, James V. 1970. *I Choose Prison.* New York: Knopf.

Bessler, John D. 2003. *Kiss of Death: America's Love Affair with the Death Penalty.* Boston: Northeastern University Press.

Bright, Stephen B. 1996. "The Electric Chair and the Chain Gang: Choices and Challenges for America's Future." *Notre Dame Law Review* 71 (July): 845.

Bright, Stephen B. 1999. "Death in Texas." *Champion* 23 (July): 16.

Dow, David R. 1996. "The State, the Death Penalty, and Carl Johnson." *Boston College Law Review* 37 (July): 691.

Greenhouse, Linda. 2005. *Becoming Justice Blackmun: Harry Blackmun's Supreme Court Journey.* New York: Times Books.

Hawke, David F. 1971. *Benjamin Rush: Revolutionary Gadfly.* Indianapolis: Bobbs-Merrill.

Lawes, Lewis E. 1969 [1924]. *Man's Judgment of Death.* Montclair, NJ: Patterson Smith.

Margulies, Joseph. 2002. "Memories of an Execution." *Law and Inequality: A Journal of Theory and Practice* 20 (Winter): 125.

Nygaard, Richard L. 1988. "Crime, Pain, and Punishment: A Skeptic's View." *Dickinson Law Review* 102 (Winter): 355.

Prejean, Sister Helen. 1993. *Dead Man Walking: An Eyewitness Account of the Death Penalty in the United States.* New York: Vintage Books/Random House.

Prettyman, Barrett, Jr. 1961. *Death and the Supreme Court.* New York: Harcourt, Brace and World.

Williams, Daniel E. 1993. *Pillars of Salt: An Anthology of Early American Criminal Narratives.* Madison, WI: Madison House Publishers.

Index

About the Authors

Dr. Joseph A. Melusky, professor of political science, director of the SFU Center for the Study of Government and Law, and coordinator of Public Administration/Government Service, has been a full-time member of the teaching faculty at Saint Francis University since 1980. He has received a number of teaching awards, including the Swatsworth Award, the Honor Society Outstanding Faculty Award, and the Alumni Association's Distinguished Faculty Award. He has served as interim vice president for Academic Affairs, chair of the Department of History and Political Science, chair of the Education Department, and dean of General Education. He is a former president and vice president of the Pennsylvania Political Science Association; former president, vice president, and executive director of the Northeastern Political Science Association; and former member of the Executive Council of the Pennsylvania Humanities Council. He serves as director of Employment Services of the Northeastern Political Science Association and judge of elections for Blair Township, Hollidaysburg East, Pennsylvania. He earned his MA and PhD degrees in political science from the University of Delaware and has done postgraduate work at the University of Delaware, the University of Michigan, and Carnegie-Mellon University. With Keith Pesto, he has coauthored *Capital Punishment* (Greenwood, 2011) and *Cruel and Unusual Punishments: Rights and Freedoms under the Law* (ABC-CLIO, 2003). Melusky also authored *The Contemporary Constitution: Modern Interpretations* (Krieger, 2006); *The American Political System: An Owner's Manual* (McGraw-Hill, 2000); *The Bill of Rights: Our Written Legacy,* with Whitman Ridgway (Krieger, 1993); *To Preserve These Rights: The Bill of Rights, 1791–1991* (Pennsylvania Humanities Council, 1991); and *The Constitution: Our Written Legacy* (Krieger, 1991).

Keith Alan Pesto graduated from Johns Hopkins University in 1980 with a BA in economics and in 1983 from the University of Pennsylvania Law School. He practiced law in Philadelphia, served as a law clerk to Judge D. Brooks Smith, and was an assistant district attorney in Blair County, Pennsylvania. Pesto has been a federal magistrate judge for the U.S. District Court for the Western District of Pennsylvania since 1994. He has also been a lecturer in the Political Science Departments at Saint Francis University and Juniata College for the past two decades and from 2004 to 2007 was appointed by Chief Justice William Rehnquist to the Federal Judicial Center's Magistrate Judge Education Committee.